THE LIVELY COMMERCE

The Lively Commerce

PROSTITUTION IN THE
UNITED STATES
BY
CHARLES WINICK
AND PAUL M. KINSIE

CHICAGO : QUADRANGLE BOOKS : 1971

Library of Congress Catalog Card Number: 79-130382
SBN 8129-0161-4

Typography and Binding Design by Lawrence Levy

PREFACE

This book presents a picture of prostitution in the United
States during the last half-century. It is based on extensive
interviewing of all elements in the social system of prostitution and of those in the community who attempt to cope with
it. Findings from the behavioral sciences and other fields are
incorporated as appropriate. In as much as there are relatively few recent empirical studies of prostitution, and because its current characteristics can only be understood in
the light of previous history and development, we frequently
refer to studies conducted several decades ago.

Even though the United States has developed its own
unique impressions of and approaches to prostitution, the
experiences of other countries are cited where relevant. We
use references to prostitution from mass communications
and popular humor where germane, because of the importance of such materials in helping to mold and convey attitudes toward the subject, and because of the paucity of more
traditional kinds of data on public opinion.

Where generalizations are made or information cited without reference to any source, such material has usually been

derived from more than two thousand interviews with prostitutes, customers, go-betweens, auxiliary personnel, judges,
probation officers, and others directly or indirectly associated
with prostitution. These interviews were conducted by the
authors or their assistants in every part of the country during
the past ten years. Actual names of specific respondents and
other persons are given wherever possible. All the American
communities discussed have been visited at least once since
1960.

We have written this book in order to improve understanding, clarify alternatives, and bring together what is known
about a problem which places a considerable burden on many
communities in the United States. Policy decisions about
prostitution have often been made on the basis of minimal
information and irrational appeals. It is our hope that this
book will help to shed light on the subject and facilitate ra-
tional consideration of a phenomenon which has been considered important enough to be called "*the* social evil."

C. W.
P. M. K.

New York City
January 1971

ACKNOWLEDGMENTS

We have been fortunate in having access to the files of the American Social Health Association and its antecedent organizations, and we appreciate the critical comments of Conrad Van Hyning, formerly executive director of the Association, on an earlier version of the manuscript. We benefited greatly from discussion with the Honorable Raymond B. Fosdick, who was gracious enough to read Chapter IX, "Prostitution and the Military." The Honorable Charles P. Taft kindly consented to read the discussion of World War II. Dr. James S. McKenzie-Pollock read and commented on the discussion of venereal disease.

Several other persons have commented on various parts of the manuscript. Dr. Jacob Goldstein called our attention to relevant psychoanalytic literature. James Pozoli and Joseph Rosner contributed information on mass media. Elliot Horne pointed up some problems dealing with the use of humor. Josephine V. Tuller and Geraldine Rasmussen helped to prepare the section on international cooperation. Judge Morris Ploscowe clarified the status of prostitution laws in Nevada. The Staff of the National Health Agencies Library, especially

Bernice Casier, provided sustained and imaginative assistance in solving many thorny bibliographical problems. We are grateful for the discussions we had with the late Dean Joseph D. Lohman of the School of Criminology at the University of California, and with Professor Leslie T. Wilkins, formerly of the British Home Office and now at the State University of New York at Albany. Professor Edward Sagarin of the City College of New York called our attention to some aspects of the literature with which we were not familiar.

The Russell Sage Foundation provided a grant for the preparation of an examination and evaluation of literature and expert opinion on prostitution by Gilda Moss Haber, on which we have freely drawn. We especially acknowledge the continued interest of Philip R. Mather. Dr. Joseph H. Douglass of the National Institute of Mental Health and Earle G. Lippincott of the American Social Health Association helped to clarify our thinking on many aspects of the problem. Ned Polsky and Jan Pennar provided some valuable suggestions, and Gershon Legman identified many helpful avenues for discussion. Raymond Clapp and Dean Snyder of the Office of Health, Education and Welfare helped us by recalling the work of the Division of Social Protection. Emanuel Geltman made helpful comments on the manuscript.

We gratefully acknowledge a manuscript typing grant from the Law Enforcement Assistance Administration of the U.S. Department of Justice. (Points of view or opinions stated in this book do not necessarily reflect the official position or policy of the Department of Justice.)

The authors alone, of course, are responsible for their use of others' work and for any errors of omission or commission.

CONTENTS

ix

THE LIVELY COMMERCE

I. VIEWS OF PROSTITUTION

Prostitution has long been a problem which has provoked and disturbed Americans. They have sometimes preferred to treat it as if it did not exist. On other occasions they have displayed great vigor in trying to combat it. For many decades it was regarded as the single most important social problem. It remains a significant problem today.

There have been a number of different definitions of the practice,[1] but it can generally be defined as the granting of nonmarital sexual access, established by mutual agreement of the woman, her client, and/or her employer, for remuneration which provides part or all of her livelihood. In earlier definitions, prostitution was the giving or receiving of the body for sexual intercourse for hire. The prostitute may be male or female. In most states a prostitute is legally defined as a person who offers to or does engage in sexual intercourse or "lewd and indecent" acts for hire; in nineteen states a prostitute is a person who engages in "indiscriminate sexual intercourse" for fee or anything else of value. In other societies the payment for prostitution may be in barter.

Prostitution can be discussed as a legal, social, or moral problem, and each approach requires a different perspective and its own set of different considerations.[2] In order to evaluate precisely how serious a threat prostitution poses to the social order, it would be necessary to have comparative data, which do not now exist, from other countries. We can, however, approximately assess the role of prostitution in America in terms of the number of persons who are involved in it.

How many prostitutes are there in America today? One reason for difficulties in fixing a number is that prostitutes only become known to the authorities as a result of violations of the law, and may be arrested for a variety of reasons. A prostitute who is arrested may be charged with vagrancy, disorderly conduct, or prostitution. Many prostitutes, of course, may never be arrested at all. Even if arrest figures were precise, uniform, and systematic, they would not provide a complete picture. Trends measured in terms of the number of arrests reflect the relative activity of law enforcement groups rather than any changes in the number of prostitutes. But data from law enforcement sources, with all their limitations, provide the best information available on incidence.

During the fairly typical year of 1968, there were some 95,550 arrests for violation of prostitution or related laws.[3] An arrest does not, of course, mean that the person was actually engaging in prostitution. Some persons may have been arrested more than once, and many prostitutes may not have been arrested at all. Balancing such factors, it is likely that the figure of 95,550 is a very conservative approximation of the number of full-time prostitutes. There is every reason to believe that a substantially larger number of women work as part-time prostitutes. The average full-time prostitute today works six days a week and has three clients daily, so that perhaps 286,650 men daily or some 1,719,900 weekly use such services.

If we assume an average fee per contact of $10, we can speculate that all full-time prostitutes earn about $894 million a year. The average full-time prostitute, in a six-day work week, may have a yearly gross of $9,300, of which she nets between $5,000 and $6,000. There is little reliable information on the earnings of part-time prostitutes.

Our estimate of 95,550 prostitutes who earn $894 million annually is extremely low when compared with other figures that have been suggested. The problems in estimating the incidence of prostitution are similar to those in evaluating the trends in narcotic addiction and help to explain the lack of agreement. Perhaps it is reasonable to analogize the number of arrested prostitutes to the number of identified heroin addicts. Just as the 64,000 known heroin addicts are only a fraction of the probably millions of drug abusers whose number can only be estimated, so the known prostitutes represent a fraction of the total number of full- and part-time prostitutes. Some students of the subject have suggested that somewhere between 250,000 and 550,000 women work at prostitution on a more or less full-time basis and that many more are part-time prostitutes.

The extent of prostitution appears now to be fairly stable, so that the proportion of men of each socio-economic group who visit prostitutes is perhaps substantially the same as it was in the 1930's, although more recent clients participate in only one-half to two-thirds the incidence of contacts reported by the earlier generation. The men in a representative community of 100,000, interviewed in the late 1930's and early 1940's, had some 3,190 contacts with prostitutes in a week. Some 69 per cent of the white male population at that time had been clients of prostitutes.[4]

One major change in prostitution in the last three decades has been a shift from an organized business activity involving a substantial number of third persons to more of an individual entrepreneurship. With the brothel's decline, prostitution is less likely to be organized than it was in the 1930's. This lack of organization also makes for difficulty in estimating the extent of prostitution, because individual prostitutes are far less visible than brothels used to be.

The only comparative figures on the incidence of prostitution over a period of years can be found in the community studies conducted by the American Social Health Association.[5] These studies provide a comparative index of commercialized prostitution. The association has developed a weighted scale for evaluating the relative amount of prostitution in a community. The scale considers the size of a community, its socio-economic level, the amount and type of prostitution as well as the extent to which it is flagrant or clandestine. When these dimensions are weighted and combined into a single numerical index, a maximum score of 100 is possible. Each quartile can also be expressed by the letters A through D. A score of 76 to 100 (D) describes a community that has a great deal of flagrant prostitution. A score of 51 to 75 (C) means that a community would be regarded as having much overt prostitution. A score of 26 to 50 (B) connotes some visible prostitution, and 0 to 25 (A) means practically no commercialized prostitution.

The surveys are conducted periodically, so that a community may not have the same rating from one year to another. These ratings, of course, reflect values that prevail at the time the survey is conducted—for example, New York today is classified as D, but in another time might have fallen into a different category.

If the different decades since World War I were to be classified and averaged in terms of this scoring system on a national basis, the 1920's would receive 95. From 1930 to 1938, the mean score was 92. In 1939, 43 per cent of the communities scored between 76 and 100. The country's national average during the World War II years was 49. In the late forties there was a sharp upsurge and a mean score of 74; every third community had widespread prostitution. The decade of the 1950's showed a considerable decline which was reflected in a score of 35. By 1957 every fourth community had overt prostitution. Ten years later, 27 per cent of the communities studied had conspicuous prostitution activity and the average national score was 37.

Prostitution flourished not only in the prosperity of the 1920's but also during the depression of the succeeding decade. In very few communities during the 1930's did prostitutes complain about the effect of the depression or leave their work as the result of a decrease in customers. The decline in their earning power probably made some men keenly aware of their maleness, and a visit to a prostitute represented one way in which they could assert it at a time when their ability to manifest masculinity by earning a living might have been difficult. The depression also created problems and irregularities in men's sex lives with their wives, many of whom became unresponsive to their husbands. Unemployed men also had more time for visiting a prostitute.[6] During the depression, prostitutes charged less. In many cases, no "reasonable" offer was refused. For these and other reasons, prostitution seems to have increased somewhat as unemployment soared in the 1930's. Many amateurs became professionals during this period, because of difficulties in finding other work.[7]

PROSTITUTION AND SOCIAL STRUCTURE

Prostitution can only be understood in terms of the social structure within which it occurs. The established sociological explanation for society's hostility toward prostitution suggests that people link sex activity to some stable relationship, usually the family.[8] Sex is thus related to the survival of the society, and when it is not so directed the community is disturbed and condemns the practice. Our social structure is threatened by people who engage in sexual activity for pay. But when the community attempts to regulate sex behavior, it helps to create opportunities for breaching the regulation.

If we classify social systems in terms of the variables of (a) open discussion of sex, and (b) acceptance and encouragement of nonmarital sex, such variables can be related to attitudes toward prostitution.[9]

	Acceptance of Nonmarital Sex	Open Discussion
1	+	+
2	+	−
3	−	+
4	−	−

Social system 1 would endorse discussion of sex and acceptance of nonmarital sex relationships and have practically no prostitution—for example, the Tikopia people of the Solomon Islands. Social system 2 provides for no discussion of sex but acceptance of nonmarital sex on the part of men, as in most Latin American countries. In social system 3 there is discussion of sex but little acceptance of nonmarital sex, as in the United States up to fairly recently. Social system 4 is based on minimal discussion and little sexual activity before marriage, as in Spain. A full understanding of each social system's attitudes toward prostitution would require knowledge of its larger role and institutional structure.

In different regions of the United States there appear to be varying degrees of acceptance of prostitution. The South was and to some extent still is our most tolerant section, and the Southeast has been more liberal than the Southwest. Prostitution in the South has been a somewhat special case because of the heritage of slavery and the long tradition of the Negro woman as a chattel. The sexual relationships of the white master and his slave covered a tremendous range, and the master could do practically anything he pleased.[10] For many a young white man, the Negro girl represented his initiation into the world of sex; he might thereafter regard her primarily as a sexual vessel who was a vassal.

The Pacific Coast and the western United States used to be much more hospitable to prostitution than is the case today. New England, with the exception of Boston, is generally unfriendly. Larger cities tend to have comparatively more prostitution than smaller communities. The relative ease of mobilizing public opinion in a small town has made it a place in which prostitution can be eliminated fairly easily if the citizenry is interested in doing so.

The twentieth century has seen a variety of attitudes toward prostitution translated into laws and procedures. In terms of their degree of endorsement and acceptance of the practice, these attitudes have ranged from complete prohibition to the acceptance of prostitution as a socially desirable service occupation.

PROHIBITIONISM

The prohibitionist viewpoint is implemented in the United States, where the prostitute as well as all persons who act as intermediaries to the client are violating state laws. Prohibitionists assume that effective law enforcement can lead to the reduction of prostitution.

The prohibitionist attitude toward prostitution has reflected the same values that characterize the American approach to other "vices." Prostitution is regarded as a degradation of natural appetites which should be subject to will. We have adopted ever-stricter laws and made prison the main means of rehabilitation. Most state laws implicitly assume that prostitutes will not want to seek other work and therefore provide no alternative to prison.

REGULATION

Regulation is based on the community's recognition of existing houses of prostitution. Although prostitutes are not individually licensed, restrictions are placed on how they may operate. The community's tacit assumption is that prostitution is necessary but ought to be controlled in some way. Regulation reflects the traditional view that prostitution has a stabilizing influence on society, suggested by, among others, the Roman Senator Cato. He was always pleased to see a man leave a brothel because "otherwise he may have gone to lie with his neighbor's wife." St. Augustine had a similar intent in his comment that suppression of prostitution would mean the ruin of society. The historian Lecky called the brothel a "bulwark for the home." Such earlier justifications of prostitution held that even though prostitution was an evil, it helped to sustain the virtue of "good" women.

In recent years, regulated brothels have usually been expected to be a minimum distance—often a quarter of a mile —from schools, churches, and similar institutions. Sometimes the prostitute must register with local authorities or receive a physical examination. Approximately one-fifth of the prostitutes in such a situation typically comply with the requirement that they make their activities known to local authorities. The regulated countries today are in the Middle East, the Far East, South America, and the Caribbean.

Although national data on attitudes toward prostitution have not been collected for over a quarter of a century, earlier polls suggest that regulation, rather than prohibition, was once favored by a majority of Americans.[11] In 1937 a sample of three thousand Americans was asked its attitudes toward controlled prostitution. Over half (50.5 per cent) felt that controlled prostitution should be legalized; 30.9 per cent did not agree, and 18.6 per cent had no opinion. Slightly more men than women and more persons under than over forty agreed with the proposition. In 1942 another sample was asked whether it would prefer to have medical examination of prostitutes or rely on police action to get rid of prostitutes around army camps. Fifty-five per cent selected medical examination and 45 per cent favored police action. More men than women preferred medical examination. By 1943, 68 per cent of the population preferred medical examination and 32 per cent favored police action.

Advocacy of regulation has come from some unexpected quarters in the United States. In 1961 in Philadelphia, a federal grand jury endorsed it, and in the previous year a large group of Los Angeles women also publicly supported regulation because many of the city's automobiles were being stopped by prostitutes who solicited their occupants. Such soliciting activities had become so flagrant that the women urged that one part of the city be specifically set aside for prostitution.

LICENSING

Soon after the turn of the century, Dr. Abraham Flexner went to Europe in order to examine the state of prostitution in various European countries.[12] Flexner concluded that licensed prostitution could never work effectively because most prostitutes did not register. Paris recorded six thousand prostitutes, but the director of the licensing program estimated that at least sixy thousand had not registered.[13] The unregistered women, though subject to arrest and detention, were working at the same brothels and hotels and walking the same streets as their licensed colleagues. On Berlin's Friedrichstrasse and Unter den Linden, and along Vienna's Kertnerstrasse, where even licensed prostitutes were forbidden to ply their trade, the same situation prevailed: registered and unregistered prostitutes walked side by side and encountered minimal interference from police. Flexner's study of the difficulties of licensing contributed to its ultimate abandonment by all civilized countries.

In recent years, registration of the prostitute as an individual entrepreneur has usually been called the "neo-regulationist" procedure.[14] Most neo-regulationist systems require women to have a periodic examination for venereal disease, the results of which they are expected to make known to customers and other persons asking for such information. Prostitutes may not seek their clients in certain areas, but there are no limits on where they may take them. Geographic restrictions generally bar prostitutes from the heavily trafficked business districts that are likely to provide the best opportunities for customers, but women often ignore the prohibition and solicit in such areas. France, which formerly practiced the neo-regulationist system, closed its brothels in 1946, and Italy and Japan closed theirs in 1958. Nineteen countries, mostly in the Far East or South America, currently follow this approach.

ABOLITIONISM

Abolitionism, which derives its name from *abolition of the regulation* of prostitution, does not call for its elimination. The abolitionist view—implicit in the film *Never on Sunday* —holds that the prostitute has the same right to choose her work as any other person. Abolitionists oppose open soliciting and emphasize that pimps and madams should not be able to make money from prostitution. On a world-wide basis, the abolitionist system probably enjoys more acceptance than any other and is recommended by the United Nations. It is especially popular in Europe and in countries which have had contact with the European powers. All the English-speaking nations, except the United States, are abolitionist, perhaps in recognition of the reality that a man who is desperately eager to locate a prostitute can probably find one if he has the time, money, and energy to devote to the search.

The efficacy of concerted legal action in curbing prostitution can be seen in the substantial decrease in the international traffic in women and children as a direct result of action initiated by the League of Nations. The United Nations has not engaged in similar action.

TOLERATION

Toleration involves recognizing the existence of prostitution and a tacit understanding that anti-prostitution laws will not be enforced. Toleration may result from public apathy, reluctance to enforce laws, lack of interest, bribery, or the effects of special pleading. The United States before World War II represented a conspicuous example of toleration.

A recent example of toleration is provided by West Germany, where some 200,000 women work full time as prostitutes and every third man between twenty-one and sixty-five is a regular client. Typical of German cities is Dusseldorf, where a large wall encloses an area within which prostitutes are permitted to operate. The city's brothels were abolished in 1927, so the area on the Bahndamm is actually a prostitute's hostel. Although no one can legally make money from a prostitute's earnings, building a hostel and charging rent for the space do not violate any laws. Each of the 450 women in the area pays $1 a day for rent plus additional charges for laundry, meals, and drinks. They eat in a large dining room, earn approximately $140 a night, and pay income tax on their earnings. The women are examined by physicians at least twice a week.

Other communities in West Germany also tend to believe that prostitution cannot be eliminated and should be made available under reasonably sanitary conditions, with police supervision, and without offense to the young. Such communities locate the facility as far as possible from the center of town. Authorities in these cities have helped prostitutes get space in comfortable quarters and argue that such arrangements protect the public from soliciting and protect prostitutes from pimps. In 1967, Wilhelm Bartels developed Eros Center in Hamburg as a "rationalized brothel" or sex supermarket. It is a four-story apartment house entirely devoted to prostitution. It even provides underground parking for clients and contains 136 one-room apartments. A branch of Eros Center opened in Bonn in 1968.

Every West German community with condoned prostitution also has clandestine prostitutes. In addition to the 450 controlled prostitutes in Dusseldorf, there are approximately 3,200 other women plying the trade. West Berlin has 4,920 women whose activities are controlled and some 18,000 who are working on a free-lance basis. There are 1,000 clandestine prostitutes in Bremen and 500 women whose work is regulated.

PROSTITUTION AS SEX SERVICE

The most liberal school of thought holds that each person ought to be guided by his own conscience with respect to prostitution, and that there is no need for laws to regulate people whose actions harm only themselves. Harry Benjamin has suggested that prostitution can be approached impartially and objectively or morally condemned by the Judaeo-Christian ethic.[15] He deplores prostitution's being regarded as so horrendous.[16]

Benjamin and others have recommended that prostitution is an issue so emotionally charged in our society that it should be replaced by a phrase like "sex service." Those opposed to a moral view of prostitution suggest that its ability to survive in the face of all attempts to eliminate it would appear to make most efforts at suppression very unlikely to succeed. They also note that women may derive many advantages from prostitution. They may gain a nonsexual goal by selling sexual favors; economic rewards may be fairly high; the life may be adventurous; girls may discover a true romance in the course of their work; highly sexed prostitutes enjoy their vocation; some women can act out a neurotic impulse; others may be unable to hold regular employment; and working as a prostitute may permit achievement of a temporary goal.

Persons who oppose a moral viewpoint about prostitution also speak of its advantages for the male, including such factors as variety; relief for those who are unable to get a sexual partner on a more established basis; an opportunity to satisfy unusual sex requirements; a means for those who wish to avoid entangling obligations; and a chance for relaxation. Proponents of the nonmoral view recommend that the problem of prostitution be treated with scientific neglect. They note that it has often flourished in societies that are outwardly very ethical; they question whether private morals are proper concerns for public law. According to this viewpoint, prostitution is a moral offense which does not militate against the common good and should therefore not be part of the criminal law.[17]

Prostitution as sex service is also said to be "natural," although some opponents of the nonmoral approach have questioned its naturalness.[18] Other opponents have noted that prostitution is one of the few occupations in which mobility is almost always downward and is negatively correlated with age. Some medical authorities who oppose the nonmoral approach have said that prostitution itself is unnecessary because continence causes no harm in either men or women.[19]

Some recent studies of prostitution have urged that the reality of its existence be acknowledged and that certain practical steps be taken that accord with such a view. Such action might include guidance in effective contraception and anti-venereal-disease techniques for prostitutes, encouragement for their filing income tax returns and making social security payments toward a retirement income, and modifications in laws which prohibit the use of apartments and homes for prostitution.[20]

DIFFICULTIES OF A POINT OF VIEW

One of the problems of arriving at a point of view toward prostitution is that proponents of different approaches usually consider only their own conclusions seriously. They tend to give very short shrift to other approaches. As a result, discussions of the subject often are one-sided. It is, moreover, not easy to achieve a balanced approach to a subject which is so complex and emotionally freighted, and in which attitudes are so deep-rooted and difficult to change. Nonetheless, it seems clear that the stridently moralistic approach of the nineteenth century is completely inappropriate for our times. The many urgent and desperate problems of American society make it impossible any longer to regard prostitution as "*the* social evil."

On the other hand, prostitution *is* beyond doubt a social

evil because it uses up women in a very rough way. In a theoretically good society, where sexual fulfillment ought to be as possible as other kinds of personal satisfaction, no one would be a prostitute or a client. Examining the American experience as well as those of other countries may help us to promote a civilized and reasonable point of view.

PROSTITUTION IN THE ARTS AND MEDIA

The proliferation of books, plays, movies, and humor about prostitution since the end of World War II suggests that the subject has been assuming greater salience in America at the very time suppressive measures have been most extreme. Public attitudes toward the discussion of all sexual matters have become much more accepting, and books by Morris Ploscowe, Alfred C. Kinsey, and William H. Masters and Virginia Johnson have facilitated a more open scrutiny of sex behavior. Court vindication of the American publication of D. H. Lawrence's *Lady Chatterley's Lover* and Henry Miller's *Tropic of Cancer* and *Tropic of Capricorn* in the early 1960's was another indication of attitude change.[21] During the same period *Confidential* became the magazine with the largest newsstand circulation in history as a direct result of its articles on the sex life of the famous.[22] *Playboy* also reached a huge circulation, probably as a result of elaborate picture stories on "Playmates" who were shown in street clothes on one page and nude on the next page—allowing the reader mentally to strip the girls.

The recent "explosion" of sexual freedom has deep roots in literature and the arts. Our sharing of language with the British makes the portrait of the prostitute in English literature of special interest. One of the world's most famous prostitutes is Nell Gwyn, who may be the most popular woman in English history and has been the heroine of many plays. Nell was born in a brothel, the bastard child of a prostitute who drowned in a fish pond. It was said that if the pond had contained brandy instead of water, her mother would have drunk herself out of it. Nell, who began her career at the age of twelve and became the mother of a semi-royal duke, was celebrated for her cockney humor and unusual freedom of language. Perhaps the first famous British prostitute to publish her autobiography was Harriette Wilson, who entered the vocation at the age of fifteen in 1786 and whose clients included the Duke of Wellington and Beau Brummel. The substantial income from her autobiography was exceeded only by the money received from former clients who had paid to have their names *not* mentioned in her book.[23]

The prostitute's life has been a subject of fiction in England at least since *Fanny Hill* was first published in 1749 under the title *Memoirs of a Lady of Pleasure*. A New York court ruling in 1963 made it possible for the book to be sold openly to the American public instead of under the counter. The brothel in which Fanny Hill worked for several years was a relatively gracious place, frequented by discreet and tactful men. The madam was like an enlightened sorority housemother.

Woman as prostitute and degraded creature had a special fascination for Samuel Richardson, founder of the English novel in the eighteenth century. His Clarissa Harlowe is rejected by her family and works in a brothel before being driven to her death. Although many novelists after Richardson had treated prostitution, the first major American writer to write a novel about the subject encountered many problems of censorship. When Stephen Crane had finished *Maggie: A Girl of the Streets* in the 1890's, no publisher was willing to risk handling the book. The opposition to *Maggie* helped to make it a rallying point for the later representation of prostitution in literature.

In practically no fiction is the prostitute presented as having strong sexual interests, and she is frequently idealized. Prostitution may appeal to writers for the same reason that an unusual case appeals to a surgeon, as an opportunity to clarify general truths by studying an exacerbation of behavior. The novelist may also use the prostitute to comment on what he regards as an unhealthy society.

The consistent interest of the novelist in the prostitute has been exceeded by that of American dramatists. One analysis of the dozen best performances by Broadway actresses concluded that half involved prostitute roles such as Jeanne Eagels in *Rain* and Florence Reed as a madam in *The Shanghai Gesture*.[24] One reason for the popularity of such parts is that a "bad" woman is more likely than a "good" girl to figure in dramatic conflict, to have interesting and provocative lines, and to provide the kind of strong role that actresses covet. The famous actresses who played the roles have helped to strengthen the belief that prostitutes are thrilling and attractive. Producers as well as playwrights may be attracted by the established formula that bad girls make good box office.

Some of the leading American playwrights have created prostitute characters. Eugene O'Neill wrote about prostitutes in a number of plays, especially those dealing with the waterfront. Other dramatists who have dealt with prostitution are Zoe Akins (*The Varying Shore*, 1921), Sidney Howard (*Morals*, 1925), Robert Sherwood (*Waterloo Bridge*, 1930), Jack Kirkland and John Steinbeck (*Tortilla Flat*, 1938), Marc Blitzstein (*The Cradle Will Rock*, 1938), William Saroyan (*The Time of Your Life*, 1940), Tennessee Williams (*A Streetcar Named Desire*, 1947), and Arthur Miller (*Death of a Salesman*, 1949). Since the end of World War II, each Broadway season has had at least one play featuring prostitution.

Only during the war period of the 1940's was the subject of prostitution hard to find in American films, perhaps because of the contemporary interest in patriotic themes and a desire not to disturb American audiences whose sons were overseas. The last twenty years have seen the movies take a much greater interest in the subject, with the prostitute generally presented as an interesting person, sometimes bizarre and sometimes hard, but a woman with whom it is not difficult to identify.

Some impression of the changes in American attitudes toward prostitution can be inferred from the successive versions of the play and movie made from Somerset Maugham's short story, "Miss Thompson." The first dramatic version (*Rain*) provided a vehicle in 1922 for the exciting and vivid personality of Jeanne Eagels. The prostitute who tempts a minister had become a more mundane sinner in the 1932 movie version with Joan Crawford as a sympathetic Sadie Thompson. In contrast, Rita Hayworth was singing and dancing to "The Heat Is On" in the newly titled *Miss Sadie Thompson* (1953).

The film representation of the prostitute has been moving in the direction of greater daring and of making her work increasingly explicit. The police inspector who is a client of the prostitute in *Irma La Douce* (1964) could not have been tolerated fifteen years ago. Some of the charm and attractiveness with which prostitution is presented in many films could represent a lingering feeling of regret that the "good old days" of the brothel have disappeared.

Until World War II, prostitution was not only regarded as an important social evil but as an institution which was related, in popular stereotypes, to alcoholism, gambling, and disorderly premises.[25] The prostitute was less undesirable, perhaps, than such other "evils," but her activities were not condoned. Today the media adopt a much more accepting attitude toward prostitution.

The near universality of prostitution fantasies may be one reason for the subject's recurring popularity in the arts. Another reason may be that Americans often admire the grifter who thrives while violating the law. The film roles of W. C. Fields, the Kingfish in Amos 'n' Andy on radio, and Groucho Marx and Phil Silvers on television are rogues who have had enormous popularity.[26] P. T. Barnum, who regarded the American as a sucker, is still a leading American folk hero.

Celebrities may satisfy a variety of needs in their publics, including some of the less orthodox aspects of personality.[27] The prostitute in the popular arts has the additional appeal of lubricity. Her eminence in a pantheon that also includes confidence men ("Yellow Kid" Weil), gangsters (John Dillinger), murderers (Billy the Kid), and train robbers (Jesse James) should not be any more surprising than is the great appeal of singer Elvis Presley, whose fame may have originally stemmed more from his being regarded as a roisterer than from his vocal techniques. The prostitute may be perceived as a member of a similarly picaresque group and is romanticized *because* she is an outsider. She may also be seen as one of the last vestiges of individualism in American life.

Like the mass media, jokes represent a vehicle for the voicing of attitudes that may not otherwise be easily communicable. We could expect jokes to be especially sensitive indicators in the case of a subject like prostitution. A content analysis of orally communicated jokes suggests that prostitution is one of their most popular subjects.[28] And omissions in content are as significant as what the jokes contain. There are few jokes about the marital status of the client or about the status of the woman (for example, the difference between a call girl and a streetwalker). Very few stories deal with the importance of clients, "perversion," or sexual initiation. It is almost as if the creators and tellers of these jokes respond to the anonymity of the prostitute-client relationship and express the most neutral aspects of contact with prostitutes. Hardly any distinguishing trappings of the customers are mentioned, although one function of orally communicated jokes is to permit the expression of otherwise forbidden themes. The prostitute is usually the victim of the witticism and is sometimes a foxy creature who has hidden insights into the frailty of her customers.

The incidence of jokes about celebrities visiting prostitutes has risen substantially during the last decade. There is no way of knowing whether the increase is related to an actual expansion of prostitution or to other factors. Like the increase in mass-media preoccupation with prostitution, it may represent another aspect of our increasingly voyeuristic interests in sex.

Many American newspapers have followed the lead of the famous British journalist W. T. Stead, editor of the *Pall Mall Gazette*, who pioneered in the personal exposé approach to prostitution. In 1885, Stead was able to buy a thirteen-year-old girl for five pounds and place her in a boarding house. He then "sold" her to a brothel, after having a physician examine the girl in order to confirm her virginity, and took her to Paris, just to demonstrate that it could be done.[29]

Newspapers, jokes, and the arts and media have mirrored this country's changing approaches to prostitution, at the same time providing significant materials for an understanding of the life of the prostitute. The extreme paucity of field studies of the prostitute since the 1920's makes them, in many instances, the only available sources.

II. THE PROSTITUTE

The prostitute's occupation is more central to her way of life than is the work of most people. Sociologists know that a person tends to identify with the image he thinks others have of his work role. In studies of socio-economic status, more than four-fifths of variability can be explained in terms of the single dimension of occupation.[1]

Prostitution may differ from most occupations in the image of the prostitute's work that others have and in her own lack of emotional or psychic attachment to the work. There is probably little likelihood of the prostitute's relating emotionally to her work or client. The vocation differs from others in that the sales person rents herself. But it is similar to service occupations in that the prostitute has a service to sell.

As in many businesses, the prostitute does not choose her clientele with discrimination. Society considers such a practice promiscuous because of the nature of the service, though it is perfectly acceptable in ordinary business. Employees in many other fields do not have an emotional attachment to their work, and may be disaffected and continue in it. The onus attached to the prostitute for having no involvement with her clients is a function of society's expectations about the sexual relationship—that it should occur only within marriage.

By the very nature of the work, there are no formal criteria of what constitutes a poor or a good performance as a prostitute. Neither prostitute nor client is likely to discuss such matters very freely. The special qualities of the work make it difficult for the prostitute to have an orderly career and develop the kind of investment in long-term goals that we take for granted in other occupations.

In spite of its traditional designation as the "oldest profession," prostitution has usually been a trade and only occasionally a profession.[2] At one time the prostitute wore a special costume, like students and surgeons. Although the latter occupations have since achieved high status, the prostitute has not done so. She freed herself from the indignities of the ancient caste and the brothel's zoological conditions, but has not advanced her activities in the eyes of organized society. She did not improve her trade practices or add to its arts. George Bernard Shaw's suggestion that prostitutes form a union has never been adopted.

Empirically based generalizations about how prostitutes regard their work are difficult to make. One experienced observer has said, "Only one woman out of several thousand ever told me that she liked the work. They all said they wanted to leave and would like to do something else." When the observer saw the women months and even years later, they had a variety of rationalizations to explain why they continued their careers. Other prostitutes, however, express few misgivings about their work, saying, "I would do exactly the same thing if I had my life to live over. I have no regrets." Enough women have made such remarks to suggest that a self-selection is operating and leads to a reasonable balance between what these women expect and what they find in prostitution.

For such women, prostitution represents a better way of

life than has been or might otherwise be available to them, and they are relatively well adjusted to it. Others may find the work unpleasant and uncongenial. Whether their unhappiness is a reflection of their work, their personality structure, or of a combination of the two, varies from one woman to another. The possible intensity of the unhappiness is suggested by the famous folk song "Rising Sun Blues," said to have been sung by young prostitutes. It was given fresh popularity in a version by Libby Holman in the 1940's:

> *There is a house in New Orleans*
> *They call The Rising Sun*
> *It's been the ruin of many poor girls,*
> *And me, O Lord, for one.*
> *. . . One foot is on the platform,*
> *The other one on the train,*
> *I'm going back to New Orleans*
> *To wear that ball and chain.*

This song was composed when New Orleans was the prostitution capital of the South.

Even if the women do not dislike their work, they may not derive gratification from it. Many tell an interviewer that they "don't mind the work," but such a reply may mask a certain numbness. It is ironic that the French expression for prostitute is *fille de joie*, for joy would seem to be the least likely emotion for the prostitute to experience. American folk songs, which tend to mirror underlying attitudes, usually present prostitution as an unpleasant activity. In none of the songs is the prostitute presented as a passionate person, but rather as one who has listened to the wrong man and consequently drifted into "the life." The woman who has "dyed her petticoat red" is sick or dying or discouraging a younger sister from following her example.

The work of the prostitute can be as routine and as boring as that in any other occupation. One prostitute recently said: "Ever since I turned out, I have regarded the work as being a little more boring than the work I used to do when I was a file clerk. The customers look like each other, what we do with them is pretty much the same, and it doesn't bother me or even reach me. I may have been shocked or disturbed or hurt with the first couple of guys, and I seem to remember that I felt terrible about it, but I can barely recall those days, and now every day is like any other and the last guy is like the thousandth one to me." A wide range of relationships is likely between the prostitute and her client. It may be pleasant, or feelings of hostility can be expressed or masked by either party to the transaction.

Many younger prostitutes today do not work with the vigor of their predecessors. Some streetwalkers and brothel inmates of the 1920's and 1930's were busy around the clock. Part of the earlier motivation for long working hours was the prodding of pimps. Contemporary prostitutes may also have shorter working hours than their predecessors because they are more conspicuous at later hours than they might have been in the past, as a result of changes in patterns of law enforcement. Even today, however, many streetwalkers often average about twelve hours a day.

Central to any evaluation of how prostitutes feel about their work is their attitude toward sex. The devaluation of sex by many prostitutes is implicit in a remark made by a Chicago woman: "I feel rotten about the work I do. There is nothing else I can do, so I really feel that I have no skill that I can sell. I envy the gal who can do other work and also hustle on the side."

The low monetary value that is attributed to prostitutes' work is the basis of a story about a man who sent his wife out to work as a prostitute one evening. She returned the following morning with $7.10. He said, "I can understand the $7, but who gave you ten cents?" The woman replied, "Everybody did." The low esteem that such stories ascribe to prostitutes' sex may also affect the prostitutes' own traditional coldness toward customers. Many prostitutes are revolted if they are expected to respond. A prostitute engages in sexual activity with a number of men in the course of a day, so there is little time for her to develop an emotional response to each customer. Prostitutes often speak of "jiving" clients by simulating a response. The irritation that some prostitutes exhibit at clients' desire for affection can be seen in occasional complaints about clients who want to kiss and otherwise dawdle. As one put it, "Some of these fellows would like to diddle with my breasts all day."

One way for a prostitute to show her negative attitudes toward men is to engage in petty deceptions, like setting an alarm clock to go off before the agreed-upon time. Stealing from clients is another way of expressing hostility and was once so common that there were many "panel houses," in which each room had a second door. The door would blend with the wall and be quite invisible. While the prostitute and her client were on the bed, her accomplice would quietly use the second door to enter the room, take money from the client's trousers, and slip out. A client who complained was assured that he must have made a mistake, because the door had been locked.

Some prostitutes worked "the badger game." A woman would take a customer to her apartment or hotel, where both disrobed. Just about the time they began intercourse, there would be a knock on the door. It was the woman's "husband," who began denouncing them and produced a knife or gun. He made it clear that he was humiliated and disgusted enough to kill them both. The woman would cry and tell her customer, "He means what he says. My husband is insanely jealous. His weakness is money. If you give him money maybe he won't kill us." If the customer had no money, the prostitute might try to get him to give his ring or other jewelry to her "husband." Very few customers would object or later lodge a complaint with the police.

Some prostitutes have associates ("creepers") who do not need the second door of the panel house to tiptoe into the prostitute's room. The "creeper" quietly goes through the client's trousers and takes his money without the client knowing that anyone else is present. A "creep house" is a place to which men are taken by prostitutes to be robbed. A client approaching orgasm is usually so preoccupied that he is relatively uninterested in what is going on around him.

Some prostitutes who "roll" a client only take part of his money in order to minimize the client's resentfulness and keep the theft legally petty if it is reported to the police. A prostitute is more likely to steal from a client who is an unpleasant cheapskate than from one who shares her impersonal and businesslike manner.

SOME CLASSIFICATIONS

One method of classifying prostitutes is based on the degree of their public visibility; it has four categories.

1. *Flagrant.* The flagrant prostitute taps on a window with a nail file or ring, or calls loudly, or stands in a window or doorway, in order to attract the attention of potential customers. The less expensive houses in many cities obtained much of their patronage by such solicitations.

2. *Semi-flagrant.* The semi-flagrant prostitute does not engage in window-tapping or calling. But she is readily available as soon as a customer contacts her in a bar or on the street or knocks on the door. She makes no attempt to conceal her vocation.

3. *Semi-clandestine.* The semi-clandestine prostitute gives no overt evidence of her vocation and insists on some kind of identification from the client. The prospective customer's appearance plays a large part in determining whether the woman will recognize him.

4. *Clandestine.* The clandestine prostitute, such as the call girl, is very cautious about admitting her identity and may require proof of the client's identification. She may ask him to show his driver's license or actually check at the hotel where he says he is staying.

On the question of visibility, some prostitutes prefer the anonymity of the established setting of the brothel. The brothel prostitute can walk almost anywhere without fear of being recognized. The call girl, who has a selected clientele, is less visible and generally feels free to socialize in almost any context. The streetwalker is relatively overt but can pretend she is just taking a walk. The bar girl must solicit fairly aggressively in order to make it clear that she is a prostitute rather than a pickup.

Another method of classifying prostitutes is by the personal satisfactions afforded by the different locales of their work. Some prostitutes prefer to work in brothels because they enjoy respectability when they are not on the premises. The call girl can believe that she is known only to her customers and can thus feel relatively free to mingle in other circles. The streetwalker is looked down upon by the brothel prostitute and the call girl. Prostitutes who work in hotels often look down on streetwalkers and bar girls who flaunt their profession.

Mobility in prostitution is usually downward. When brothels in some communities close, prostitutes often invade hotels and become resident hustlers or call girls. Former brothel prostitutes also often resort to bars and streets in an effort to acquire customers. But finally the conventional criteria of occupational status may be meaningless to many prostitutes. Thus a woman who works as a call girl appears to enjoy high status but must seek out clients and is more subject to police harassment than the brothel prostitute.

BEAUTY, SOCIAL GRACES, AND AGE

Contrary to the way they are usually represented in mass media, prostitutes tend to be physically unattractive, and some have fairly flagrant defects. Her appearance may be a factor in the woman's desire to enter "the life." There is no way in which a prostitute can be unmistakably recognized by appearance. Although many prostitutes bleached their hair during the 1930's, tinting hair is so popular today that it has lost its distinction as a mark of identification. In the 1940's some prostitutes dyed a few front strands of their hair blonde, but such "streaking" was also later adopted by fashionable women. The wearing of colored stockings was another way a prostitute called attention to her vocation, but it, too, began to receive general acceptance from other American women around 1957. Many aspects of female dress are now so free that the prostitute has hardly been able to retain any distinguishing features of clothing or appearance.

Prostitutes in large cities have traditionally been better dressed and more attractive than those in smaller communities. Probably clients in big cities are more demanding about standards of appearance. Competition among prostitutes may be greater in urban centers. When a prostitute in a large city has to leave it because of police action or other reasons, she generally goes to another large city.

Over the last three decades, many prostitutes apprehended by the police tend to be overweight and short. They often have poor teeth, minor blemishes, untidy hair, and are otherwise careless about their personal appearance. Docility and indifference are common. This leads one to conclude that such women may feel inadequate to compete in more traditional activities and thus more readily accept a vocation that involves the sale of something they may not value highly.

Today's prostitutes may have more social graces than their predecessors, but even markedly unattractive women can still make a living at the vocation. One madam says, "Customers used to be choosy in the old days; now there's more tripe around, and some of them are getting $25 where some of our girls got a dollar." Another madam observes, "The girls nowadays aren't as good as the old ones. They don't know what real hustling is, especially with so much money around."

Some prostitutes may be exceptionally naive, in spite of the wisdom with which they are often imbued by mass media. An example of such naiveté was provided by a Springfield, Illinois, brothel prostitute who complained to the police that she had earned $50 but only received $25 from the madam. The girl was so inexperienced that she did not realize a brothel prostitute was expected to turn half her earnings back to the madam, and naive enough to assume that the police could adjudicate her complaint. This case received so much newspaper publicity that it led to the closing of the Springfield brothels.

How old are prostitutes? The median age of working prostitutes is probably somewhere between twenty-five and forty. One suggestive source of data is the age of women arrested for prostitution, as recorded by the FBI Uniform Crime Reports. Averaging figures cited in the Reports in the last several years, the proportion of women arrested in each age bracket is:

Under 21:	16 per cent
22–29:	53 per cent
30–39:	19 per cent
40–49:	7 per cent
50–59:	3 per cent
Over 60:	2 per cent

We do not, of course, know the extent to which these age trends reflect the ages of prostitutes who are not arrested.

A number of prostitutes who began in their teens are still working at sixty or seventy. Prostitutes who specialize in sadism or masochism are likely to be older than others, perhaps because with age they realize that such services yield more money, or because "straight" customers become more difficult to find.

SOME STEREOTYPES

The arts have presented prostitutes in various ways, and some representations have become stereotypes. Many readers, both in America and abroad, were introduced to the prostitute as an intense seeker for redemption who figured prominently in the work of Tolstoy (*Resurrection*) and Dostoevsky (*Crime and Punishment*). A popular fantasy about redemption is presented in Anatole France's *Thais*, in which a sinning prostitute ultimately becomes a saint, and a saint who has sinned loses his original role in the process of redeeming her.

In the film *A Walk on the Wild Side* (1962), which is a substantial rewriting of the novel by Nelson Algren, an extremely naive young man searches for his lost beloved for three years before finding her in a New Orleans brothel.[3] With the help of another prostitute who has a heart of gold, he finally takes her away and redeems her. Redemption is also the theme of earlier films like *Resurrection* (1931)—based on the Tolstoy novel—in which a pregnant woman ultimately saves the aristocrat who seduced her. Both find salvation in pity and an understanding of each other in this film. The theme's appeal for Hollywood can be seen in the film's five different versions, beginning with D. W. Griffith's in 1909.

Perhaps the first major network television presentation of prostitution on a nondocumentary program was made in 1963, when a prostitute was the heroine of the initial program of the "East Side, West Side" series. It dealt with an attractive, intelligent, sensitive, and appealing prostitute who had been driven to her vocation when her husband deserted her. She was a superb mother, even though scorned by her neighbors. At the end of the drama, her child is taken away by a social agency because she is a prostitute. This program succeeded in including almost every cliché about a prostitute that had ever appeared in the arts.

Movies have often reflected the male fantasy about rehabilitating the prostitute. *The World of Suzie Wong* was a book and a play (1958) before it became a movie (1960), all of which were financially successful.[4] It is the story of a good-hearted Hong Kong prostitute who meets an attractive American man who is curious about her way of life and tries to reform her. Another American man who wants to rehabilitate a prostitute is the hero of *Never on Sunday* (1961). Its heroine is an amiable Piraeus prostitute who refuses to join the group of prostitutes working for a local vice lord.

An American decides to rehabilitate her. She falls in love with him but learns that he was paid by the vice lord to reform her so that she would stop competing with the syndicate prostitutes. She and the other prostitutes go to jail, but are finally liberated and continue their work. The American leaves, presumably a wiser man.

Television has also dealt with the rehabilitation of the prostitute. In February 1964, on "The Eleventh Hour" dramatic series on the National Broadcasting Company network, a program dealt with a fifteen-year-old girl who has been led into prostitution by her mother. A court-appointed psychiatrist arranges for the daughter's placement with a foster family. The overall emphasis of the story is on the possibilities of rehabilitation as well as on the psychological difficulties the girl encounters before she is able to function in a new environment.

One kind of prostitute that has become familiar in literature is the genteel and charming woman presented in the play *I Am a Camera* (1955), made from Christopher Isherwood's *Berlin Stories*. Sally lives by her wits in pre-Hitler Berlin and makes her living by accepting money from a number of men. Less familiar but also popular is the woman who functions successfully in another profession, as a psychologist, for example, but is primarily a prostitute.[5] A prostitute who is not even promiscuous is the heroine of the play *The Owl and the Pussycat* (1964). She is an ideal example of the "good-bad girl" who figures in much American dramatic and other literature. The theatergoer can experience all the pleasures of watching the prostitute on stage but balance his enjoyment by the realization that she is actually highly moral. The heroine of *The Owl and the Pussycat* claimed to be a high-fashion model who "took a few tricks on the side." She fell in love with her customer—another popular fantasy.

The prostitute's attractiveness for playwrights could be seen especially graphically during the 1961 New York theater season, when five different plays offered a wide range of types and actresses, each playing a prostitute. Tall and vigorous

Salome Jens dressed like a horse to please a client in *The Balcony;* unsullied gamin Elizabeth Seal was *Irma La Douce;* Avis Bunnage played a bizarre figure in *The Hostage;* Angela Lansbury was a raffish and brazen charmer in *A Taste of Honey;* the brassy but good-hearted prostitute was represented by Eileen Rogers in *Tenderloin.*

Probably the most popular type of the prostitute in literature is represented by Donna Reed's Academy Award role in the movie *From Here to Eternity* (1953), made from the novel by James Jones.[6] She works in a Honolulu brothel but favors one soldier (Montgomery Clift). Miss Reed plays an earth goddess whose warmth and decency show her to be more of a woman than the ostensibly more respectable females in the film.

Jokes about prostitutes, like other humor, mirror truths about our society and reflect something of the quality of the prostitute subculture. The prostitute is seen as being antipodally ignorant or shrewd, ruthless or generous, evil or good, cruel or kind, bored enough to read a comic book in the midst of intercourse or ravenously passionate. Part of the appeal of so many jokes about prostitutes is that their characters are unidimensional and exaggerated, like the heroes of fairy tales, each one of whom also is the embodiment of a hyperbolic dimension. Jokes about prostitution are seldom told either by prostitutes or madams, who are also not about to laugh at such jokes. Their work is not a subject of amusement to them. Many stories express the hostile side of community ambivalence about prostitution.

Domestication of the prostitute may have been advanced considerably by the film *Kiss Me, Stupid* (1965), which deals with an amateur songwriter who hires a prostitute as a substitute for his wife in order to expedite selling his music to a celebrity. The songwriter succeeds in selling his songs and the prostitute gets a new car, suggesting that lack of virtue is more than its own reward.

The arts have portrayed the prostitute in many different lights—as a person to be redeemed, a source of salvation, a sweet and generous person, a sophisticated woman, an earth goddess, and an asexual neurotic. The nature of the prostitute's representation in the arts has reflected such factors as the availability of prostitution, the prevailing morality, the status of women, and similar dimensions which vary from one place and time to another. The preoccupation of the artist and his audience with the prostitute suggests that the need to fantasize about her is strong and continuing.

BACKGROUND

Previous studies reveal little about the backgrounds from which prostitutes come, and there are no recent data. More than two-thirds (71 per cent) of an early sample of 302 brothel prostitutes regarded their parents as adequate providers.[7] Farming constituted the largest single category of fathers' occupation (12 per cent). Carpenters, saloon proprietors, tailors, and barbers were also represented. Italy and Russia were frequently found to be the father's country of origin, along with France, Germany, and Ireland. Such findings must be interpreted cautiously today.

Few prostitutes are well educated, in spite of all the jokes about college graduates working in the field. ("How did a college girl like you end up in a place like this?" "Just lucky, I guess.") Some intermediaries claim they can provide a college graduate, but few actually do. Almost half the 302 brothel prostitutes interviewed had reached the sixth grade in elementary school, and approximately one-sixth had achieved the first year of high school. In the 1930's almost 60 per cent of a sample of prostitutes had had an elementary education. Only one out of a hundred prostitutes interviewed in 1942 had finished high school.[8] More successful prostitutes may share approximately the same educational background as the middle class, and less successful ones may have educations comparable to their socio-economic counterparts in the general population.

There is some evidence that the prostitute's intelligence is not below normal. One study of 147 girls concluded that poor home conditions were more positively correlated with prostitution than was intelligence or feeblemindedness. But contrary results emerged in another early study of prostitutes in a reformatory, 49 per cent of whom were mentally defective, while 16.5 per cent had dull normal intelligence. Other studies have reported the proportion of prostitutes with subnormal intelligence to range from 35 per cent to 53 per cent. One autobiographical account links prostitution with a generalized intellectual deterioration.[9]

The only systematic information on the religious background of prostitutes goes back over half a century. Of prostitutes in a New York State reformatory, 41.1 per cent were Catholic, 38.9 per cent Protestant, and 19 per cent Jewish. Of prostitutes in Philadelphia institutions, the largest number were Catholics, with Protestants next most heavily represented.[10] More recent data suggest that some prostitutes are fairly consistent in their attendance at religious services.

The work done by the woman before she became a prostitute tends to be fairly unskilled—domestic service, waitress, and so forth. The sectors of the entertainment industry which produce some prostitutes involve little status. Inadequate income is common in the immediate previous work background of prostitutes.[11]

One early study concluded that two-thirds of the prostitutes in a Philadelphia reformatory had unfavorable family lives as children, and more than half had lost at least one parent through death. One-fourth of adolescent prostitutes in a reformatory had relatives with tuberculosis. (There appears to be a considerable incidence of tuberculosis among prostitutes, even in recent years.) In France prostitutes seem to come from homes with a history of alcoholism and paternal instability. Approximately one-third of French prostitutes in detention had mental, emotional, or physical abnormalities and were in the lower socio-economic groups. One study of French prostitutes concluded that most were mentally subnormal, came from a bad home situation, and had friends who were relatively unwholesome. Prostitutes in India also seem to come from poor families.[12]

Many prostitutes refer to their mothers as having been very strict and complain that they never shared the freedom of other girls. If their friends could stay out until ten at night, their mothers usually required them to be back by nine or an earlier hour. Other prostitutes have gone to a strict religious school.

Ordinal position and size of family may be related to a girl's becoming a prostitute. A girl in a large family may be forced out by want or receive inadequate attention.[13] On the other hand, an only daughter may be pampered and have difficulty in deferring gratifications. If the mother is often away from home and her daughter associates with persons connected with prostitution, such association may be related to entering the vocation.

Indicators of disease such as alcoholism in prostitutes and their parents are found more frequently in earlier studies than in more recent investigations. There are no data to confirm that prostitutes of today have more disturbed personalities or backgrounds than nonprostitutes. The high proportion of pathological characteristics in earlier prostitutes may be a function of the lower level of education at that time, the measuring devices used, and the samples studied.

It is unlikely that there is only one cause for a woman's becoming a prostitute. We might expect it to be a decision based on growing up in a subculture or in a particular family situation, and on how the woman herself perceives both. The likelihood is that the decision to become a prostitute is based on many factors, and that different factors affect different women.[14]

Many of the previous vocations reported by prostitutes were solitary. Perhaps there was a self-selection of the solitary occupation, as a reflection of underlying tendencies that later showed up in the choice of prostitution. Occupations like domestic work and waitress require the woman to work by herself and often place her in contact with men, but it is hardly likely that women enter restaurant work or domestic service for their sexual opportunities. More probably, a very small minority of the women who drift into such work later drift into prostitution.

One weakness of most studies of the earlier life of the prostitute is that they are retrospective and based on recollection. The prostitute may give answers which she thinks are wanted by the investigator. The more verbal respondents to such studies may also be overrepresented. Many prostitutes do not answer questions, even in the earlier studies. Other reasons for the inadequacy of data include the defenses of the women, a lack of facilities for verifying case information, and the poor record-keeping practices of agencies dealing with prostitutes. Very few studies have attempted independent confirmation of interview data. The prostitute's work may also create problems that were not significant in determining her selection of occupation, and some researchers have confused such problems with her original motivation.

Rather than concentrating on the problems of the prostitute, or the key episodes which led to her vocational choice, or the propensity of some women to respond to specific opportunities, it may be more useful to view entrance into prostitution as a process of interaction, with each stage contingent on the result of a previous stage. It is likely that the career sequence involves three contingencies: (1) a tendency toward sexual promiscuity, (2) limited opportunities which include prostitution as one work option, and (3) recognition of the money to be earned by prostitution.[15]

THE SUBCULTURE

Working as a prostitute involves membership in a special subculture with its own values. Perhaps as a way of maximizing the in-group implications of the career, a prostitute is frequently called "a working girl" by her associates. She has a job, just like other people. Many prostitutes believe they are honest and that the rest of the world is corrupt. They often rationalize their own reversal of traditional social values by regarding most "square" human relationships as a "con," while the honest prostitute eschews hypocrisy. Such feelings are understandable in as much as the prostitute daily sees men in circumstances which violate the norms of their society. Different standards of enforcement of the prostitution laws may reinforce the woman's cynicism about social relationships. For many prostitutes it is relatively easy to identify with the contraculture of the criminal world.

There have been some changes in the ethnic backgrounds of women who become prostitutes. From World War I through the 1930's many prostitutes were immigrants from Eastern Europe, France, and Italy. In the 1940's there was an increase in the proportion of Negro prostitutes, especially in Chicago, Detroit, Los Angeles, Pittsburgh, San Francisco, and Washington, D.C. From the 1950's to the present there has been a major influx of Puerto Rican prostitutes in Chicago, New York, and Philadelphia. Many tend to be actively religious and have paintings of a patron saint, a crucifix, and other religious symbols in their rooms. (Mexican prostitutes in American border communities, similarly, often have a picture of the patron saint of Guadalupe on the wall.)

The Negro prostitute usually seeks white customers, except for some who cater to Negro soldiers. Typical of such military specialization was the monthly migration of Negro prostitutes to Junction City, from Kansas City, around payday, in order to accommodate the many Negro soldiers stationed at Fort Riley. Negro women represent a substantial proportion of arrested prostitutes, perhaps because they operate in a conspicuous manner. There may, of course, be police selectivity in making arrests. Any figures on the incidence of Negro prostitution can only be understood in the light of relatively high Negro rates for other violations of the law as compared with whites. In a typical recent year, approximately one-third of the total arrests in the United

States were of Negroes, although they represent only 11 per cent of the population. Even a generation ago, Negro women accounted for more than half the prostitution arrests in New York City. More recently, the rate at which Negro women in New York are arrested for prostitution has been ten times the white rate. Of another sample of Negro women in prison, 56 per cent had been convicted of prostitution, in contrast to 21 per cent of the white inmates.[16]

Some Negro prostitutes used to apply makeup in order to look white. A Cleveland pimp recently commented, "I remember when all of the Negro girls used to whiten their faces and look out of the windows to see if they could fool their customers." The women would use whiteface makeup on the assumption that a man who walked into a brothel would not leave even after he had discovered the deception. They would cope with any reluctance on the customer's part by energetically fondling and otherwise stimulating him. Deception of the customer in other ways is fairly frequent, and "to turn a trick" may have developed its currency as a phrase because the prostitute regards sexual intercourse with a customer as a kind of hoax.

The Negro's marginal status, so similar to that of the immigrant, may be a factor in the Negro role in prostitution. As recently as the 1930's there seemed to be more white than Negro prostitutes in our large cities, but the ratio has been reversed over the last thirty years. Most Negro prostitutes have been economically deprived, recalling William W. Sanger's finding, over a century ago, that "destitution" was the single most important reason for prostitutes' having entered "the life."[17]

On the subject of a subculture's special language, the argot of prostitutes was limited even when most worked in brothels and their opportunities for developing an in-group language were relatively good. Some of the argot today has a curiously old-fashioned quality: "my old man" is a pimp; to "sit for company" is to wait for a client to appear; the "professor" is the house musician in a brothel. A prostitute who steals from her clients is called a "mush worker"; a "lush worker" specializes in clients who are drunk.

One reason for the relatively limited argot of the prostitute is that the trade lacks group solidarity. The prostitute has little feeling of pride in work, few incentives to classify customers, little opportunity to advance up the ladder of her profession. Such characteristics are usually found in criminal groups that have developed an argot.[18] The prostitute's current activity on a relatively individualized basis further decreases the likelihood of expansion of any private language.

It is relatively rare for a prostitute to refer to herself as a "prostitute," although she may use the term to refer to another woman in a disparaging sense. She generally talks about herself as a "hustler," which has also become a generic term for an illegal way of making a livelihood. Ever since the Civil War, "hooker" has been a synonym for prostitute. The name derives from the camp followers of General Joseph Hooker's division at a time when troops were quartered on Pennsylvania Avenue in Washington. Historians have commented on the irony that many Americans only hear of "Fighting Joe" Hooker in terms of his completely accidental connection with prostitution.[19] "Hustler" began replacing "hooker" around 1940, although the latter term is still used. On the West Coast a prostitute was often called a "puella." In some Southern states prostitutes were called "strumpets," but similar literary designations ("trull," "bawd," "harlot") are rare. "Biffer," "prossie," "she-she," "pig-meat" are some other slang designations. Fat prostitutes are often called "blimps."

The words used by the prostitute to describe her services are often ambiguous: "How about a date?" "Would you like to have a good time?" "Let's have a party," or "What about some fun?" From World War I through the mid-1930's she might ask, "How about some jazz?" "Date" is probably the most popular euphemism today. Prostitutes call their clients "johns," "suckers," or "trade." "Sucker" seems to derive from the woman's feeling that anyone who spends money on what she sells is "out of his mind." Some prostitutes say they would continue "hustling" even if they could earn the same money in another occupation because anyone who works legitimately is a "sucker."

The names that prostitutes assume have not changed very much over the years, except that colorful names like Bird-Leg Ruth are less common. Many women assume a new name and seem to feel that as long as they are making up a name, it ought to be somehow fancy. Several popular names taken up by prostitutes are sexually undifferentiated: Jackie, Billie, Jerry, Jo, and Willy. Frequent names in the South include Beulah and Joann. Elsewhere favored names include Marie, Sally, May, Margie, Olga, Peggy, and Bertha. Some women are reluctant to give a customer their full name, even an assumed one, and counter with some phrase like "What's in a name?"

Few names are modeled after movie stars, but many are related to the color of their wearer's hair. "Everybody calls me Blondie." "I'm Red." Some women have several different names, and occasionally are confused over which one they are currently using. One recently identified herself: "My name is Mary, no! it's Jackie. Jackie is my name. I don't know why I said Mary." Some tell a customer they have a "real" name *and* another one: "My real name is Mary Jo, but I am called Josie." Others will make it clear they are giving a false name: ". . . My name is Johnnie. That's not my real name."

In money matters, the traditional generosity of prostitutes is personified in what New York's Mayor William J. Gaynor told the Rev. William Parkhurst of the Committee of Fifteen: "You want me to close the brothels, and if I close the brothels the girls will move into your own apartment houses where they will become the most desirable tenants since they will give the janitor a dollar a day where you give him only a quarter at Christmas." Such generous tipping is one reason for prostitutes' difficulties in saving money. They also lack foresight and are frequently overcharged. Prostitutes in large cities have been observed to be especially kind to beggars, hoboes, and other unfortunates. By giving them a substantial tip, the prostitute may express her superiority while hoping to stave off any such fate for herself.

The prostitute's generosity may be one reason for the "heart of gold" legend. On another level, her generosity may be an expression of guilt and penance via good works. Generosity may also permit an expression of tenderness which has few other outlets. Another manifestation of tenderness is the frequency with which prostitutes own a dog, cat, or bird, perhaps because they feel that with a pet they can have a genuine relationship.

Competition within the trade can often be brutal. Sometimes a prostitute may disparage a colleague to a customer or potential customer: "That old whore is a 'hard leg'—she's got a million miles on her." She may even say that "She is burned up" (has venereal disease). Such a comment is especially likely to occur in a bar: "I saw you talking to ———. Lay off her, she's burned up." The warning may be made because its subject actually has venereal disease, or because one prostitute has had a quarrel with another. Sometimes a prostitute will praise her own services in terms of price: ". . . I don't believe in overcharging my customers like that girl over there . . ." Such remarks suggest that a prostitute's relationships with her colleagues often involve hostility.

Like other subcultures, prostitutes have their own peculiar folklore. Prostitute folklore has, for example, dealt with the relative attractiveness of legs. A number of madams and prostitutes have been known to spend large sums on expensive stockings, on the assumption that men are more interested in legs than faces. One madam noted: "Girls don't walk on their faces, and when a man follows you he is stalking legs." Folklore has also included stories about situations in which the prostitute wins out over conventional society. One episode that is discussed to this day occurred during the hurricane of 1938 in Albany, Georgia, where the red-light district was called Ragsdale and its leading madam was a highly respected citizen. The hurricane destroyed the community's church, firehouse, school, and every other important public building, but Ragsdale was completely undamaged. Discussion of this incident in prostitution circles was usually associated with the comment, "Virtue is its own reward."

One superstition of many prostitutes is that using one's real name will bring bad luck. Another superstition is that a cat should not be allowed to remain in a brothel because it may bring trouble. Sprinkling powder or placing urine on the sidewalk in front of the house, and readjusting the position of the wall mirror are both believed to be ways of attracting customers, according to prostitute folklore. Bad luck for the rest of the evening is said to await a prostitute whose first potential client does not want her. Bad luck is also supposed to befall a prostitute who does not get a coin from every visitor, even one who does not engage in sexual relations. Any coin will do, but not a bill. The woman who does not spit out the sperm after fellatio, it is said, will get bad teeth or rot her stomach. Such occupational folklore varies from region to region.[20]

Mobility patterns among prostitutes have changed over the years. Except for their travel to convention sites and military communities around payday, prostitutes before World War II were more likely to remain in one community than they are today. The brothel prostitute had less motivation to travel than the contemporary entrepreneur who is alert to such specialized work opportunities as a convention. Women who are ambitious enough to go to another community may have a higher motivation for making money than colleagues who remain in one place. Few prostitutes "hustle" in their home towns.

OTHER WORK EXPERIENCE

There is much folklore in society at large about the previous vocations of prostitutes. One popular joke deals with a man who went to a brothel where the madam explained, "We have girls who have done all kinds of work before entering 'the life.'" She took him to one floor and said, "These girls were all telephone operators." One of the inmates said, "I really would like to show you a good time. I allow three minutes." The women on the next floor were all identified as former stenographers. One greeted him, "I'll give you what you want, but we'll have to shortarm you before we can shorthand." The client was not interested, so the madam took him to another floor with former schoolteachers. One said to him, "I would like to be with you, and we are going to take as much time as we need until you get it just right." The customer decided to stay with her.

When prostitutes are apprehended, many identify themselves as actresses or models. Such identifications are seldom accurate, though there are undoubtedly aspiring actresses who come to Hollywood and New York and later drift into prostitution. Some women may drift into full-time prostitution as the result of part-time work at conventions and similar meetings. They may have begun by doing clerical or hostess work for a company or groups connected with the convention.

Other part-time prostitutes have a wide variety of occupations: ". . . I'm a telephone operator. I usually come in here after 11 P.M. when I finish working." ". . . I'm a stripper. My boss said I should take a rest, that's why I'm up in this hotel for two weeks." ". . . I ride horses in a rodeo during the summer in Arkansas and Oklahoma. I have two horses of my own. In the winter time, I just take it easy and do what I'm doing now. It helps to pay my expenses when I'm not in the rodeo." ". . . I work for an insurance firm. You can call me where I work." ". . . I don't make a living this way. I came here to dance and look for a husband. I want to get married."

Such women are semi-professional prostitutes; they have other jobs and an infrequent number of contacts, often on evenings and weekends. How meaningless the distinction between full- and part-time prostitution can be is epitomized in one apocryphal story attributed to George Bernard Shaw. He asked a titled English lady, "Madam, would you go to bed with me for a million pounds?" The lady was taken aback, but said, "Well, for that kind of money, yes." Shaw continued, "Well, would you go to bed with me for two pounds?" The lady answered, "Heavens! What do you think I am?" Shaw answered, "We have already established what you are, Madam; we are now merely trying to establish the price."

PREVIOUS ACTIVITIES

The customer's traditional interest in how the prostitute enters her vocation has a parallel in the concern of many students of prostitution. Many of the studies of prostitution conducted after World War I, and even through the 1930's, however, must be interpreted very cautiously today. Changes in social conditions and the near disappearance of white slavery and procurement suggest that a woman who becomes a prostitute today does so more or less voluntarily.

Likely, the decision to enter the vocation is not made quickly; but women who become prostitutes probably have not been satisfied with the way things are going for them. The dissatisfaction may have many different causes. One may be a distaste for discipline. Some girls move toward prostitution because they believe they are ugly and that nobody wants them. Others seek to meet men whom they would otherwise never know, and some enjoy the opportunity for sleeping with a wide variety of men.

One avenue to prostitution may be a lack of training in the normative sexual behavior of our society. Women who grow up in a subculture in which sex only within marriage is not a visible goal, and without a conventional mother figure with whom to identify, may not regard prostitution as degrading.

In some cases there may be no immediate discernible reason for the woman's entering into prostitution. The prostitute's career choice may be the end result of a long process of personal and social disorganization and a feeling that she does not belong anywhere; but the very selection of prostitution may help to make her feel that she is needed by someone. Although this is probably a major appeal of the pimp for the prostitute, clients' continuing need may reinforce her feeling of being wanted. Ironically, the prostitute may achieve a social identity from a vocational choice made because she lacked such identity.

Peer groups often play a major role in familiarizing a woman with prostitution. Women who have difficulty in functioning in the ordinary labor market may become prostitutes as one result of association with women in "the life." They may try some "dates" for pay, gradually get used to the idea, and then become a full-time worker. To the extent that association with other prostitutes is used as a major reason for entrance into the field, it resembles criminologist Edwin H. Sutherland's theory of "differential association," which seeks to explain how a person comes to engage in criminal behavior as a result of learning to value such behavior favorably through his associations with others.

A prostitute who observes an amateur ("chippie") may point out that she could be earning money instead of "giving it away": "Ruth gave away $1,000,000 worth before I showed her she could sell it." An older prostitute often instructs a beginner in how to handle a customer, how and when to ask for money, how much time to give him, all about "perversions," and precautions against venereal disease. One woman observed: "When I found out that I was sitting on a gold mine, I decided to use it instead of being pushed around in a crummy job where you don't get any kind of decent money. By the time I was eighteen, if I still had a cherry it would have been punched back so far I could use it for a tail light. And I had nothing to show for it. I can make some real money hustling, and I enjoy turning a man on more than he's been turned on before. I buy nice clothes, live well, and I take good care of myself. Every guy isn't a great lay, but who cares? When I get a live one I remind myself that I would have put out for him for nothing not too many years ago. It's a good deal for the guy and it's a good deal for me. People lie to each other and use each other all over the country, every day. At least what I do is honest and it doesn't harm anyone."

In recent years the emergence of the emancipated "swinger," who participates in relations with a number of men or in group sexual activity has created a new source of part- or full-time prostitutes. One twenty-three-year-old Dallas woman noted: "I used to go to orgies at the home of a friend because I enjoyed them. I found out that my friend was charging men admission to the parties, and I told her I wanted to be paid. I keep my regular job in an office but take a few dates for pay each week. At some orgies there are girls who are there for fun and others who are strictly in it for the money. Because there is so much more group balling around, the johns seem to ask for a group scene more than they used to."

Women who are in contact with the trappings of luxury but who must live without them may sometimes be attracted to prostitution. Those women whose work involves beauty and physical appearance, such as some models and beauticians, could be sensitized to the rewards of an attractive appearance and alert to the possibility of selling their physical attractiveness through prostitution. The heroine of Shaw's *Mrs. Warren's Profession* asked, "Do you think we were such fools as to let other people trade in our good looks by employing us as shopgirls, or barmaids, or waitresses, when we could trade in them ourselves and get all the profits instead of starvation wages? Not likely." Even today, women often cite lack of funds as a reason for having entered prostitution: "A girl can have a lot of problems, so I 'date.' I just started doing this two months ago. . . . I have a lot of problems and need extra money. . . ."

The change in prostitution resulting from new social roles can be seen by comparing women today with their ancestors. A half-century ago a substantial number of American women might expect to become prostitutes if they did not seem likely to marry, whether for social, religious, or other reasons. Today it is taken for granted that an unmarried woman can lead a satisfying life. Prostitution is no longer regarded as a viable alternative to marriage.

The classical study by Abraham Flexner suggested that the insecurity and poor pay of their previous work led many women to prostitution. Some had drifted into "the life" when regular work was not available. Fifty years ago standards of minimum wages and job security were considerably lower, and a very large population of women who had migrated from other countries were not living with their families. The large-scale move from the farm to the city and the depersonalizing process of urban living also contributed to a potential prostitute's accessibility to offers from procurers. In an urban society an isolated girl may be readier to accept prostitution as a pattern of behavior.[21]

Prostitution can also be viewed as a career choice that enables some women to solve a number of life's problems. The women lose social status, but their work probably saves some from other forms of anti-social behavior. Lack of access to society's conventional opportunities may facilitate the movement of some women toward prostitution. Through it, some women who do not have power in our society may use their sex to achieve some of their goals.

In America today a number of girls who leave home at sixteen and seventeen drift into prostitution shortly thereafter. This is typically the age at which young people move toward drug addiction and other forms of delinquent behavior.[22] It is an age at which society's demands for decisions in vocational choice and marriage are likely to be pressing. The young woman who faces these decisions by electing to become a prostitute is, to some extent, avoiding them.

Films have frequently presented the prostitute as a woman who enters the vocation because of unfortunate early experience with men. In *Susan Lennox* (1931), Greta Garbo plays a hard-working girl driven out of her home by an unpleasant father. She is abandoned by a young man (Clark Gable), becomes a kept woman and ultimately a prostitute. Lorelei Lee, in *Gentlemen Prefer Blondes* (1953), a film based on Anita Loos's famous novel, is an example of a charming prostitute who has been "done wrong" by a man in Little Rock before learning that "diamonds are a girl's best friend." The novel *Elmer Gantry* was made into a film (1960) in which Shirley Jones won an Academy Award for her portrayal of a girl who is deflowered by Reverend Gantry in a church and subsequently leaves home to become a prostitute.[23] Another woman who became a successful prostitute after being wronged is the beautiful rose fancier and poet heroine of the film *Sylvia* (1965). Raped by her stepfather, she was also the victim of two different ministers.

The decision to enter the vocation as one over which the woman has little control is a theme that crops up again and again in films. Helen Hayes plays a "good girl" who becomes a "party girl" and then a streetwalker in *The Sin of Madelon Claudet* (1931). The "sin" of her vocation is a decision beyond her control. Greta Garbo in *Anna Christie* (1931) is a barge captain's daughter who inevitably moves toward a career as a prostitute. Another film which suggests that a woman enters "the life" as a result of vast impersonal social trends is Jean-Luc Godard's *My Life to Live* (1963). The heroine Nana, like Zola's heroine also a victim of blind forces, is finally murdered in a fight between two groups of pimps.

In Europe many women each year drop out of sight and are believed to have entered into some aspect of prostitution, not necessarily in the country in which they disappeared. In Paris alone approximately eight thousand women disappear each year and cannot be found. Many such women are believed by French authorities to have been forced into prostitution. But it is unlikely that any substantial number of American women still enter "the life" in such an involuntary way. Very few, if indeed any, madams solicit girls to enter prostitution. Although organized rings at one time did seek out women and force them to become prostitutes, this is most unlikely today. A typical madam probably has more applicants for work than she can accommodate.

One typical pattern of recruitment into prostitution is that of a woman seeking some other kind of work in a larger city. For a good many years there was a continuing flow to the North of women from the poorer Southern states. The woman's lack of vocational skills made it difficult for her to obtain work, and she often found herself pregnant or in other difficulties. Contact with someone in "the life" facilitated her entrance into prostitution.

Today a prostitute has often grown up in a slum neighborhood, or in a broken home, or in an unstable family life. She may have been born out of wedlock, be a school dropout, and member of a minority group, perhaps with teen fantasies of wanting money and clothes, and a member of a crowd of young people who live loosely. As an impressionable adolescent she has probably seen girls in her neighborhood working as prostitutes. Her father may have frequently beaten her, or left home, or been weak. She may have had unfortunate experiences with a boy friend or husband, difficulty in finding work, or a bad experience on a job. Needing money, she becomes a prostitute and may indeed drift into lesbian relationships which strengthen her feelings that men ought to be exploited.

The initiation into prostitution need not necessarily have traumatic effects on the prostitute. One noted: "I can recall the day that I became a whore. I didn't feel guilty and I didn't feel any remorse. I don't really think that I changed very much, because the sex just didn't mean that much to me. So I took money from a man to let him ball me. It didn't really bother me." A new prostitute may have an unusual asset that she will never have again in the course of her career: her novelty for the customer. Her initial success because of her "newness" may provide an incentive for continuing in the occupation.

The initial sex experiences of some prostitutes involve rape, although few women are likely to have as brutal an introduction to sex as the heroine of *Sanctuary*, the novel that was William Faulkner's first popular success.[24] *Sanctuary* presented the story of Temple Drake, who was abducted and forced into a life of prostitution by an impotent procurer called Popeye. In one of the most famous scenes in modern fiction, he rapes her with a corncob. Incest or sexual relations with a relative other than a member of the immediate family is fairly frequent in the sexual development of girls who subsequently become prostitutes.

A combination of reasons for her own entrance into prostitution has been provided by an insightful English woman named Sheila Cousins.[25] She notes that a prostitute generally has some insecurity in her family life, a vein of laziness, an incapacity to say no, and inability to resist the parasitism of others. The very characteristics which make her a prostitute, Miss Cousins observes, are precisely the qualities that she ought not to have if she is to be successful in her work.

One psychiatrist has tried to link prostitution among young girls to their reading of comic books. He cites the case of a ten-year-old girl who engaged in sex play for money.[26] "This girl read about twenty comic books a day. Some of them she read over about three or four times." In spite of such charges there appear to be very few girls in their early teens who work as prostitutes. One investigator who has studied prostitution for decades in many cities said recently that "the only Lolita-type of girl I recall is a deaf mute in New York City a few years ago. She walked along Broadway, passed notes to men, and invited them to a 'date.'" During the last fifteen years, very young "Lolita-type" girls have been available, in spite of the legal risks they pose, because of their special attractiveness to some customers.

During the last decade, "baby pro" has been widely used to refer to a prostitute who is less than sixteen or seventeen years old. They tend to work conventions, expensive hotels, and resorts. One fifteen-year-old in Chicago reminisced: "I've been in the racket since I was twelve years old. There are lots of guys who are kinky for young girls. Most of the baby pros I know are about thirteen or fourteen or fifteen. Some of them are so busy they travel a lot, especially to resort towns.

"I started in Illinois coal country. A guy came to visit my family and convinced my father he could help me. He did, by taking me to Chicago and teaching me how to turn out. Every few months I had to French him, but otherwise he left me alone. He wanted me to be as tight as possible.

"Quite a few kiddy freaks think they have small organs, and they want to make it with a young girl because they expect her to be small and tight. Part of our attraction to some old johns is that we don't respond, because we are supposed to be inexperienced. They expect a kid to be pretty passive. A lot of the johns don't want to do much but stinkfinger. They like to hold me tight, cuddle up, and talk.

"Because it's so dangerous for an old guy to get busted with a kid, the uncle doesn't send me out except to johns he knows or who know him. There's a kind of a circuit; the uncle finds the johns somehow. Johns recommend me to their friends. I always lie about my age. The johns want you to be young, but they want you to say you're older.

"When I need a john in a hurry I go to a place like a fancy hotel lobby where there are a lot of old guys. I look very classy in white gloves and no makeup. I flash [showing the genital area], accidentally like. The easiest way is to wear an over-the-shoulder bag and then arrange it so that when you comb your hair, the bag accidentally pulls your skirt up and you're sitting so the guy can see up it. We call that 'the pin,' when you get the guy's attention. You pull your skirt down and wait for the john to come over and ask about your parents and all that. I look so innocent that I pretend to be embarrassed about my skirt going up. If the guy is interested, he'll come over and start talking to me, and I take it from there. I figure I'm good for about another year as a baby pro and then I expect to quit, for good."

The alertness of potential clients to the subtle cues offered by a "baby pro" is documented in Joyce Carol Oates's novel *Them*, which won the National Book Award in 1970.[27] Maureen is a pretty fourteen-year-old who lives in Detroit with her mother and stepfather. Maureen discovers that how she sits, turns an ankle, or moves a leg can alert a potential client to her availability as a prostitute—even while she is reading in the public library. She usually picks up her clients at the library and goes with them to a motel or car. Maureen is like other "baby pros" in that she makes a great deal of money, remains numb through the sexual experiences, and does not really listen to her clients' conversations.

Very young prostitutes have assumed a new importance since the publication of Vladimir Nabokov's *Lolita* in 1958.[28] The witty story of Humbert Humbert and his twelve-year-old mistress received enormous attention. Coincidentally, the book was published one year after the appearance of the prototype mannequin doll. "Barbie," a sexually aggressive teen-age doll, was introduced in 1959 and soon became the most successful and popular doll ever marketed in the United States. Sales of mannequin dolls have averaged six million per year. In 1955 *Susan Slept Here* had been the first Hollywood film to present a sexually emancipated teen-age heroine. In recent years, women's fashions have been stressing the teen drum-majorette look, as women of all ages have turned to boots and miniskirts which display their knees. Such developments in popular culture may have helped to reinforce the interest of older men in young prostitutes.

STORIES

Most prostitutes are used to being asked, "How did a girl like you get into this business?" They usually have developed one or more stories designed to elicit sympathy and extra payment. The traditional story may involve seduction by an older relative or a clergyman. Prostitutes often say they were innocent at the time but that the disgrace forced them to leave home and ultimately go into prostitution.

It is difficult to tell how seriously to take such stories, because many prostitutes have a considerable ability for self-delusion and rationalization. The reality of their lives can be so painful that it may be almost necessary for them to lie. They may see no reason to tell the truth to a casual customer, and it may seem to their advantage to lie to an interviewer or probation officer. The lies may coincide with the contents of puberty fantasies.[29]

Brothel prostitutes had more leisure to chat with clients than is likely today, when extra time spent with a client can increase the likelihood of arrest. Today most women are eager to have a customer finish his business as quickly as possible: "Do you or don't you want to go with me—I haven't any time for gabbing."

It is still relatively common for prostitutes to volunteer their ethnic background—"I'm half Dutch and half Cherokee." The customer may be curious about the woman, and such information is one way of coping with his interest without divulging too many details. Curiously, few prostitutes will attempt to lie about or conceal their age. Men who feel a little uneasy about being with a rather old prostitute may try to reassure themselves that she is not as old as she seems. One such man said to a prostitute: "You look pretty young— I would guess you're not even thirty." Much to his surprise the woman said, "Oh, my goodness, no. I'll be forty-three on July 7th." The advanced age of the prostitute appears to be a subject of continuing folklore interest. One story is concerned with a customer who tells a sixteen-year-old girl in a brothel, "I'd like to go with you." She points to a much older woman sitting nearby and asks, "Why don't you take her?" The client exclaims, "But she's sixty!" The girl says, "Yes, but this is a union house and she has seniority rights."

Many prostitutes claim that the person with whom they live is unaware of their vocation, as in typical comments from recent interviews: ". . . I live in an apartment, but I share it with another girl. She doesn't know that I do this." ". . . I can't have you come to where I live because I live with my grandmother." ". . . I have my own place, but my sister is visiting with me and she doesn't know I do this. She will be out shopping."

INITIAL SEX EXPERIENCE √

The traditional mass-media story of the virgin who is brought to a house of prostitution by an evil man is extremely difficult to substantiate. Over half of a sample of prostitutes interviewed around World War I had their first sexual experience between the ages of fourteen and eighteen, and became prostitutes between seventeen and twenty-two.[30] At about the same time, a sample of 420 prostitutes who averaged 21.6 years of age at entrance into prostitution reported their initial sexual experience to be at the mean age of 17.4.[31] One generation later, a sample of prostitutes had initial sex experience between fourteen and eighteen, and age at entrance into prostitution ranged from fifteen to thirty-four.[32] During the 1930's a number of other studies concluded that the typical age for the first sexual experience of prostitutes was eighteen and a half, and twenty was the modal age at entry into prostitution. Although some students have claimed that it is the second sexual experience which leads to promiscuity or prostitution, it is hard to accept the conclusion that any specific number of sexual experiences is linked inevitably with a future fate.

There appears to be an average period of about two years between the initial sexual experience and entrance into prostitution. Through the 1930's prostitutes perhaps were having initial sexual experience and introduction to prostitution at an earlier age than today. The younger age in earlier decades may have been a result of the large number of very young immigrants and domestic workers from rural areas who drifted into prostitution.

Interviews with a substantial number of prostitutes suggest that relatively few have received any sex education. Typically, the mother communicates nothing about sex until the onset of menstruation, at which time the mother often warns her daughter about the hazards of sex and the need to be very cautious with men. Sex is identified as something to be avoided, and pregnancy is presented as a kind of degradation. Such a reaction from the mother helps to make the menarche revolting to the daughter.[33]

RESPONSE TO SEX

How frigid are prostitutes, and to what extent do they derive sexual gratification from their work? Such questions are difficult to answer because prostitutes' relationship to sex is likely to be affected or modified as a result of their work.[34] Their lack of response may be one means by which they can express superiority to or contempt for customers. Without the woman yielding, she has forced her customer to respond in the form of his ejaculation.

Prostitutes often experience sex on a more intense level with a pimp, husband, or boy friend than with clients. Such women may adapt to their work by relating more intensely to men with whom they maintain a traditional relationship, and in a detached manner to clients: "With a john, it was not happening to me but just to my body." When unmarried prostitutes go out with their boy friends, they may engage in characteristic feminine resistance. Their egos are involved, and they may use feminine wiles appropriate to the norms of their society. If they do have intercourse, their response can be more complete because they feel involved. But prostitutes' long-range attachments sometimes involve a reversal of the prostitute-client role by providing the woman with an outlet for her hostility toward men.

Typically, the prostitute displays lack of involvement in the sexual act with her client. She may chide a customer for trying to excite her, feeling that she has been paid to submit and should not be seduced into enjoying it. As long as the act is not pleasurable, she can feel less guilty that she is doing anything wrong.[35] Occasionally a prostitute may request a man to engage in sexual intercourse with her and insist on paying him handsomely. The money probably helps to create an impersonal atmosphere in which the woman can feel more comfortable or less guilty.

Psychoanalytic studies stress prostitutes' frigidity, immature psycho-sexual development, and severely deficient object relationships. Experiencing full sexual sensation tends to bind a woman to a man; she is likely to go from man to man primarily when it is lacking. Just as Don Juan presumably avenged himself on all women for the disappointment he received from his mother, the first woman who entered his life, the prostitute may be avenging herself on every man for the love she had expected to get but did not receive from her father. Her frigidity can be regarded as involving a humiliation of all her clients and therefore a mass castration on an unconscious level. Another reason for frigidity is that it may represent an unconscious striving to diminish the importance of that part of the body which is used in sexual intercourse.[36]

Although popular fiction has suggested that many prostitutes are nymphomaniacs, there seems little reason to believe that this is the case. Some nymphomaniacs may enter prostitution, but there are no data on how the proportion of nymphomaniacs among prostitutes compares with that in the general population. Highly sexed prostitutes may have been under-represented in earlier studies, and only 23 per cent of a sample of thirty-one call girls reported never having experienced orgasms with their customers.[37] If this finding were confirmed on a larger sample, it would suggest that prostitutes are more sexually responsive than most psychoanalytic studies imply.

Prostitutes may develop lesbian relationships because they distrust men and find it easier to develop affection for women. Lesbianism may be appealing to prostitutes who get tired of a continual round of men and turn to their colleagues for relaxation and a sentimental relationship after work. A woman with a strong personality and another who is submissive may develop a relationship based on their complementary needs. Men are ultimately paying the bills for such liaisons, adding a dimension that heightens the pleasure afforded by the relationship itself.

Some prostitutes who have a lesbian relationship work together as a team. An Indianapolis prostitute recently approached a man and asked: "Would you be interested in having a nice time? I'll go get my girl friend to join us here. Maybe you'll like her too. We try to help each other out. We have a package deal. For $25 each, we'll put on a good show for you, and after we finish you can have a straight date with me and anything you like with her. The whole thing will take an hour. I thought you'd like to have a nice party with both of us instead of just a date with me." She later explained that she and her chum were lesbians.

A person whose emotional relationships with others are diffuse may have many such relationships, in contrast to someone who has an intense commitment to one other person and probably has little libido left for others. In as much as a prostitute may not give much of herself to any one person, she can carry on with a pimp and a lesbian girl friend and perhaps even one or two "special" customers. A lesbian prostitute who has a male pimp may not encourage him to engage in sexual relations with her. She may have him do household chores and errands while she maintains a sexual relationship with her lesbian girl friend. She can participate in an emotional exchange with the latter while expressing hostility toward her pimp and customers.

CHILDREN AND MARRIAGE

Most studies have concluded that prostitutes have fewer children than other women. One investigation around World War I found that only 18 per cent of white and 15 per cent of Negro prostitutes had children, and another reported thirty-one illegitimate children born to a sample of 420 prostitutes. In a group of Danish prostitutes in the 1930's, 63 per cent had children, most of whom were illegitimate. Approximately one-third of a sample of May Act violators had illegitimate children.[38]

Some prostitutes induce abortions by treating themselves with ergot, hat pins, and similar techniques. In other cases, abortions are performed by midwives or by the physicians who examine the women. Married Finnish prostitutes had children only one-tenth as frequently as normal women of a comparable age group, as a result of the consequence of changes in genital organs caused by gonorrhea, criminal abortions, or both.[39]

The Indiana University Institute for Sex Research concluded that married prostitutes who were serving time in prison had a variable conception rate and an extraordinarily high proportion of pregnancies that aborted spontaneously.[40] There were so many spontaneous abortions that relatively few were induced. The relative infertility of these women and their proneness to abort spontaneously may have been caused by the syphilis which some had.

The seeming infertility of prostitutes may be related to the functioning of the Kristeller plug, a mucous plug at the mouth of the uterus which opens and descends to a certain degree into the upper vault of the vagina. It does so as a result of the contraction, at orgasm, of the sphincter muscles, a contraction that is shared by the vagina and rectum. As a result of this contraction, there is a ladder of entry that facilitates the rendezvous of the spermatozoa with the ovum. The ladder is a highly developed part of the mucous elaboration of the vagina and has the consistency of honey that is dropped from a spoon. Extensive sexual intercourse may lead to fatigue of this facilitating action of the Kristeller plug. The plug does not descend and thus does not facilitate movement of the spermatozoa.[41]

There may also be a self-selection of women who become

prostitutes because they have conscious or unconscious feelings of resistance to having children. Some prostitutes may express their lack of interest in children in emotional or unconscious responses such as antibodies and hormonal or other chemical systems that inhibit conception. A number of yet undiscovered factors may be responsible for prostitutes' apparent infertility.

The availability of reliable contraceptive information among prostitutes varies widely. Many believe that contraception is unnecessary because different strains of semen destroy each other. But other prostitutes do not share such beliefs, and there seems to be a considerable exchange of information on anti-conception measures. Some prostitutes have even had permanent pessaries fitted. In recent years an increasing number of prostitutes have been using birth-control pills. Some prostitutes take the pills daily in order to stop menstruation so that they are able to work every day of the month.

Many prostitutes use an antiseptic solution for their hands. Some douche with bichloride of mercury, permanganate of potash, proprietary preparations, vinegar, or soap and water after each client. The desire for a douche is one reason many prostitutes do not like to work away from their established place of business. The vaginal suppository and diaphragm are used relatively infrequently, even today.

In years past the peddler who sold jewelry and grooming products to brothel prostitutes often stocked condoms. Sometimes a peddler would approach a customer on the street and offer to sell him a condom. Some brothels did not offer a condom to a client because their madams felt that doing so would make him suspicious that the prostitutes had venereal disease. A customer who asked a prostitute for a condom was generally given one, at no charge. If she did not have a supply, he might obtain it from the maid or madam. Most customers did not wish to use a condom. Few worried about the prostitute's becoming pregnant, and most believed that she could "take care" of herself. A prostitute who was afraid of becoming pregnant might sometimes ask the client to use a condom. Such a condition was considered enough of a potential deterrent to clients so that the woman would generally say, "My price is ——, but you've got to use a rubber."

American prostitutes who become pregnant usually continue working and lose little trade. The United States is one of the few countries where pregnancy is often an asset to a "working girl." Many prostitutes speak freely of the children whom they are supporting: "... I take all I can get. I have one big reason for doing this—my little girl, who means everything to me. I need the money to raise her. I want her to have the best of everything. I'm divorced from my husband and he doesn't contribute a cent towards her support. She stays with my mother." "... I do it because I have bills to pay and a small daughter to raise." "... I have my own apartment, but I have a six-year-old daughter, and I don't like to have different men come to my place when she's home." "... I date, but I can't go right now. I have four children at home and I would have to make arrangements for a baby sitter here tonight." Most prostitutes who identify the sex of their children indicate that they have daughters. Customers often seem to be willing to pay more if they believe the woman is supporting her children.

It is difficult to get reliable information on the proportion of prostitutes who are married, because many who are single say they are married. Some who do so believe that customers feel more comfortable and less guilty with a married woman who is supplementing her husband's income. A prostitute who has been arrested may claim that she is married in order to obtain greater leniency from law enforcement authorities. A probation officer may recommend special consideration for a married woman, especially if she has children. Twenty-seven of the fifty prostitutes studied by the League of Nations and more than half a sample of one hundred women who had been accused of prostitution during World War II had been married.[42] Half of a sample of 405 New York City prostitutes interviewed by the authors in 1968 were married.

Many prostitutes may avoid marriage as part of a generalized contempt toward legitimate society.

Some prostitutes have become so uneasy about police action or lack of customers that they have gotten married as an alternative to continuing in "the life." Others may be in common-law marriages. One prostitute who had already committed bigamy was eager to get married to a third man so that she would be "respectable"! Where a prostitute mentions a husband to a client, the traditional story is that he is working out of town or overseas in the armed forces.

Occasionally a man marries a prostitute both because of her bad reputation and in spite of it.[43] He may expect to discard the prudery with which sex is so frequently invested and feel comfortable in the presence of a woman of no pretenses. He may also prefer a woman who has been possessed by others. A man may marry a prostitute because his sexual relationship with her will have a minimum of romance. Such elements may have contributed to the marriage of Auguste Comte, who sired positivism and sociology. Comte married a young girl who had been a prostitute, although he was fully aware of her prenuptial career. Far from being a Bohemian, Comte was a fairly strict defender of moral views.[44]

VENEREAL DISEASE

Venereal disease used to be a significant occupational hazard for the prostitute, but is far less likely to be so today. A syphilitic streetwalker whose portrait is etched in acid was played by Claire Trevor as the despairing anti-heroine of the movie *Dead End* (1937), adapted from Sidney Kingsley's well-known play (1935). The movie even showed the syphilitic sores on her face.

For many years it has been routine for prostitutes to examine potential customers for a chancre as a sign of syphilis or for a discharge, which would be a clue to the possibility of gonorrhea. They generally tell the customer, "I want to look you over," and he usually knows the meaning of the request.

Some relatively naive prostitutes may not recognize the symptoms of gonorrhea and feel that it is "just the whites" (leucorrhea). But others are so aware of venereal disease that they regularly take penicillin or other antibiotics and get frequent medical checkups. Many madams covered all the medical expenses of a known customer who contracted venereal disease in their brothel. Madams often justified their work on the basis of alertness to venereal disease. As one said: "We have just as much right to be in our business as you have in yours. Not only do we have the right, but we also perform a useful social service. Our girls can take care of themselves. Venereal disease is spread by chippies and not by our girls. A pro won't hook you with a disease."

Venereal disease was once so widespread that 23 per cent of the prostitutes studied at the time of World War I had outward signs of syphilis, and 74 per cent showed a positive Wassermann test. Half of a later sample of prostitutes could not work adequately because of ailments related to venereal disease. Before 1939, three-fourths of all venereal disease could be traced to prostitutes. Even in the post-penicillin era, 128 out of a sample of 418 prostitutes had gonorrhea or syphilis.[45]

A declining proportion of venereal disease in some populations is still contracted in brothels. Approximately 5 per cent of current American cases can be traced to prostitutes. Of 4,700 alleged prostitutes examined in connection with the New York City Women's Court in 1966, four cases of infectious syphilis and 619 cases of gonorrhea were found.[46] As many as 90 per cent of all professional prostitutes are infected with venereal disease at some time during their career, and each can infect an average of twenty men before her disease is discovered.

The more frequent a customer's exposure to an infected woman, the more likely he is to get a venereal disease. The folk adage that "if you go to a prostitute, go to an old one," probably reflects the decreased likelihood of infection from a mature prostitute who has a chronic case of gonorrhea or has passed through the infectious stages of syphilis. The client's chances of acquiring gonorrhea are greater when the woman has an acute early infection than when she has a chronic condition. Similarly, the infectiousness of untreated syphilis is greatest during the first year and diminishes thereafter. There is great variation in the incidence of infection among groups of men who visit prostitutes with venereal disease, for reasons which are not fully understood.

An infected prostitute with a large clientele may expose a large number of men to the possibility of infection. An example of this possibility was provided by a California interstate truck driver who was recently diagnosed as having primary syphilis. Upon interviewing the prostitute whom he had identified as the probable source of infection, the names of 310 sexual contacts were obtained. The contacts were interstate truck drivers who lived in thirty-four states, Canada, and Mexico, and whose names were obtained because the woman kept a diary. A number of early cases of syphilis were found in the men.[47] Such dramatic examples of the spread of syphilis by one prostitute who has infectious lesions are very rare, but they do occur.

Spot checks in military areas during World War II demonstrated a sharp decline in venereal disease rates when prostitution was curtailed. In San Antonio the rate of soldiers infected was 89 per 1,000 in November 1941. One year later, after the closing of the brothels and cribs, the rate was reduced to 13.8 per 1,000. The German army in World War II set up a system of forty-two brothels in Paris, with each inmate inspected twice a week and a prophylactic station situated near each house.[18] From January to August 1944, despite these precautions, there were 3,106 new cases of venereal disease in the German garrison of forty thousand troops. Eighty-four per cent of the infections came from prostitutes in the official houses. A comparison of the World War II rate of venereal disease between the German and American armed forces over a comparable period suggests that the "controlled vice" policy of the German army resulted in a venereal disease rate four times greater than in the American armed forces, which had an official policy of suppressing prostitution. Differences in national character must of course be considered in interpreting such differences.

There seems to be considerable cross-national variation in the role of prostitutes in spreading venereal disease.[49] Australia reports that the closing of supervised brothels in recent years has evidently not significantly affected the incidence of venereal disease, and that the most usual source of infection with syphilis is still the professional prostitute. The Austrian government, on the other hand, downgrades the importance of prostitution in the genesis of venereal disease. Ceylon found that prostitutes are a major source of venereal disease infection. The decline of syphilis incidence in Greece can be attributed to changes in the living arrangements of prostitutes and to the increased frequency of sanitary checkups. Japan reported syphilis in 1,058 of a sample of 9,452 prostitutes examined. In Pakistan prostitution is a major source of venereal disease. Portugal regards the major source of venereal disease to be prostitutes of low socio-economic status. In Thailand the large number of inadequately supervised brothel prostitutes has resulted in a greater spread of infection and difficulties in treatment. In some countries, closing the brothels has led to an increase in venereal disease: Italy had more cases in the 1960's than it did before its brothels closed in 1958.

In view of such inconclusive statistics, it is no wonder that some countries view prostitution as an important factor in the spread of syphilis while others did not assign it a significant role. Such cross-national differences include anti-prostitution laws, requirements for medical examination of prostitutes, efficacy of law enforcement, the proportion of prostitutes in the population, cultural traditions, and the role of women. The relative immunity of a population to syphilis as a consequence of a high incidence of yaws is also relevant.

In the United States there is no doubt that penicillin has very sharply reduced the likelihood that a prostitute will be a source of syphilis and, to a lesser extent, of gonorrhea. Many prostitutes now regularly take prophylactic doses of either oral or injectable penicillin and thereby minimize the possibility that they will contract either disease, if the dosage of penicillin is sufficient. Insufficient dosages can, as in Vietnam and Thailand, lead to the development of resistant strains of the gonococcus. One reason for concern in this country is that a number of prostitutes who take daily doses of penicillin develop resistant strains of gonorrhea which they pass on to customers. Physicians are only now beginning to deal with this problem.

DRUGS AND ALCOHOL

Narcotics addiction and drug abuse among prostitutes have increased greatly since 1939. Before World War II the typical prostitute working in a brothel was under the close scrutiny of its madam, who was generally very alert to and opposed to the use of drugs. The brothel provided personal and social relationships that are less available to the prostitute today; their absence could be one reason for the increase in addiction among present-day prostitutes.

Some cities are more likely to have prostitute addicts than others. In Philadelphia it was possible during the 1930's to buy heroin, opium, cocaine, and morphine on the corner of Vine and Eighth Streets quite openly. Division and Green Streets in Albany, New York, were narcotic centers. New York was, and still is, a center for addict prostitutes. At present perhaps half the prostitutes in our large cities are addicts. Most prostitutes who use drugs prefer heroin, though some mix it with cocaine to get a lift that eases sexual activity and balances the emotional apathy of heroin. In as much as the life cycle of the addict is often characterized by periods of abstention, it is likely that many women return to prostitution when they return to drug use, so that their involvement in prostitution has a cyclical quality.

Drugs can make it easier for the woman to ply her trade by

enabling her to feel less guilty, less vulnerable, and better able to socialize with potential customers. By narcotizing herself, she may be better able to cope with her work. Both prostitution and addiction may represent choices made by women struggling with similar problems. Some prostitutes regularly go through periods of profound depression, during which they may be especially susceptible to the appeal of drugs. Prostitutes may also use drugs in order to cope with the waiting and boredom that are characteristic of the vocation. Some pimps have been instrumental in their prostitutes' drug use because they assume that a woman who always needs cash must continue working at prostitution. Some call girls have been forced to work streets or bars because of their urgent need for money for drugs.

The same drug may serve a variety of purposes, depending on the user and circumstances. For some prostitutes who are severely impaired psychologically, heroin may block the eruption of symptoms and permit minimal integration of the personality. One Detroit addict noted: "I take heroin before I go out on the street at night. It calms me down and makes it easier for me to trick and to forget what I'm doing. The hours go by quicker. But when I ball with my pimp, the heroin makes it nicer for me with him. It peps me up and I can enjoy being with him." Prostitutes who are heroin addicts are likely to have minimal problems in engaging in anal intercourse, because the drug seems to relax the anal sphincter muscles.

A substantial number of young women drift into prostitution and drug addiction at about the same time, as part of a larger pattern of anti-social behavior. Many have grown up in an environment in which they see others engaging in prostitution and drug use. It is not possible to say with any certainty what proportion of prostitutes became drug addicts before or after their entrance into the vocation. A study of women arrested for prostitution in New York City concluded that 8.5 per cent of first offenders, 25.5 per cent of those with five arrests, 52 per cent of women arrested from eleven to fifteen times, and 70.8 per cent of those charged twenty or more times were narcotic addicts.[50] Certainly the correlation between incidence of addiction and recidivism may be a function of the women's need to earn money for drugs, suggesting that drug use antedated prostitution.

Relatively few prostitutes have felt that drugs interfere with their ability to work with clients.[51] But there are cases in which a call girl has been sent back by a customer who was able to detect that she was "on" and said, "You're no good to me." A brothel, hotel, or bar prostitute who had taken opiates probably would not be rebuffed by a client. In as much as it is all but impossible to detect the presence of drugs in a user by nonlaboratory methods, only an experienced and sophisticated client who has more than a hasty contact with a woman is likely to be aware of her drug use.

There is little reason to believe that many prostitutes drink heavily. Among the reasons for their not drinking may be a belief that they will be too drunk to work or fear that their employers will be irritated. Even women who work in bars seldom drink heavily, although some take an occasional drink in order to deaden themselves or as a response to tedium.

HAZARDS

A prostitute does assume a certain risk in going with a strange man, especially when she goes to his room. The man may be a sadist or plan to rob her. In order to guard against such events, some prostitutes tell girl friends or pimps where and for how long they are going. They may leave instructions about what to do if they do not return from an assignation by an appointed hour. Some carry knives, teargas pistols, and other weapons for protection.

One kind of incident that can occur was reported by a prostitute who visited a man in a hotel in Beaumont, Texas. When she entered his room he locked the door and took out a knife. He explained that he enjoyed carving patterns in women's skin. She feigned enthusiasm and said, "That's wonderful.

I like blood-letting myself. It really gives me a thrill. But let's have some drinks so I can really get excited." When the bell-hop came with the drinks, she screamed and fled.

No matter how hazardous the conduct of such patrons might be, many prostitutes will continue to ply their trade. In London the naked bodies of six strangled prostitutes were found in a fifteen-month period during 1964–1965. The murders all seem to have been the work of one person, whom Londoners dubbed "Jack the Stripper." During the time the women were murdered, there was no abatement in the incidence of prostitution. One woman said, "It's a chance, one takes, you know, and if you're going to be afraid you might just as well give it up." When asked about the effect of the activities of "Jack the Stripper," another prostitute said, "The murders make no difference to me."

Among other occupational hazards of "the life" is the chance that an excited client may exceed the limits of the prostitute's capacity by suddenly choking her or engaging in other unexpected behavior. The streetwalker has the greatest likelihood of getting a customer who engages in violence. She also is most likely to be robbed and therefore typically carries very little cash.

A different kind of occupational hazard found among many prostitutes is a characteristic gynecologic pathology resulting from hyperactivity. It is a chronic pelvic congestion characterized by a copious discharge from the cervix and vaginal lining, and a sensation of tenderness and fullness of the side walls of the pelvis. This congestion is frequently found in the prostitute because she seldom relieves her pelvic turgescence by orgasm. About half the prostitutes who consult physicians because of pelvic discomfort take narcotic drugs for relief of this symptom.[52]

Because of such hazards and the general character of her trade, the prostitute finds it difficult to get insurance of various kinds. One Texas woman unsuccessfully sought work-men's compensation payment because her breast had been bitten by a client. Prostitutes in Gary, Indiana, could not collect unemployment insurance after a cleanup, though the gamblers who were thrown out of work were able to do so. Prostitutes can but are unlikely to report their income and thus are unable to contribute to social security and other retirement plans. One madam, in Rome, Georgia, reports the income of her inmates as well as her own income to the Internal Revenue Service, but this is an exception.

SOME CASES

Myra R. is a prostitute of forty-six who has been working in New York in recent years. She has spent thirteen years and nine months in prison as the result of eighty-six appearances in court since she "turned out." Most of her prison time has been served in sentences of ten to ninety days. Born in Brooklyn, she left school at twelve and drifted into drug use three years later, just about the time she began to work as a waitress. She had a series of relationships with men for periods of as little as a week and as long as a year. A girl friend encouraged her to go on dates with servicemen for pay, and Myra found she could earn much more money by dating than from her restaurant job. Myra feels that prostitution is the only way she can earn enough money to buy drugs.

Bobbie, a prostitute addict who grew up in a San Francisco slum and is still working in the city's Tenderloin section, is exactly half Myra's age: "I was brought up in the Fillmore like a lot of the kids there are. I was one of seven and my home life was pretty shitty. My father was in a lot of the operations in the Fillmore and quite often we didn't see him for weeks at a time. My mother was the real boss in the family. By the time I was eight years old she had started hitting the bottle. What with the kids, and the lousy school, and nothing to do and not knowing where to go, I started hanging around with some older kids. As part of my initiation into a local gang when I was eleven I was screwed.

"By this time I couldn't take school and I had begun popping pills. I took mainly 'bennies,' 'dexies,' 'reds,' and 'yellows,' so by the time I was twelve I was really hung up on the 'freak' scene. One of the kids in the gang started to pimp me off in part of the Fillmore around Webster Street. He used to take most of the money I made off the tricks who cruised by in the cars. I first turned on to Smack when I was fourteen. I thought it was an absolute gas and swung out for about a month and then my connection was arrested. I didn't know anyone else to get the stuff from, so my first comedown was quick. A little later I got another source and by the end of the year I had about a $30-a-day habit.

"With the heat in the area I decided to move to the Tenderloin. My old pimp dropped me and I made a connection with a new guy who organized my business a lot better. Now most of the money I get off johns goes to the pimp for his cut and my habit. The dope doesn't get in the way, because as long as I am up I can have all the sex they will pay for and those screws wouldn't know the difference anyway. I never tried to get a job because if you are black you can't get much of a job beyond cleaning a shit house and I can make a lot more pushing my ass."[53]

Quite a different background characterizes Joan T., a prostitute of the 1940's who grew up in Morgantown, West Virginia. She left home at eighteen to work in a cigar factory in Lancaster, Pennsylvania. Her parents were considerate, but she got bored living at home. After losing her job she met a madam who talked her into entering a brothel. Joan had a large scar on her face, which made her feel socially inadequate and depressed about her appearance. She left the brothel from time to time but always returned to it.

Yet another kind of prostitute was Sue F., a thirty-five-year-old woman who worked at a Baltimore nightclub in the 1940's. The stock market crash and the depression left her penniless with two children after her husband died. "Since I was never prepared for any special kind of work, I naturally fell back on my music. Beethoven, Bach, Rimsky-Korsakov, Paderewski, Schubert, and the rest of the masters can't help you very much when you want to capitalize on your music.

I went in for light operettas of the Victor Herbert type, which were quite popular at the better nightclubs. But I developed laryngitis, and my voice cracked. I've gone to throat specialists and they say it's nerves.

"When my voice cleared up, I went to a local booking agent who sent me here. The boss liked me but the late hours, the drinking and general worriment soon put me down. My voice cracked again. The boss asked me if I wanted to be a hostess and told me all that it involved. He told me he would pay me a small salary and large commissions. He told me the worst characters in Baltimore came to this place and would try to get hold of me; that I should take care of myself."

Sue said her salary and commissions were not enough to maintain herself. "I've considered it all, and if it were not for my children I'd follow some of the teachings of the philosophers and end it all. The two kiddies need me and I have to carry on, even though it's a hard and extremely hopeless task."

LEAVING "THE LIFE"

How do women "square up" and leave prostitution, and how many do so? A number get into a "respectable" work or family situation. A much smaller proportion drift into marriage with a former customer. One marriage resulted after a New York publicist was asked by a client to hire several call girls and arrange hotel rooms for four businessmen who were coming into New York, without the men's having to sign a hotel register or be otherwise embarrassed. The publicist was able to make such arrangements with a hotel and paired one call girl with the company's president, who married her within a few weeks.

Women arrested for prostitution are substantially younger than persons arrested for other crimes, perhaps reflecting the greater skill of older prostitutes in avoiding arrest. Stepped-up law enforcement has helped to drive many young women out of prostitution since World War II, especially as they are relatively able to get other work. The formerly high incidence of young prostitutes can be seen in the story about a man who visited a brothel and was uneasy about the very youthful appearance of the inmate assigned to him. He asked the madam her age and was told she was thirteen. When he refused to go with the girl, the madam indignantly asked, "What's the matter with you? Are you superstitious?"

Special situations in some communities lead to older or young women being more prevalent among the community's prostitutes. In Detroit, 65 per cent of the arrested prostitutes are under eighteen, 30 per cent are between eighteen and thirty, and 5 per cent are over thirty. It is not clear whether the woman over thirty tends to retire or marry, or whether competition drives the older woman out of business.

A popular legend has it that the typical prostitute leaves her career after a few years, but there is little reason to believe that this is necessarily so. Considerable evidence suggests that many prostitutes "stand up" for decades and continue working indefinitely. The older prostitute who continues working into her sixties and seventies may be reduced to seeking clients on the local Skid Row and end up as a "flea bag."

Some women leave the vocation after severe illness, because someone wishes to keep them, or for other relatively unusual occurrences. Police activity may become strong enough to drive others out of "the life." Those prostitutes who have set a specific financial or other goal may leave after the target has been achieved.

Many prostitutes of the post-World War II years are drug addicts and may quit prostitution when their addiction loses its urgency. Approximately two-thirds of drug addicts seem to "mature out" of addiction at an average age of thirty-five. Female addicts may leave prostitution when they no longer require large sums of money to buy drugs. If this hypothesis is correct, we might expect to find substantial numbers of women leaving prostitution around their thirties, and the scanty data available suggest that such a phenomenon is occurring.

A large proportion of nonaddict prostitutes may also leave their work during their thirties as an expression of the same kind of "maturing out" which appears to occur not only in addicts but also in psychopaths, delinquents, and others who have been behaving in an anti-social manner.[54] A significant number of such people seem able to modify their behavior patterns and adapt to the larger society. Their adaptation is often the end product of a combination of forces. In the case of the prostitute in her thirties, she may also recognize her age and its concomitant of lower fees. A call girl or hotel or brothel prostitute may find it increasingly difficult to get clients and have to work in a bar or on the street for less money. Such a reminder that she is moving into a more difficult phase of "the life" may spur a prostitute to leave it.

No matter how long she has been in "the life," many prostitutes tell a customer, "I 'turned out' a few weeks ago and am planning to leave in a year and go back to a different job." Such a statement is intended to give the customer the feeling that the prostitute is relatively inexperienced and has not become hardened.

One fantasy about leaving prostitution is suggested in the film *Ada* (1961), in which Susan Hayward plays a prostitute who becomes the first lady of her state and then its acting governor. In this adaptation of a novel she marries a guitar-playing musician (Dean Martin) who is elected governor because some politicians believe he will acquiesce in their wishes. He rebels and decides to run an honest administration but becomes ill, and Miss Hayward becomes acting governor.

Other prostitutes, at least in folklore, have become pillars of society. How a prostitute can develop into a lady and not be embarrassed by her past is the burden of the movie *Kitty* (1946), played by Paulette Goddard. Kitty is a street girl who is taught manners and elegance by a man with whom she continues a liaison even after her marriage to someone else. When her necklace breaks at a social event and she lets fly a bit of profanity, her associates are delighted with her "charming" freedom of speech.

Suicide is the most drastic way of leaving the vocation. An early study concluded that 11 per cent of brothel prostitutes had attempted suicide at least once. Three-fourths of a sample of call girls had attempted suicide.[55] As many as 15 per cent of the suicides brought into large public hospitals may be prostitutes. Some prostitutes detained in prison for several months, while awaiting trial, have attempted suicide. A woman may also try to do away with herself in reaction to the departure of her pimp. Investigators are likely to under-represent suicide by prostitutes because of their reluctance to sully a dead woman's name. But a substantial proportion of suicide attempts may be made by prostitutes *before* they enter "the life"; their work may actually counter feelings of anomie.

Some prostitutes may not try suicide but nevertheless feel they have entered a hopeless situation. As one said, "Once you start, you can't stop . . ." A street girl who cannot leave the streets is depicted in the film *The Asphalt Jungle* (1950). Fellini's *Nights of Cabiria* (1958) presents a prostitute as a member of a subgroup from which it is impossible to escape. Cabiria believes she can marry and be happy, but her fiancé is ready to murder her for her pitifully small savings. She is so virtuous that the film audience knows she will survive in spite of her total rejection by society and even the Church.

Very few prostitutes are likely to emulate the heroine of the film *Girl of the Night* (1960). She is a call girl being victimized by a pimp, but seeks psychotherapeutic help. She finally develops sufficient inner resources to leave prostitution. The theme of *Girl of the Night* is not farfetched in the light of British experience which suggests that there may be a substantial number of young prostitutes who can be helped to leave the vocation, if it is regarded as a condition which, like addiction, requires treatment. Such treatment might not only include psychotherapy but also, and perhaps even more importantly, vocational retraining. In many cases the retraining would be the first formal preparation for work that the woman has received. Psychotherapy can have little effect if the woman's situation does not include a possibility for work other than prostitution.

The need for useful vocational rehabilitation was demonstrated in Japan in the 1950's after prostitution was outlawed. The vocational retraining that was provided included arts and crafts, homemaking, and similar activities that did not interest many women and seemed relatively unlikely to produce much income. As a result of the women's boredom and belief that the training would be financially unrewarding, many would slip out at night and engage in prostitution after a day of vocational retraining. The Japanese experience suggests the need for a total and realistic treatment plan in any attempt at rehabilitation. Vocational retraining would appear to be the most direct way of bringing a prostitute back into the traditional structure of society.

As recently as the nineteenth century there was a common belief that a prostitute's soul was more important than anything else in rehabilitating her. Rehabilitation efforts have foundered for other reasons than an undue emphasis on religion, among them the prostitutes' problems with authority and their difficulties in using welfare services.[56] Men might be more acceptable than women case-workers to a prostitute client. In any case, social agencies in most communities are geared toward handling traditional problems, and few are ready or able to provide proper treatment to a prostitute. It may be more realistic to speak of treating a severely disturbed total personality than of treating a prostitute. The fairly high incidence of addiction and lesbianism among prostitutes suggests that many lack the resources of personality that are needed in rehabilitation.

The reluctance of social agencies to develop programs for the rehabilitation of prostitutes may reflect the larger unspoken attitudes of the society. Prostitutes are regarded as bad women who violate the code of chastity. On the other hand, because they perform a necessary function for the maintenance of the double standard, they are not without some oblique prestige.[57]

Most case-work agencies regard the client who voluntarily seeks help as being more likely than an involuntary client to find a favorable outcome. Few prostitutes, however, seem to request help. Lack of interest in rehabilitation of prostitutes on the part of civic leaders is another reason for the inactivity of social agencies. Their inertia also reflects the community's reluctance to acknowledge the existence of its prostitutes and give them an opportunity to find another way of living. War represents one of the few occasions when the community is willing to do something because of its uneasiness about the large number of military personnel who might be in contact with prostitutes.

At other times the prostitute usually gets rehabilitation from the community only through her contact with the courts. The typical arrested prostitute is charged with a misdemeanor and appears before a lower court. Such courts seldom have adequate probation personnel and many have no probation service at all. Some few police departments (for example, the District of Columbia) have women's bureaus staffed by policewomen and social workers who specialize in working with prostitutes. The few effective women's bureaus are found mostly in large cities.[58]

In some jurisdictions a first offender gets no rehabilitation because of a policy that other women who are institutionalized for a longer period of time should get whatever help is available. Even the latter, however, seldom get much retraining. In fact, the younger "first offender" may be the likeliest candidate for rehabilitation.[59] The Isaac T. Hopper Home in New York City obtained encouraging results during 1946 and 1947 by assigning social workers to first offenders, most of whom were young prostitutes. Among the services provided were railroad fare, clothes, contacting relatives or friends, and referral to social agencies.

In many large cities prostitutes are processed by the courts in a revolving-door manner. They are arrested, given a prison sentence, serve their time, are released, and return to prostitution. They seldom seek other work, and some time after they return to "the life" many are arrested again. Young prostitutes may meet older and experienced colleagues while in jail and learn about previously unfamiliar aspects of the vocation. Few penal institutions have facilities for giving prostitutes the education they could use to get other work.

One of the few specialized rehabilitation programs was opened in Baltimore in 1943 when the Protective Service of the City's Department of Public Welfare was established to help prostitutes make a new start in life.[60] The program accepted the police task of apprehending prostitutes and the health department's responsibility for treating venereally infected patients. The Service's role was to help prostitutes accept responsibility for their behavior and learn a more satisfying way of living. Any woman who sought help from the Service would receive it so long as she wished to stop being a prostitute. Women might be referred by social agencies, the police department, or physicians. The median age range was between seventeen and twenty-five, and the majority of women were white.

The social worker tried to help the woman develop good habits of work and recreation and provided money until the client earned her first paycheck. The case-worker continually pointed out the work options available and concentrated on helping the client achieve relationships that had meaning and continuity. Once the client learned to trust the worker and the agency, she was on her way to trusting other persons, and ultimately even men. The goal of the program was not to isolate the client from men but to help her establish meaningful relations and strengthen her capacity for resistance to the point where she could accept responsibility for her own actions.

One of the most dramatic cases in the Baltimore project was provided by Mrs. Laurene Stecher, a twenty-six-year-old married prostitute with two children. After her arrest, her great difficulties in establishing a relationship with the caseworker were compounded by her husband's being in jail for pimping. In spite of such problems, she was helped to establish an adjustment and become more self-sufficient. Her relationship to her husband changed for the better. She ultimately got a job as a waitress and began with her husband to cope with the new situation.

A Louisville program during World War II permitted part of a prostitute's sentence to be replaced by counseling and social case-work. San Francisco's Women's Court was established in 1943 to provide special services for women arrested for prostitution and related misdemeanors.[61] Of the first 859 women seen at the court, 44 per cent were sent to the county jail, 18 per cent were given suspended sentences under special conditions, 23 per cent were dismissed, and 4 per cent were referred to the juvenile court. The remainder were committed to the psychiatric ward of the county hospital or a state mental hospital.

Another type of rehabilitation was attempted in New York City by a special court for wayward girls. Judge Peter M. Horn was largely responsible for the creation of the Girls' Term Court, which was later absorbed by the Family Court. In an average year eight hundred girls between sixteen and twenty-one appear in the court on petitions that they are engaged in anti-social behavior, much of which consists of prostitution. The judge is available at all times; social workers evaluate the case before the girl gets to court, and she may be referred for appropriate remedial treatment.[62] The judges do not find the girls guilty or not guilty, but prescribe treatment for each case. The Girls' Term Court is one of the few genuine American reforms in the handling of prostitution.

One comparatively successful rehabilitation program has been mounted in Detroit by the Legion of Mary, a lay volunteer program which began in 1964 under the spiritual direction of a priest. Thirty-five volunteers staff the program. The volunteer develops a relationship of trust with the young prostitute. If the woman needs a place to live, three halfway houses are available. They offer room and board and help in obtaining work training or an immediate job. Religious discussion is available but is completely voluntary. After its first year of full operation, 74 per cent of the girls were working at a "square" job or attending school, 15 per cent had returned to prostitution, and 11 per cent could not be recontacted. Flint and Houston have developed analogous halfway-house programs.

Canada has also developed a halfway-house approach to helping prostitutes. Street Haven in Ontario was started in 1965 as a nongovernmental facility for the rehabilitation of women caught in the web of prostitution and petty crime. It is a voluntary residential center which processes over 250 women a year. Many of these have given indications of rehabilitating themselves. They participate in recreational activities and discussion groups and publish a newsletter. Their self-confidence is enhanced slowly but regularly by such small victories as realizing that other teams are willing to compete against them in the Ontario ladies' baseball league. Street Haven, without any professional staff, provides a way-station back to the "square" world.

A typology of prostitutes can be drawn in terms of their response to rehabilitation. One type of woman has been in the business only briefly and has not established habit patterns or personal involvements that are difficult to break. In such cases, referral to a social agency can be very successful. The second group is disillusioned with respect to the satisfactions derived from prostitution or may never have really wanted to engage in the work. Many of these women have a history of sexual delinquency, and others have become prostitutes in order to get money for drugs. This group needs considerable rehabilitation because it includes women with severe emotional problems. A third group of women engages in prostitution primarily to earn a livelihood, and may be receptive to alternate methods of doing so. Many younger recidivists are in this category. A fourth group is not likely to respond voluntarily to any rehabilitation plan. This includes women for whom prostitution is a very successful way of making money as well as those whose satisfactions from the work are exceptionally binding.[63]

Some prostitutes seeking rehabilitation may do so more effectively through established community channels rather than special programs.[64] Forced peonage and "white-slave traffic" are relatively infrequent today, so there is less need for formal "rescue" work. A prostitute who is motivated for rehabilitation may feel more comfortable about going to a mental hygiene clinic or to similar community facilities without the stigma that may be attached to a special prostitution program. Still, very few prostitutes do seek out community facilities.

Another approach to the rehabilitation of prostitutes seems to be effective in England. Under the National Health Act a woman who is convicted for soliciting or overt prostitution may be transferred from jail to an open mental hospital. There she is treated like any other patient; she can go home on leave and may even get a job outside the hospital. The prostitute is transferred from the jail on an "order of residence," a probation order calling for her to remain in the hospital for a specific period of time. If the hospital staff feels that the woman is ready to be returned to the community before the expiration of her original term, it may recommend such a change to the magistrate who originally sentenced her. This procedure makes it possible for a prostitute to move out of the penal setting into nonpunitive psychiatric treatment.

A representative case of successful treatment in England is provided by a woman named Rose.[65] She started truanting from school at twelve, was put on probation, and was then sent to a reformatory, from which she ran away at fourteen. She thumbed a ride and was picked up by a long-distance truck driver and taken to a coast town, where she worked out of a local café as a prostitute. She ultimately had a baby. Rose was arrested and sent to Holloway Women's Prison, from which she went to a mental hospital on an "order of residence." She received individual psychotherapy three times a week for a month, and then this was reduced to once a week. Rose also received occupational therapy, got a job in the hospital, and was paid for her work. She spent ten months in the hospital, which then granted her a leave to live with her mother in London. She did sales work for about a year, got married, and now has a child with her new husband. Originally diagnosed as having a character disorder, Rose clearly profited from her treatment and shows no sign of returning to prostitution.

Denmark and Italy have been able to conduct successful programs for the social rehabilitation of prostitutes by careful employment of social-work techniques. Both countries have expressed cautious optimism about the use of probation and welfare services in resocialization.[66]

So little has been done in attempts to rehabilitate prostitutes in America that one must use a trial-and-error approach in order to determine which kind of woman can profit most from a particular kind of treatment. It is reasonable to assume that there is a wide range of personality and other types found among prostitutes, and that each is likely to respond differently to various kinds of help. Extensive follow-up studies would permit identification of the characteristics of the women who respond to each kind of intervention.

One possible direction is that of intensive probation supervision. Probation could improve the self-concept of prostitutes and strengthen their positive feelings about themselves. Many feel they are so worthless that they conclude, "What else can I do?" Effective probation experience could give them a stronger sense of themselves so that they would be more highly motivated to get other work. Experiments in giving parole officers relatively small caseloads of former drug addicts suggests that such supervision can be effective. An intensive probation effort with small caseloads, perhaps twenty-five to thirty, might be similarly effective in helping young prostitutes. Even a dedicated probation officer who believes firmly in his work cannot engage in more than a token effort when he has a caseload of over one hundred young prostitutes, as in New York City. The success of the Girls' Term Court with girls from sixteen to twenty-one sugguests that a similar intensive effort on the probation level, with older women, might be effective.

Even though it seems difficult to generate community support for rehabilitation of prostitutes, such programs might be mounted on a demonstation basis as part of an overall anti-poverty effort. There is no reason why anti-poverty funds could not be used for experimental approaches in the rehabilitation of prostitutes, especially since poverty contributes so heavily to the conditions that breed prostitution.

PSYCHOANALYTIC VIEWS

Prostitutes studied by psychoanalysts are likely to be unusual because of their very presence in the office of a psychoanalyst. Such prostitutes may be more self-aware and questioning than their colleagues, so that any generalizations about them could have only limited application to their colleagues. Prostitutes who come for help are also unrepresentative because their seeking out such treatment suggests that they may have reached an extreme conflict or other impasse in their career. They may not necessarily seek treatment in order to leave prostitution, but there is likely to be an element of desperation in their motivation for wanting help. They may represent the most disturbed prostitutes, and those who are adapting least effectively to their work. Psychoanalysts have, however, suggested some of the possible personality factors in prostitution and helped to minimize moralistic discussions of "fallen women."

The endless sexual episodes of the prostitute's later life may reflect an urge to make a mockery of parental love. One pattern is a disappointment with the father because of a failure to charm him, a failure ending in frustration. The child may exhibit self-debasement and self-destruction. The prostitute's displacement of sexual interests from the one to the many serves the purposes of her defense by denying that originally there was a parental love object. The displacement may also provide a form of revenge against the father and against the men who represent him symbolically. Some prostitutes may never have had an extended relationship with a father figure and therefore lacked the opportunity to participate in a relationship involving one man.

Revenge against parents seems to be a factor in the decision of some girls to become prostitutes, especially those of "good" family. One such girl was intelligent but decided to take revenge for the injuries she felt she had suffered. Some girls enter prostitution because it represents a "negative identity," which is an identity perversely based on all these identifications and roles which, at critical stages of development, were presented to them as most undesirable or dangerous and also as more real.[67] Such a case was personified by the daughter of a brilliant showman who ran away from college and was arrested as a prostitute in the slum quarter of a Southern city.

At least two kinds of fathers of prostitutes can be identified. One is the "castrated" man who is intermittently capable of affection for his daughter but will not intercede on her behalf with his wife. The daughter who seeks closeness with such a father becomes angry and frustrated and believes her father has failed her. She may become a prostitute and seek vengeance upon every man for childhood disappointment in the relationship with her father. She can express revenge and a feeling of humiliation resulting from the revenge. More typical is the brutal and forceful father. Many prostitutes' tomboyism reflects identification with such a father.[68]

A variety of relationships with the mother may be psychodynamically relevant to a woman's entering into prostitution. Some women seek escape from a situation of great involvement with a mother.[69] One prostitute's mother was an intense person who "owned" her. As a result of her mother's possessiveness, she wanted to avoid subservience and sentimental attachments by becoming a prostitute.

Retardation in emotional development seems to character-ize some prostitutes and has been reported among prostitutes in England, Italy, and France. Infantilism was studied by ad-ministration of the Szondi test to twenty-three streetwalkers in Paris, a matched control group of normal American women, and a group of fifty seven-year-old American public schoolchildren of both sexes. The basic personality pattern of the prostitutes tended to be much closer to those of the seven-year-olds than to the adult control group. Children and prostitutes lived compulsively on a concrete level, completely engrossed in the concrete world of real objects. The imper-sonal relatedness provided by prostitution may be analogous to the developmental stage of the first six months of life, dur-ing which others provide relief from the infant's physical tension.[70]

Acting out may be an important component of the emo-tional factors that lead to prostitution. When women act out in the course of psychoanalytic treatment, they sometimes engage in prostitution, threatening their socio-economic status as well as the continuance of their treatment. A twenty-six-year-old housewife had an amnesic episode which in-volved a living-out of a prostitution fantasy. Condemnation of this fantasy by her superego was completely suspended dur-ing the amnesic period in which the woman turned into a streetwalker. Under sodium amytal, the patient was able to recall everything that had happened in her period as a prosti-tute. Parents may find vicarious gratification of their own un-integrated forbidden impulses in a child's acting out, through their unconscious permissiveness or inconsistency. Accusa-tion, detailed questioning, and warnings could actually con-stitute unwitting permission for prostitution.[71]

For some women, the prostitute's role represents a com-bination of sexual gratification and moral humiliation that is an extreme of masochistic self-abasement. The injurious con-sequences of prostitution suggest that it may have an uncon-scious masochistic component, along with strong guilt about early sexuality. The prostitute may unconsciously seek punishment for incestuous strivings by denying herself normal adult love and marriage.[72]

Prostitutes may become tattooed as one expression of their masochism, thereby giving themselves more reason for self-pity by undergoing the pain of tattooing.[73] Prostitutes' tattoos reflect a cynical humor. One New York prostitute had the inscription "Keep Off the Grass" above her pubic hair. She married a man who did not know of her past but discovered the inscription immediately after their marriage and nearly murdered her. Another woman had "Admission 50¢" over the same part of her body. Although she charged more for her services, the humor of the inscription involved humiliation and self-pity. Contemporary prostitutes favor flower and tree designs in tattooing.

There is reason to suspect that a number of prostitutes are functioning emotionally on an oral level. One unconscious motive possibly relevant to such cases is a hunger for the "sweets" of love. Sexual hunger which is displaced in the oral sphere may be resisted by loss of appetite, which preserves the symbolic dependence on the mother and permits release of aggression toward men in prostitution fantasies. Another dimension of orality is suggested by the analysis of a forty-eight-year-old prostitute who derived great pleasure from circumstantial talk that was almost indiscriminately communicated to clients.[74]

Anality seems to characterize a number of prostitutes. These women regard semen as excreta that could hurt and perhaps even kill them. Such mechanisms produce the delusion of persecution. They also lead to jealousy, as these women unconsciously want their pimps or husbands to seek out other women in order to spare themselves from the destructive effects of the husband-pimp's semen-feces.[75]

Fear of the streets, or agoraphobia, seems to be important in a number of women who may be attracted to prostitution. Agoraphobia involves repression of the impulse to take the first man who is met on the streets and can be regarded as a form of identification with the prostitute. Agoraphobia may represent a defense against the temptation of becoming a prostitute. Such fantasies can represent a displacement of incestuous desires from the father to a stranger.[76]

A good many women seem to have fantasies about becoming prostitutes. Such fantasies are not limited to any one class or group in the population. One twenty-three-year-old girl had fantasies in which she appeared as a seductive woman who used men as impersonal sexual tools and blamed them for "perversions." In some women the fantasies appear to result from real or imagined subjection by the husband, while in others they help to provide security.[77]

A patient with prostitution fantasies identified with a prostitute in de Maupassant's story "Boule de Suif," which takes place during the Franco-Prussian War of 1870. A Prussian officer refuses passports to the passengers of a coach until one of them, a fat prostitute, submits to him. What attracted the patient was the fact that all the women passengers were participants in the sexual adventure of the prostitute with the officer. Under the guise of a heterosexual act, it was actually a homosexual one in which she exhibited before these women and made herself the object of a Peeping Tom in the emotions of the spectators. The women are interested in what the prostitute does in order to get their passports and unconsciously envy the girl because of her adventure. They also respond to the element of "sacrifice" with which the prostitute contributes to the fate of the women.[78]

Since it is impossible for the relatively few psychoanalysts to help the many thousands of prostitutes, psychoanalytic ideas can best be viewed as aids to understanding rather than as directly applicable techniques for mass treatment. Psychoanalytic studies conducted in many Western and Eastern countries tend to agree on a number of the characteristics of the prostitute's personality. Psychoanalysis is an internally consistent system, but we might have expected countries as diverse as Italy, India, and the United States to show differences in the needs met by a woman's participation in prostitution. The lack of such differences suggests that the psychoanalysts may be tapping a significant substratum of personality.

MALE HOMOSEXUAL PROSTITUTION

The male prostitute who services other males is sometimes called a hustitute and usually prefers to be called a hustler. The extent of male prostitution is difficult to gauge, not only because of the secrecy and furtive character of the pursuit, but because it involves large numbers of youths who engage in it only on occasion.[79] If prostitution is defined as the sale of sexual access as an occupation, the number of males participating at any one time would be rather small. If it is defined as the exchange of sexual favors for cash, on an indiscriminate basis and with no emotional involvement, the number would be much higher.

Few communities become concerned about homosexual prostitution because it is fairly concentrated and offends relatively few people. In almost all large cities of the United States there are street corners, parks, public bathrooms, and other locations where young men look for customers and older men seek temporary partners. Sometimes the same areas are used for "cruising," a search for homosexual partners by persons who are neither seeking to pay or be paid. Generally, if there is a considerable age disparity it is understood that the older person will pay the younger; if both are fairly close to the same age level, one or both may be hustling, as they quickly discover.[80]

The street encounter between the hustler and the "score" is fraught with difficulty. The female prostitute must always suspect that the man she is approaching, or who is approaching her, may be a detective. In an all-male encounter both sides harbor such a fear. An arrest is much more significant for both. The female prostitute is seldom living with a family or holding down another job in the workaday world, so that she tends to regard an arrest as an unfortunate nuisance. The male hustler could very well be living with parents or other family members, working at another job or going to school, or visiting on a weekend pass from the local army post. For him, arrest looms as a disaster. It is even more so for the customer, who is often a middle-aged man with a clerical or semi-professional job.

Homosexual client and prostitute meet on a "meat block," a section where men seeking such services are likely to be found, such as West 42nd Street in New York City. They look at each other on the street, each unsure of the other's role. The younger may put his hands in his pockets, where he ostentatiously moves them in a manner to draw attention to the fact that he is handling his genitals. The men hold each other with a stare, and one of them smiles slightly. Each is on guard lest he be making an error. The conversation starts innocuously: "Nice day, isn't it? Do you have a cigarette? How you doing, fellow?" Then it continues, with less caution: "Looking to make a few dollars? What are you doing tonight? Do you live around here?"

This sparring takes about three or four minutes until the two men arrive at an understanding: there will be payment for a homosexual encounter. There is a little bargaining over price, with the hustler demanding more or offering himself for less, depending on the age and physical attractiveness of the score. The hustler expresses a willingness to participate in various types of sex if more money is offered, insisting that he cannot participate "all the way" if the amount is small. For example, if the score insists that he can pay only $5 (the current standard fee) while the hustler has asked for $10, the latter relents and accepts the five. He will permit fellatio to be performed, and nothing more. "But, if you'll give me $10 . . ."

Bargaining over price and who does what to whom gives the hustler an opportunity to reinforce his own self-image as an essentially normal or straight person who is not "queer like the other guy." "I'm only involved in this sort of thing to earn a few extra dollars." If the customer is seeking an ultra-masculine type of male, as distinct from an effeminate gamin-like adolescent, the masculine image is fortified by the hustler's reluctance to be the recipient of fellatio or anal relations. A male prostitute who permits fellatio may not let the situation continue to orgasm. Some male prostitutes are very restricting in what they are willing to do, and any departure from their expectations may lead to violence against the client.

A community, like San Antonio, may have minimal heterosexual prostitution but considerable male prostitution. The West Coast seems to have more homosexual prostitution than other parts of the country. San Francisco has several massage parlors in which a homosexual can get a massage from a homosexual masseur. It also has a considerable amount of soliciting by male prostitutes, with about two hundred young men hustling in the Tenderloin area. Some male prostitutes seek customers in the downtown areas of large cities. A number may be addicts who engage in prostitution in order to get money for drugs. Many adolescent addicts are aware of homosexual prostitution as a source of funds which can be used to buy opiates.[81]

Turkish or steam baths in some large cities are popular places for making homosexual prostitution contacts. A customer wears only a robe or towel while in the baths. After taking a shower or steam bath, he generally rests in his bed, which may be in a private room or in a larger room with several other beds. Such circumstances facilitate overtures for homosexual prostitution. Some male prostitutes have no home and sleep in Turkish baths, bus terminals, or all-night movies if they do not score.

"Gay" bars generally discourage the patronage of male prostitutes. The bars fear police attention because of assaults and larcenies connected with male prostitution. Their habitués, who are often functioning effectively in the non-homosexual community, have little sympathy for prostitutes.

In a few large cities some attractively and expensively dressed male prostitutes look for customers in chic bars and in the lobbies of fashionable hotels. Some cities have male homosexual brothels ("peg houses") which are on the decline now that homosexual prostitution is generally conducted on an individual basis. Some male prostitutes look for customers in all-night movies in large cities. They move from seat to seat, hoping to find a client. Prostitute and client can quickly make arrangements for payment and engage in some form of sexual activity while sitting next to one another, in the bathroom, elsewhere in the theater, or outside.

The male prostitute is more sensitized than the female to his client's physical demeanor and dress. Many males have a sliding scale of prices, so that more personable customers pay less than relatively unattractive ones. Their concern about the customer's appearance suggests that the male prostitute is emotionally involved in his work to a much greater extent than the female.

The typical male prostitute seems to have fewer contacts during a given period of time and to be in business for less time than his female counterpart, perhaps because there is a smaller market for his services. His career's comparative brevity probably also reflects the extent to which youth is a more desirable commodity among men than among women prostitutes. The older the hustler, the less he can charge; the older the client, the more he must pay.

One reason for the relatively slight attention given by law enforcement agencies to homosexual prostitution until recent years was the substantial incidence of male prostitutes' engaging in robbery and violence against their clients. The victims seldom reported such incidents because of their embarrassment at admitting to sexual relations with their aggressors. As a result, official records showed very little homosexual prostitution. The family of the victim also often refused to help the police. There is always a possibility that the prostitute may threaten to blackmail his client, perhaps driving him to theft, embezzlement, passing bad checks, and, rarely, even to suicide.[82]

In addition to such hazards, homosexual prostitution is

probably a major cause of the spread of venereal disease. Perhaps three-fifths of homosexual prostitutes have had venereal disease. Some participants avoid anal intercourse, which they believe to be the most frequent method for infection, especially gonorrhea. There are also cases of hepatitis which have been spread by homosexual prostitution.

The typical male prostitute is between fifteen and twenty-five. Younger men may claim they are older in order to get into bars, and older hustlers often misrepresent their age in order to get larger fees. A sample of West Coast male prostitutes showed most not to be obviously effeminate. In another city, however, thirty-one of thirty-seven prostitutes were mildly to extremely effeminate in appearance and dress, five looked like "junior hoodlums," and one was a clean-cut "all-American" type.[83] The latter earned the most money, somewhat less than $100 weekly. The majority of male hustlers probably are strongly bisexual or homosexual. Only a minority are primarily heterosexual.

Some male prostitutes wear women's clothing. In September 1967 San Francisco police arrested thirty-three streetwalkers in one night, in response to the mayor's urging that the downtown district be cleaned up. Of the thirty-three, twelve were men in "drag." One man explained why he was "on the street": "Not only do you get a chance to give a blow job and get paid for it, but you get a chance to handle a lot of different organs."

Such men usually offer fellatio to a client, who cannot tell that the prostitute is male. In the last ten years there has been a steady increase in the number of male prostitutes in "drag" in many communities in all parts of the country. Such cities as Little Rock and Kansas City have a substantial number of men in "drag."

Of thirty-seven male prostitutes studied in a large American city, only four were steadily employed, usually at unskilled jobs (messenger, bellhop, busboy). Most felt that "only squares work." Only three had completed high school, and nine had been in the armed services. Twenty-two were

Roman Catholics. Eight youths were Spanish-speaking, eight were Negro, and seven were Irish-American. Five Italian-Americans, three Jews, three Anglo-Saxon Protestants, one French-Canadian, one Polish immigrant, and one person of unknown background were also included in the sample.[84]

Of thirty-three male prostitutes interviewed in San Francisco and thirty seen in Seattle, half had been in town for less than one year.[85] Most were Catholic or Protestant, and there were some Fundamentalists. The relative poverty of working male prostitutes can be inferred from the amount of money the subjects had in their pockets at the time of the interview. Thirty-four had less than $1, and only seven had more than $5. More than a fourth of the subjects had tried to commit suicide, and eight others had seriously considered it.

Most male prostitutes appear to come from intact homes but tend to be extremely hostile toward their fathers and to have experienced rejection by their families. Some have engaged in sex relations with their brothers, and a few have attempted such relations with sisters. In a substantial proportion of cases, the youth first became aware of disagreement with the father during a period of early exploratory homosexual behavior (cosmetics, for example, or wearing women's clothing, or bringing other effeminate youths to the house). The prostitute may have experienced at least one homosexual seduction as a youth.

Male prostitutes often experiment with amphetamines and marijuana, but few are alcoholics. A substantial proportion have been arrested, though comparatively few have come into contact with the police as the result of prostitution. They tend to be contemptuous of legitimate society and have a brash outer façade. It is common for male hustlers to be very mobile and to change their place of residence often. Few have permanent liaisons, though some may see the same client over a considerable period of time. A very small proportion of prostitutes become "kept boys" while outwardly working as secretaries, chauffeurs, or similar service occupations.

One book which helped to open up a public discussion of male homosexual prostitution was *City of Night*, a novel about an uneducated Texas boy who works as a homosexual prostitute in various parts of the United States.[86] As one prostitute gleefully noted, "We're a real social problem now —we even had a novel written about us." Sixty-five thousand buyers made the book's original edition into a best seller. Such a book might not have been published at all forty years ago, and would have enjoyed a limited sale only a decade ago. Genet, the famous French writer, has of course written about homosexuality for years, as did André Gide before him. The world of homosexual prostitution had previously been thoroughly explored, via case histories and epigraphy, in an earlier but unpublished monograph.[87] The movie *Jason* (1967), a frank and detailed presentation of the life of a male prostitute, was received very sympathetically in many American cities.

Programs of rehabilitation for male prostitutes are practically nonexistent. Members of the group are extremely mobile and are not likely to be in contact with or favorably disposed toward conventional treatment agencies. Their behavior affects a relatively closed minority group—the homosexual community—and is not likely to come to the attention of referral agencies because it is confined to a localized "meat block."

In a few communities, some male prostitutes have been responding to programs which offer counseling for "square" jobs and opportunities to enroll in schools and colleges. All of the thirty male hustlers who expressed interest in a "square" job in one Seattle program were placed. Psychopaths and very successful hustlers did not respond to job counseling. Many of the hustlers needed help in getting food and shelter as well as vocational orientation. A halfway house proved to be useful in resocialization. The hustlers were recruited into the program "on the street," and the interviewer avoided any social agency references.[88]

The relative success of this Seattle program suggests that

efforts to help prostitutes which are adaptable to the special requirements of a situation may achieve relative success. It also implies that such programs might offer a wide range of assistance and that different prostitutes, regardless of whether they are male or female, will seek different kinds of help—when they feel ready to do so and if it is offered in a way that is not threatening.

III. THE MADAM

Since 1945 there has been a decline in the number of auxiliary personnel connected with prostitution. Commercialized prostitution's best-known third person is the madam, who is the combination manager-hostess of the brothel. In the brothel's heyday she sometimes owned it and on other occasions was a paid employee. She acted as the head of the brothel "family." A madam running a typical city brothel in the 1920's and 1930's carried many responsibilities: to make arrangements for opening the place, attract prostitutes and customers, effect working relationships with police authorities and customers, and otherwise run a complex business establishment. She also had to be sensitive to a client's special interests and know how to praise his choice of prostitute.

Considerable tact was required to supervise a number of women competing with each other and working on a commission basis. The madam had to receive customers, encourage visitors to buy drinks, "show off" the prostitutes, collect and spend money, and keep records. She was the brothel representative who suffered punishment in case of a raid. If she were convicted and served time in prison, the brothel owner often paid her a fee for each day she was incarcerated. Although some madams regularly robbed clients who were too intoxicated to know what was happening, such behavior was infrequent.

The madam was responsible not only for keeping the prostitutes happy but for preventing quarrels and stifling jealousy. She was both friend and employer, and might have a strong emotional relationship with the prostitute. Her work made it almost inevitable that she would assume traditionally maternal functions. Prostitutes and customers often called her "mother." Many madams were practical psychologists who played on and exploited the fears and insecurities of their women.

A figure of consequence in the life of the madam was the man associated with her, usually half-lover and half-pimp. Although she regularly gave him money and other gifts, she did not regard him as a pimp. He typically spent much time gambling and had little to do with the operation of the brothel. The emotional tie between madam and paramour was similar to that between pimp and prostitute. The paramour occasionally was the man who made the administrative and financial arrangements with police and other authorities.

Fictional madams have often been presented fairly accurately in novels. A sentimentalized madam figured in the movie version of *Gone with the Wind* (1939).[1] Scarlett O'Hara refuses to engage in sexual activity with her husband Rhett Butler because she doesn't want to endanger her sixteen-inch waist by pregnancy. Rhett, unable to get into his wife's room, goes to a house run by the madam Belle, who manifests understanding and kindness and provides girls as well as gambling. Although decent women ignore her on the street, she is presented very sympathetically. A woman who uses misfortune to obtain what she wants is Irma, the lesbian madam in the film version of *The Balcony* (1962), made from the 1960 play by Jean Genet. She embodies power and evil majesty but permits her customers to have their illusions.

The author seems to enjoy presenting her humanity even though she is "bad."

The highly publicized autobiography by Polly Adler, *A House Is Not a Home*, appears to be substantially fictionalized, as was the film (1964) later adapted from the book. Miss Adler was admired by prostitutes because she had not only made a great deal of money as a madam but later succeeded in the "legitimate" world by writing a book about her illegitimate activities. Before her death Miss Adler had enrolled at a college on the West Coast and was working toward a degree. The fantasy of enrollment in a college after retiring is not uncommon among prostitutes. Although many read Miss Adler's book and decided to write their own autobiographies, few did so.[2]

Most madams are prostitutes who graduated to their new role. Some few may have been favorite women in a particular brothel, but the decision to become a madam usually depended on the availability of a backer. There appears to be a certain amount of friendship and cooperative activity among madams, even among those in different communities. They keep one another informed about changes in law enforcement that may affect their business. Some madams may have known each other in earlier careers as prostitutes.

Many madams pride themselves on being able to recognize a policeman, no matter how he disguises himself. One madam recently said, "I could spot a copper a mile away—if I don't see him I can smell him." There was a time when some policemen tended to be burly and perhaps relatively easy to recognize. There is no doubt that many madams could identify policemen in mufti by a combination of subtle clues.

Some madams enjoyed national reputations. Such a madam during the 1930's was Rose A., whose brothel straddled the state line between Massachusetts and Rhode Island. She would move her clients from one part of the house to the other, depending on which state was causing her difficulties. In Salt Lake City, "Jew Jenny" was queen of the underworld before World War II, as well as the leading "bag woman" for ten brothels. In New York, Polly Adler was the favorite of certain gangsters. Many noted madams during the prohibition era dealt regularly with gangsters who controlled the illegal liquor that was important to brothels. Other madams were involved in the illegal sale of narcotics.

One of the famous madams of Detroit was "Silver-Tongue Jean," who derived her name from skill at teaching and performing fellatio. In an interview conducted after her retirement, Jean smiled when she was asked about the hundreds of prostitutes whom she trained in fellatio: "The johns wanted it, so we gave it to them. I think I saved a lot of girls from contracting venereal disease that way. It's easier to avoid venereal disease than by the regular thing." Like many older madams, Jean once thought that gonorrhea was like a bad cold and syphilis a blood disease that could be cured at a drug store. "Now," she said, "a good hustler is well informed on venereal disease. Even in the old days I would tell the customers to show up for their inspection. If a customer looked bad, the girl would refuse to service him." Jean was like a number of other madams in not taking the prostitute's word for a man's freedom from venereal disease—she would check it herself.

Jennie the Factory in New York established a system of organization that was widely copied by other madams. She maintained seven large tenement apartments in different parts of New York. The location of the brothel would be changed from one apartment to another from day to day in order to confuse the police. Knowing that many customers did not give their real names, she would ask the customers for their birthday, jot down the date, and know which client was born, for example, on November 4. A client would call and say, "This is November 4 calling." As an additional identification Jennie would ask him for the name of the prostitute he had seen most recently. Jennie would say, "All right, today we are over in Brooklyn at———Street." Only one apartment would be in use on any one day. When the client arrived, he would be scrutinized by Jennie, who would not admit him if he seemed unfamiliar.

Similarly complicated plans were sometimes used by madams to deceive the police. In some communities a brothel customer would give his first name as well as the street number of his home address, and the city. Thus, John Smith of 17 Doe Street, Ashland, Ohio, might say that his name was John from No. 17 in Ashland. The madam would give him a card with his client number, for example 23. The card would not include the man's name in case it happened to fall into the possession of his wife. When calling the madam, he could identify himself as No. 23, giving his address. This would enable the madam to check on whether he had been a customer previously. He would go to an address designated by the madam, where she would give him the prostitute's location. In the Midwest a customer was often identified by the first three digits of his driver's license, which the madam recorded. When the man wanted a prostitute, he would telephone and identify himself, as 746, for example, and the madam would confirm his number.

Veteran San Francisco madam Sally Stanford had a succession of large and luxuriously furnished brothels which catered to a relatively well-to-do clientele. One former prostitute there recently recalled, "If your fingernail polish was not just right, she sent you home to brush it up." She developed a call-girl business when the police ended her brothel activities. In order to avoid detection she would never answer the phone herself. The man whose high-pitched voice answered the telephone at Miss Stanford's would have a standard patter: "It will be $25, honey. Do you want a blonde, brunette, or redhead, and slender, plump, or heavy?" After the client had made his choice, the man would say: "Where are you? She'll be there in a half-hour. Remember, you will have to pay the taxi fare both ways." Miss Stanford's telephone number was listed in the local telephone directory, and she made no attempt to conceal her business. After considerable harassment by law enforcement officials, she opened the Valhalla, a Sausalito restaurant and bar that has been quite successful. She ran for city councilman several times between 1962 and 1970 but was defeated each time. Many citizens campaigned for her, saying that her experience in running a successful brothel could be adapted to managing Sausalito. The writer Hilary Belloc recommended the slogan: "A chick in every cot." Other supporters said they wanted to be able to address her as "Madam Councilwoman."[3]

She was arrested seventeen times in the course of her career. Miss Stanford says that she was especially active in supplying women to the diplomats who founded the United Nations. "I did the best I could for them," she recalled. "There was a lot of money around, a lot of Arab princes. Once they came, I always remembered them. I was always at the door." She regards the current sexual scene with dismay. "There's been a general breakdown in morals," she laments. "If we had more prostitution today, we wouldn't have so much trouble."

Another madam who prided herself on being one of the first to use the honkey-tonk for prostitution had two daughters working in the establishment. She was a reigning madam from 1935 to 1941 in Phenix City, Alabama. Her honkey-tonk consisted of a bar with women who were available for dancing as well as sexual intercourse. The customer would express his interest in a woman, who then took him to one of a series of cribs near the bar. The women charged $5 for fifteen minutes.

Another well-known madam, whose brothel enjoyed special cachet because her daughter and granddaughter worked in the house, flourished in St. Louis during the 1920's and 1930's. The madam had been the mistress of one of the state's congressmen. When he left her nothing in his will, she opened a brothel in St. Louis after his death. While living in Washington with the congressman she had established a considerable reputation because of her ability to secure women for his colleagues. She was already well known by the time she opened her own establishment.

Lena Hyman (Mother H.), a madam who moved to Toledo, Ohio, from New York in the 1930's, had made over a million dollars, but died a pauper after being "taken over" at the age of sixty-five by a gambler-pimp who was many years younger and with whom she fell madly in love. She was famous for her skill in teaching various "perversions." Her elegant Saturday night chicken dinners for the police were quite well known. She would leave a cash "donation" under each policeman's plate. She always managed to have "connections" wherever she operated, and never complained about having to divide her earnings with those who made it possible for her to function.

Jealousy and greed between prostitute and madam sometimes led to disagreements that resulted in cleanups. In a southwestern Texas city during the 1930's madam Lucy Tatum claimed she had the vice squad "in the palm of my hand." When Lucy happened to discuss her "connections" with one of her prostitutes named Billie, both claimed the same protector. The argument reached a climax when Billie announced that she was tired of working for Lucy—and that she intended to become Lucy's competitor and open "the best house in town." Lucy lost no time in contacting her protector at the vice squad. Lucy fired Billie, who went to work at a rival house but talked to the press. As a result, practically all of the city's brothels were closed.

Other madams had a benign attitude toward their competitors. Tana Wallace, who had a brothel in San Antonio in the 1930's and 1940's and then reopened it in the guise of a poodle kennel outside the city limits in the 1950's, always cooperated with other madams. She used to shrug her shoulders and say that "there's enough business for all of us" when a competitor would "steal" one of her customers. Miss Wallace was well liked not only by competitors but also by customers. She was the first madam in the Southwest to make it generally known that she would pay all medical expenses for any customer who contacted a venereal disease from any of her prostitutes.

A madam had to remain on the alert not only for disgruntled inmates but also for customers who felt they had been badly treated. A customer might be irritated because he had been turned away when drunk, and might subsequently inform the police about the brothel's existence. Many madams, knowing the police were interested in the names and addresses of their customers, would use code for their "little black book." The customer usually called his list of prostitutes and madams a "little red book."

Through the 1940's some madams used lists of buyers' arrivals in various newspapers in order to reach potential clients. Many such lists gave the name of the hotel at which the buyer was staying. The madam would mail the buyer a printed note or card informing him that he might be interested in looking at some "new models" that could be inspected by calling a telephone number. Those buyers who were interested usually got the message.

Only in scattered communities, like Seattle and Pensacola, did the madam pay much attention to what a client and a prostitute actually did together. Many madams in Seattle used a one-way screen which appeared to be a mirror but was actually a transparent glass through which she and others could see without being seen. In Pensacola it was common for a madam to drill a small hole in the door of each room in her brothel, and peep through the hole from time to time in order to check on the prostitute. The precaution was necessary because some prostitutes performed and received extra money for fellatio but told the madam that the client had only engaged in coitus.

Some customers were eager to "date" the madam on the assumption that she was "good." Relatively few madams serviced customers directly because they did not want to violate the clear lines that separated them from their employees. There have, however, been cases of a madam engaging in lesbian relations with one of her prostitutes.

A frequent theme in prostitution folklore is the madam who marries a substantial businessman. When Miss Stanford married Robert Livingston Gump, a member of the prominent San Francisco merchant family, their wedding supper was held at Miss Stanford's brothel. A cartoon of the time showed the women chatting as they passed the Gump store. One said, "There's the famous Gump store. They're getting very prominent, aren't they?" "Yes," replied her friend. "One of them recently married into the Stanford clan."[4]

Prostitution folklore attributes alertness and shrewdness to madams. A story told about Sally Stanford illustrates these qualities. Her assistant had received a telephone order from some Arab leaders who wanted girls, but "no Jewish girls." When the assistant recorded the order she didn't connect the vertical lines of the letter "N," so that her notation looked like "110 Jewish girls." Miss Stanford rounded up a large number of prostitutes and gave each one a mezuzah to make them look Jewish. Shortly after the Arabs arrived, Miss Stanford learned from the clerk that "110" really should have been "No" on the order. An Arab asked Miss Stanford, "What are those things the girls are waving at us?" She quickly explained that they were "the latest and most wonderful American contraceptives." The clients accepted her explanation and enjoyed their visit.

Madams who go to jail usually return to their vocation after release. Madams may pride themselves on their ability to avoid the law, and some will even not admit to previous arrests. Ironically, many madams could not be convicted of prostitution but were successfully prosecuted for income tax violations. One brothel proprietor in South Carolina was fined $50,000 for failure to report her true income.

The average pre–World War II madam operated for approximately three to five years and then closed her establishment for one reason or another. Some went to prison, others lost out to racketeers, and some became restless and moved to another community. Today's madam is likely to be connected with any one brothel for a shorter period of time, because of the shifting nature of the contemporary situation.

Many madams pride themselves on behaving honorably. One of the best-known madams in Kansas City still lives in the city in which she worked for many decades. She recently said, "I never exploited a girl and always gave the customers a break." She had come from a small town in Kansas, married a man who later deserted her, and was influenced by some of her friends to become a prostitute. She ran a massage parlor with three or four women and became so familiar with local political influentials that she operated it without a license. She was arrested often but retired only because of illness.

A brothel was usually named after its madam. She had to try to become well enough known to attract a clientele, but avoid being so notorious that the community would seek to close her house. One of the best-known madams was Nell Kimball, whose career was fairly typical of the successful madams of the brothel era. She worked in a St. Louis brothel after being seduced by a man with whom she ran away from home. She was a prostitute for many years and mistress of a businessman for several years before she started her own brothel.

It was a profitable operation until one of her prostitutes accidentally killed a client, forcing her to close the brothel. She opened another in New Orleans, which also became successful. She was married several times. Her last marriage, to a much younger man, ended when she found him in bed with another woman. Miss Kimball made some unfortunate investments and died poor.

A story is told about Nell Kimball which has also been attributed to a number of other madams and summarizes the relationships between money and sex in prostitution. According to the story, a young woman noticed Miss Kimball, then in her fifties, at a restaurant with a handsome young man. The young woman initiated a conversation with Miss Kimball, who mused, "When I was young, I gave it away. When I was older, they paid me. Now, I have to pay them for it."

Miss Kimball was typical of other madams in her tolerance of almost any kind of request from her clients and of many kinds of unusual behavior among the prostitutes who worked for her. She was fairly rigid, however, in her distaste for lesbian activities among the women, believing that a woman who had become too involved in homosexuality could not be enthusiastic in servicing men clients.

Miss Kimball was representative of madams who "took care" of their employees. "And I made them wash, do their hair before they came down, and wear clean robes or peignoirs. I saw they had a good meal. No la-dee-da-ing. . . . One of the problems with whores is constipation. I insisted they stay regular and use cascara and rhubarb. At first most didn't like the daily bath I made them take, but I didn't put in all that plumbing just for show."[5]

Until World War II some madams provided a variety of special services. One prominent Buffalo madam who used to specialize in sex circuses for conventions recently observed, "I haven't done anything in three years. I can't make a connection. The police are too honest and won't take a dime." In smaller communities the madam may still be an accepted local figure. She contributes to local charities as a respected member of society. But in communities of all sizes her role in prostitution has declined with the need for her services.

IV. THE PIMP

A pimp derives part or all of his livelihood from the earnings of a prostitute. He is sometimes called a "meat salesman." Technically, a man who is regularly in the company of prostitutes and seems to exercise control over their activities in a manner which suggests that he is abetting them is presumed to be a pimp.

It is extremely difficult to estimate the number of pimps. One student of prostitution estimated in 1935 that Chicago's population of three million included approximately 8,800 full-time prostitutes and 6,300 pimps.[1] By the very nature of the pimp's relationship to the prostitute, it is difficult to tell how reliable such figures are.

Among the pimp's roles is getting the woman's cash, being on the alert for police, attempting to bribe the police, posting bail, and obtaining a lawyer if one is needed. Pimps are available when "things happen." A drunken or disgruntled customer who causes trouble may be handled by the pimp, who can get other pimps to join in beating the customer.[2] Pimps generally have their own code of ethics, which involves their not stealing or seducing another pimp's prostitute.

The pride and affection that some prostitutes have for their pimps may not be beautiful to outsiders, but it is genuine. In as much as the prostitute's body is for sale, her giving it to the pimp is one expression of her commitment to him. There is some reciprocity between the prostitute's attitude toward her client and her pimp's attitude toward her —each uses the other for money while conveying a semblance of emotion. One pimp noted, "She's a whore and I'm a whore too—I don't put out unless I get paid by her, except that I'm the one who decides when I put out. It's a tough game but you have to go by the rules."

Several different sexual relationships are possible between pimp and prostitute. They may share an interest in specific "perversions." Some pimps may engage in cunnilingus and thus be able to service several women within a short time. (Orality may be easy for a pimp in that it may reflect the passivity that is an important factor in his personality. It satisfies sucking needs, does not require touching, and does not challenge potency.) Although pimp and prostitute may complement each other's sexual needs, the sexual relationship between the two often diminishes with the passage of time. Stories about the great sexual prowess of pimps are very likely false.

A pimp may also be a bookmaker, confidence man, or otherwise engaged in criminal activity. Such a man, who presumably has underworld connections, provides special security for the prostitute against robbery and assault, for given the nature of her profession she is usually reluctant to call in the police after she has been the victim of a crime.

One appeal of the pimp can be seen in a remark by a veteran prostitute. After her pimp had left town for a few weeks, she said, "I will find it very difficult to live without him. He has always made me feel very good about myself. I was only a prostitute, but he treated me like I was a real lady." The pimp may be the only sustained object of affection for the woman and is a surrogate husband or relative. She can relax and discuss her work with the pimp, who provides stability and discipline, and is simultaneously an audience, employer, and manager. He is available at odd hours to accompany the woman to bars and restaurants where others "in the life" gather. Pimps tend to seek out each other's company in order to avoid embarrassing questions from others about the sources of their income.

For some women the pimp represents a major appeal of prostitution. If a woman wants to abandon prostitution, she knows that the pimp will also leave if she gives up "the life." The woman generally does everything possible to avoid causing trouble for her pimp and often takes the initiative in resolving a dispute with him. She will deny that she gives him money and often claim that he is working at a legitimate vocation. She may identify him as her "boy friend," with whom she happens to be living. When asked if her "boy friend" knew about her work, one woman said, "Sure, he doesn't mind. Why should he? We're not married."

The ability of a prostitute to believe well of a pimp can be seen in those situations when she is sent to jail for as long as a year or two. Although she knows that her pimp will be consorting with other prostitutes during this period, she is likely to say, "I know he will be seeing those other girls while I am away, but I don't mind. I know I am really the only one he cares for." She says this although fully aware that she is of no value to the pimp while she is in prison. Many prostitutes have spent months and even years in jail rather than divulge the names of their pimps. One pimp with five women recently observed, "They don't believe you're really using them, even if you have other girls. Each girl thinks that in a few years it'll be just you and her."

Often a man becomes a pimp by meeting a prostitute who falls in love with him and gives him money. He finds the life pleasant and associates himself with another prostitute when the first relationship lapses. The pimp may appear on the scene after the woman has already "turned out," but some help to start the young woman in her new vocation. "I was a young kid and I met this guy in a big car who took me to an after-hours club," one woman said recently. "He was sweet to me and I liked him. He suggested that we could swing if I did a little balling with some fellows. It didn't really bother me and I liked the guy, so I figured why not?" Pimps often try to associate themselves with a prostitute as soon as she has entered "the life," because during this period she is often least sure of her commitment and needs assurance that she has done the right thing.

Some pimps try to recruit new properties by going to court and observing those prostitutes who do not have money for bail. The pimp may then put up the bail and leave the courtroom with the unattached woman. One pimp observed: "I put up bail and walk out with the girl. I then psych her and use psychology when I'm turning her out to work. Show her nice things, swinging friends that I have, attention, and she's mine."

A pimp's previous work may have provided occasions for him to function as an intermediary with customers—as bellboy, elevator operator, or barman. He may have drifted from there into a subsequent career as a pimp. During the 1930's a number of men entered the vocation when they could not get other work.

The women working for the pimp are generally described as his "stable" or his "wives." Several women working for the same pimp often refer to themselves as "wives-in-law." A pimp with several women usually has a favorite or "number one" or "bottom woman."

A pimp often tells his woman that her career as a prostitute is going to be relatively short-lived because he will take her away from "the life" after one or two or three years, or after she has earned a specific sum of money. His "saving" her money for a future shared goal provides a justification, if one is needed, for her work. A prostitute seldom ends up with the pimp for whom she initially worked, for he is likely to leave as she grows older and less able to earn a good living.

But some pimps actually marry their women. In about half of these cases, the wife has continued as a prostitute. It is not likely that many pimps marry a prostitute in order to support her by earnings from a legitimate occupation.

On occasions in years past, there was competition between the pimp and the madam. Some pimps with their own stable of girls did not want to share income with a madam. A pimp might propose to a prostitute that she leave her madam and work for him. On the other hand, a madam sometimes worked in collusion with a pimp in driving his prostitute to work hard. Some madams preferred that a prostitute keep a pimp because he forced her to work even harder. A pimp-less prostitute was often called an "outlaw," a term that expressed the difficulties that such a woman presumably posed because of drinking, unreliability in reporting for work on time, or otherwise causing trouble for the madam.

In the heyday of the brothel, some pimps accompanied their prostitute from community to community. One function of a pimp was to keep informed about working conditions and income at various brothels so that he could direct his woman to the best place. A number of pimps lived near the brothel, not only to cope with drunkards and obstreperous or nonpaying clients, but also to check on the number of customers. The typical pimp of the pre-World War II years lived in an apartment of his own. Very few were ever permitted to live on the brothel premises.

Some lesbian pimps keep house and manage the affairs of a woman prostitute. Such a pimp generally wears men's clothes and functions as the "butch" or aggressor. The prostitute has heterosexual relationships with her clients but maintains a "jasper" or lesbian situation with her "bull-dyker."

During the 1930's and even into the early 1940's there were a considerable number of French pimps (*souteneurs*) in some large cities. They were avaricious exploiters who have gradually disappeared, a good many by deportation. Some *souteneurs* would assault women who did not bring in enough money. In one well-known case in New York, a *souteneur* began whipping a prostitute. She complained to a policeman, who gave the woman his gun and urged her to "kill him." She did and was acquitted, although the policeman got a one-year sentence.

During the twenties and thirties many pimps were of Italian or Jewish background. More recently they tend to be Negro or Puerto Rican. Pimps in big cities used to have favorite meeting places where they would play cards, gossip, and relax. Sachs' Restaurant on West 28th Street and Bernstein's Delicatessen on Seventh Avenue in New York were well-known pimp headquarters. In Washington, bars at 9th between E Street, N.W., and Pennsylvania Avenue were gathering places for pimps. Nearly all cities had similar hangouts. When pimps arrived in town, they went to these places, introduced themselves, and sought information about local conditions from their colleagues.

Pimps were seldom involved in theft or crimes of violence, except for bravura purposes. One pimp was very proud of having stolen a sable coat from dancer Lillian Loraine, the girl "with the most beautiful back in the world." Its belonging to her was more important to him than its value.

A number of pimps were young men from good families, like Max M., a famous pre–World War II pimp in New York City. He was the scion of a wealthy family but had become a narcotics addict. He used to spend most of the day sitting in a delicatessen with a fellow pimp playing the Hungarian card game of Klabiatsch.

Another representative figure in the pimp underworld of the 1930's was Anthony A. of Buffalo. Of his three women, two worked in a $5 brothel and the third in a $10 house. Each knew of the existence of the others, and they competed to see who could give the most money to Anthony. Once a woman joined his stable, she did not dare to leave until he had discarded her. Anthony required each woman to turn over all her earnings to him; he would return to them whatever seemed reasonable to him. He lived luxuriously, dressed extremely well, and drove an expensive automobile. He was influential enough to make special arrangements with the madams of the brothels in which his prostitutes worked. Most madams paid their women at the end of the week, when the women would give the money to their pimps. Anthony made weekly visits to the brothels and himself picked up the earnings of his stable.

An example of pimp morality is the case of Mack S., who was arrested in Los Angeles in 1942 for violating the Mann Act. A prostitute whom he had transferred across the state line confessed and implicated him. The famous Hollywood lawyer who represented Mack advised him to marry the woman. After Mack told her that he loved her, they did marry. The case was dismissed on the ground that a wife could not testify against her husband. Immediately thereafter, Mack took his bride back to their hotel room and beat her into unconsciousness. He subsequently moved to a large Texas city, where he resumed his career introducing teen-agers to prostitution.

During the twenties and thirties the pimp was often a drug addict, and the prostitute's earnings contributed toward supplying him with drugs. The pimp's routine typically included drug use, visiting a good restaurant early in the day, going to a prize fight, baseball game, wrestling match, or other sporting event later in the day, and some form of gambling.

One prominent pre–World War II addict pimp was Whitey Lewis, whose prostitute was known as Lillie the Bitch. She worked at a twenty-women brothel in Bethlehem, Pennsylvania, which serviced the workers at a nearby steel mill. Whitey was a well-known opium smoker and had a subsidiary business selling drugs. Ultimately convicted of violation of the narcotics laws, he died in jail.

Pimps today often are alcoholics or addicts, and some even sell drugs to their women. Pimps sometimes take drugs when relaxing in a social situation with fellow pimps. They often take them before engaging in sexual activity with their women, both to bolster their feelings of manhood and to increase their sensations of well-being and relaxation. One Los Angeles pimp observed, "I take a shot of heroin before I spend some time with one of my girls. It relaxes me and it takes me a lot longer to pop off."

Many contemporary pimps appear to get women either by faking an emotional interest or offering to help a woman make money, or some combination of the two approaches. Bob is a thirty-five-year-old Chicagoan who started as a small-time gambler and exploited his charm into a career which now produces about $60,000 a year from the five women in his stable. "I decided to get into the racket. So I went with a babe till she was all hot about me. Once she was nuts over me, I told her I had lost my job because I was sick. I had talked up what a good life hustling could be. Just dropped a hint here and there, so it was in the back of her mind. She took a couple of dates and it worked out fine. I told her that we'd have a great life together and in a month she was a real working girl. She's been gone for years, but I have five girls now."

Al is a thirty-three-year-old New York pimp who makes no pretense about what he is doing. "I don't waste time with a girl. Either she's ready to work for me or not. If not, another one will. A girl that has to be broken in is no good. Either she looks awful or is too fat or just can't handle men. I want a girl that has fooled around with guys and has what it takes. I tell her she'll get a break with me and I'll try to make big money for her and that she'll have fun and an easy life. I look after her interests. I take her to a dress shop, beauty parlor, and dentist, and remove her moles. I show a girl that she's been wasting her life working for peanuts and giving it away. My girls have what it takes. It's a good deal for them." Al has served as a pimp for "about two dozen" girls since he started ten years ago.

Many pimps develop extensive interests in a hobby or the arts. One dog trainer who was a leading Philadelphia pimp acquired the nickname of Mutt. His career as a pimp extended from 1921 to 1965. He was associated with a number of different prostitutes who worked at houses in the city's prostitution area, from Arch to Spring Garden Streets on the north side, and between Eighth and Broad Streets.

Pimps tend to have unusual nicknames. "Red Devil," "Blue," "Snapper," "Snake," and "Bomber" are the names of some pimps recently interviewed in Chicago. Many pimps who dress garishly and enjoy driving conspicuous cars have relatively young and naive prostitutes. Dressing conspicuously in extremely colorful clothing has long been a characteristic of the pimp.

A pimp who needs ready cash may sell a prostitute to another pimp. In New York City during recent years such sales have occurred for as little as $50. Pimps also exchange prostitutes with other pimps. The women usually complain vigorously about such sales or exchanges but generally comply with the arrangement. Sometimes one pimp places a woman in pawn to another pimp in order to "work out" a debt.

A pimp tends to remain in the vocation until forced out by law enforcement authorities. If he leaves pimping, he often drifts into some other illegal activity. A pimp whose woman leaves him will generally try to find another prostitute. During the depression, pimping became a temporary activity for some men because of illness, inability to find other work, and similar setbacks.

A pimp often has a "Mexican bankroll," a large bill on the outside covering a roll of singles. Although most pimps dress flashily, there are some whose source of income would be almost impossible to guess from their appearance or conversation. A pimp today is likely to be relatively discreet about pandering, like the man who recently approached an out-of-towner visiting New York City: "Can you show me your driver's license? I have my own girls. I have to make sure I'm not talking to someone on the vice squad. You look okay. I'll take you to a place where I'm sure you will have a good time."

Pimps are not especially concerned about moral stigma. The popular greeting, "Hello, pimp," seldom embarrasses its recipient. The "righteous pimp" is one who is fully committed to his work and has no misgivings about it. A "mackman" (probably from the French *maquereau*, or pimp) who has more than one prostitute may be as busy as the New York "mack" who observed: "You think I take it easy? I have to take care of my hole, keep her away from other guys, get her welfare check on 'mother's day,' and take care of myself. It's a tough life."

As for the personality of the pimp, a man's being kept by a prostitute may involve regression to the desire to be kept by the mother.[3] Castration anxiety and impotence may be other factors in the personality of the pimp.[4] Some pimps may be covering up a homosexual drive and have a feeling of self-abasement that is as strong as that of some prostitutes. The pimp's ability to externalize his aggression seems to prevent him from feeling as self-destructive as the prostitute. Symbolically, the pimp can be seen as an older brother who simultaneously protects his sister against other aggressions and subjects her to his own aggression.[5]

Many prostitutes congratulate themselves on waking up in the morning and seeing "the only thing lower than myself next to me in bed." A white prostitute who has a Negro or other minority-group member as a pimp may be reinforcing her feelings of worthlessness. Masochism seems an important part of the prostitute's relationship to her pimp. Some prostitutes have tattooed a pimp's name or picture on their skin, but such decorations can lead to unpleasant quarrels when pimps are replaced. Some older prostitutes use a lit cigarette to eliminate tattooed names of former pimps.

The prostitute's continuing association with a pimp after he has brutally beaten her has puzzled many observers. Some pimps regard a "gorilla" (beating) as the best way to demonstrate love, and there are prostitutes who share such views. For some prostitutes a beating by a pimp is a kind of symbolic equivalent of an argument between a middle-class husband and wife. The subculture of violence from which many prostitutes and pimps come has its own vocabulary of emotion. The sadistic pimp can rationalize a beating by saying that he had to do it as a lesson for some presumed error or wrong. As one said, "You can't let a girl get away with that kind of thing or she won't have any respect for you." Violence may be one way in which pimp and prostitute can cope with their problems of expression and communication.

A pimp sometimes beats a prostitute as one way of celebrating the beginning of her career with him. This is especially likely in the case of a pimp who has several women and is selecting a new "bottom woman." Some pimps believe that the best way to secure a woman's loyalty is to beat her into unconsciousness and then "hump" her. One recently explained: "I told this girl—she was nineteen years old and had lots of mileage left in her—that she was my new bottom woman but she would have to prove it. I whipped her till she passed out and gave her some head [engaged in cunnilingus]. I told her that if she wanted to see my swipe [penis] she would have to prove herself and show she was a real hustler."

It is difficult to obtain evidence against pimps that is valid in a court of law. The only activity for which they can be easily apprehended is pandering. The relatively few pimps who are convicted are usually found guilty of misdemeanors rather than felonies. On the very few occasions when a prostitute has testified against her pimp, he is generally charged with forcing her to engage in prostitution. Even when a prostitute testifies against a pimp, she needs corroborating evidence, which is difficult to obtain.

Some women are frightened of their pimp, while others are suspicious about how he spends money. He usually gives her very little money, in order to minimize her desire to leave. At first the pimp is usually grateful for the money that he receives, then he takes it for granted. The prostitute is intimidated and feels that only an increase in her earnings can enable her to keep him. When one woman takes a pimp over from another, a quarrel and even violence may result. The woman who lost her pimp typically sends his successor to rob or smash the apartment of her rival. The importance of the relationship can be inferred from the considerable number of prostitutes who commit suicide after desertion by a pimp.[6]

With the development of prostitution into an individual entrepreneurship, there are fewer pimps who "own" their women. In the last twenty years there has been increasing use of the phrases "popcorn" or "chili" or "coffee-and-cake" pimps to suggest their lessened importance to the prostitute. The decline of the brothel has made the pimp less of a business asset to the prostitute. Some pimps even have part-time "legitimate" jobs and receive only "chump change" or pocket money from their prostitutes. Whereas pimps used to select the brothels in which they wanted their women to operate, today they sometimes stay in the background. The contemporary pimp may disappear rather than help in the event of trouble. The emotional and companionship needs which the pimp meets are sufficiently strong, however, to insure that he will continue to be a significant figure in the prostitute's world.

V. BIT PLAYERS

Taxi drivers, bellboys, and other auxiliary personnel may function as panders, who aid or abet in procuring customers for prostitutes. Although a pander is seldom a pimp, many a pimp is also a pander. The booker is a pander who schedules prostitutes for specific assignments, in the same way that a theatrical agent booked performers into theaters, but his role has become negligible in recent years.

The go-between is a person who acts as intermediary between prostitute and client. A specialized go-between is the procurer, who inducts a girl into prostitution. The cadet was a procurer who seduced a young girl, often after promising to marry her. Once the woman was established in a brothel, the cadet would look for other victims, who were likely to be poor working girls and immigrants whose English was poor. The cadet helped to maintain a steady supply of prostitutes.

The procurer was sometimes called a kaftan, a name deriving from the large coats worn by some European Jewish procurers during the twenties and thirties. The name remained even though the coats were not worn in this country by procurers. Many kaftans were successful in recruiting prostitutes in Europe. Posing as marriage brokers, they would visit the European ghetto areas and promise young girls a husband. Kaftans often worked closely with a booker, who ran a central registry of brothels in his area and knew their personnel requirements.

Other go-betweens include the steerers and "wigwaggers" who once operated in larger communities. The steerer mingled with other men in places where there were likely to be customers for prostitutes, and disseminated appropriate information. They were especially active around burlesque theaters in Chicago and New York during the 1930's. They directly accosted prospective "johns" and spoke glowingly about the "nice girls" available, sometimes distributing cards with the girls' addresses. The "wigwagger," also called a "lighthouse," was a lookout for police. Some had specific assignments, like the man in Buffalo who kept the head of the vice squad under surveillance. When the police official went home for dinner, the "wigwagger" telephoned from a pay booth so that the brothel proprietors could begin accosting from windows and doorways.

If the go-between is suspicious of a prospect, he delays any overtures until certain that he is not dealing with the police. Once he is convinced that the prospect is a "true john," a high-pressure sales talk usually follows. Recent go-betweens have not been as aggressive as their counterparts of a generation ago. Although still eager to introduce prostitutes, they now usually wait to be approached by customers or are alert for some other sign.

The laws of all states provide penalties for go-between activity and any assistance in prostitution or procuring. Some jurisdictions actively prosecute go-betweens but others do not. In New York convicted steerers generally get a substantial sentence. In parts of the South they are seldom even tried. Florida and other southeastern and southwestern states are especially lax in prosecuting go-betweens. It is rare for a go-between to report a colleague to law enforcement authorities, except where the "stool" is seeking some favor from the police.

The "Murphy man," named after a legendary Tenderloin confidence man, appears to be a pander but takes money from a customer without producing a prostitute. He may approach a potential client and say, "I've got a girl for you, but let me take care of your money so you don't get robbed." Or, "Give me the money and I'll give it directly to the madam so you won't be overcharged." In both cases the "Murphy man" will disappear with the money, usually after making the classical envelope switch, in which an envelope stuffed with paper is replaced for one with money.

Sometimes the Murphy man cites fear of the police as the reason why he must receive money from the customer before the latter can meet the prostitute. One intermediary who approached a customer in New York City said: "You must pay me before you can go to the girl's apartment. She doesn't want to take the money herself. I take the money for her in case a vice squad guy should get to her. She doesn't want the vice squad guy to give her marked bills, so that I handle all the money." Many visitors from out of town have undoubtedly given the intermediary their money under such a pretext. It is unlikely that a fleeced customer will go to the police with his story.

A version of the Murphy in which an accomplice is unnecessary involves a prostitute who carries a spare dress inside her brassiere. She strips down to her underclothes and asks the client for the money in advance. When he pays, she goes to the bathroom, presumably to prepare herself, but actually puts on the dress and leaves either by the window or by running through the room.

Panders sometimes use photographs of women as an enticement, although the likeness may not be of the woman whose services they are selling. All over America, men now sidle up to a prospect and begin: "You see the picture *Never on Sunday?*" They palm a photograph of Melina Mercouri and ask, "Want to go to bed with a girl from the movie?" The man who accepts the proposal is likely to be disappointed.

TAXI DRIVERS

The taxi driver in many communities steers potential clients to prostitutes. As a taxi driver's license is a valuable asset, the driver is likely to be aware of police activities and to balance such hazards against the 40 per cent of the prostitute's fee that represents his payment. In most large cities, taxi drivers work for fleets, and a driver apprehended as a go-between will probably lose his job.

Some taxi drivers solicit a passenger instead of waiting for him to inquire about a prostitute. Others wait for the customer to ask. One way in which customers may interest a cab driver in producing a prostitute is to ask the driver what sounds like a rather casual question to which he can respond if he wishes—for example, "Where can a guy have a good time?" or "Where's the action?" Some taxi drivers have a printed card with their name and telephone number and make it clear to the passenger that he can make arrangements for some "fun" by telephoning.

Some drivers used to refuse to take a legitimate passenger to his destination because of their greater interest in delivering clients to prostitutes. Typical of many cities was Buffalo during the 1930's, when a number of independent taxi drivers derived their major income from prostitution. These men, with picturesque names like Big Fatima, Little Fatima, and Dixie, would try to accost every man going to or from large hotels. If he called "Taxi!" they would ask if he wished to go "down the line" to the red light district. If he had another destination they would refuse to take him. If hailed by a customer to go to another destination they would say, "Sorry, but I'm waiting for someone."

Scattered on Niagara Avenue in the Johnson Park area of Buffalo were more expensive brothels, which got most of their customers from independent taxis which used to "hustle" every man leaving or entering the hotel and tell him, "We've got some fine stuff if you'd like to try it." The cab drivers provided most of the customers for the higher-priced brothels in Buffalo. Practically none of the taxi drivers who were active as go-betweens are still working with prostitutes. One recently said, "If I know a guy is okay, I can arrange for a call girl, but if I don't know him, I don't even try." Another said, "If I have two liners a week, that's a lot." Each driver used to take an average of ten customers a night to brothels. One man formerly prominent in the prostitution underworld now owns a fleet of taxis, but will not permit his drivers to have anything to do with prostitution.

The driver did not always take a client directly to a prostitute. He might remove his cap and park his cab at least a block away from the brothels in order to avoid suspicion. Other drivers would telephone and receive approval from the madam or prostitute to have the client appear by himself. A madam might not accept a customer who came in a taxicab because she felt that it called undue attention to her activities.

Some taxi drivers work exclusively with one establishment and say, "The best place in town is ———," or "The place for a man like you is ———." Such a driver gets a special bonus in addition to the standard 40 per cent fee. The role of taxi drivers as go-betweens has been declining in the last decade because a number of drivers have been arrested for taking servicemen to prostitutes. Many prostitutes arriving in a new town will nevertheless still ask a taxi driver, "Where is the best place to go for a little hustling?"

In many smaller communities taxi drivers play a significant role as intermediaries. Recently a taxi driver in Georgetown, South Carolina, told a passenger: "I can take you to a house with ten nice-looking young girls. It's about four miles out from town. The cab fare is $1.50 each way and I'll wait for you ten minutes without extra charge. The house is safe and men come from all over to go to it. The girls get examined every week by a local doctor. Because it's a little past the city limits, the law never bothers the place." The passenger noted that the driver used code to tell his dispatcher that he was taking the passenger to the brothel, presumably as a precaution against any police who might be listening to the conversation. The driver said he would be happy to wait while the passenger had a "short date." Other drivers recommended the same brothel and seemed to have a working relationship with it.

BELLBOYS

The hotel bellboy or porter, like other intermediaries, receives 40 per cent of the prostitute's fee. Her fee may be increased if the bellboy senses that the customer is a "live one" who might pay more than the going rate. Some few bellboys do not take money from the prostitute but instead develop a credit which they "take out in trade." This is especially frequent in the South.

Hotels differ in their attitudes toward bellboys collaborating with prostitutes. In parts of the Southeast and Southwest, some hotels feel that providing a prostitute is part of hotel service. They do not disapprove of bellboys or porters acting as go-betweens. Some Oklahoma City hotels used not to pay salaries to bellboys because it was assumed that their income would come from prostitutes. Most hotels in other cities, however, will dismiss a bellboy who is apprehended for steering a client to a prostitute.

The bellboy may wait for the hotel guest to initiate the request by asking about the opportunities for "fun" in the city, or he may initiate the discussion himself. Some bellboys glance meaningfully at the hotel guest as they bring the baggage to his room and say, "If there is anything at all you might want, just let me know; I'm Number 14. Remember, anything at all." If the client is interested the bellboy will contact the prostitute. He might then telephone the client and report, "Sir, this is Number 14. The package you were waiting for has just arrived." The client will tell him to "Please send it up now." Some aggressive bellboys stand in front of hotels and greet men walking by with, "Hi, Captain, how are you tonight?" or a similar phrase. If the man responds, the bellboy will continue: "We've got some nice girls here—all you have to do is get yourself a room." Such a greeting is primarily for out-of-towners, as local residents usually know about such services. If the man says, "I already have a hotel," the bellboy will encourage him to rent a cheap room to take advantage of the "nice girls." A potential client may try to lower the price: "Why should I shell out money when I don't know what I'm getting? I may not like the girl." The bellboy may counter, "I'll put you in a vacant room so you can save some money." Some small hotels have "date rooms," where a client can inspect the prostitute before going to her room.

Some bellboys collaborate with prostitutes who travel a great deal and stay at a hotel only for a few days. A bellboy in a Southern city recently told a man checking into a hotel: "Have I got a girl for you! She's a blonde, nineteen years old. Just arrived in town this morning and will be around for three days. She'll be making the circuit of all our hotels, but I can fix you up while she's here."

NIGHTCLUB PERSONNEL

Steerers may be found among some bartenders, waiters, and doormen. Most receive the usual commission from the prostitute, but others furnish names and addresses out of friendship. A potential client usually has to intimate that he would like to meet a prostitute. He may ask, "What's wrong with this town? I've been here ten days and haven't seen any action." This is a sufficient cue to nightclub employees alert to such interest.

One bartender in a Los Angeles nightclub recently observed: "I make more than twice my regular pay by working with hustlers. I can tell when a guy wants to pay instead of waiting for a 'Georgia' [sexual access without pay]. When I get a live one, I give one of the girls the office by looking at the john and nodding. The girl goes with the john and levels with him—no snatch before scratch. They are honest with me. I also have a deal with taxicab drivers who bring johns to the club—we split 50-50 on the money the girl gives me. It's good for me and the drivers and good for the girls. The johns get clean stuff and it's good for them."

A Denver bartender boasted: "I'm doing the guy and the girl a good turn. I've got the girls that work my bar. If I see a guy who looks like he wants some action, I tell him that one of my girls—whoever is there—is lonely and was just divorced, and is looking for a good time but is broke right now. If he gets the message, I tell her that he wants to buy her a drink—that's how she knows he's okay, and not just looking for a pickup."

LEGAL PERSONNEL

Some bondsmen used to specialize in cases involving prostitution. At one time a "straw bond" could be made by a "reputable" citizen who appeared at the station house and vouched for a woman arrested for prostitution. For example, the owner of a bar that used to be at Seventh Avenue and 30th Street in New York City would be told by the police that they had arrested a prostitute. He would go to the station house and "vouch" for her. She was then released and would give the tavern owner $10, half of which he gave to the police. Professional bondsmen still generally charge a high fee for making a bond for a prostitute, but they are no longer likely to specialize in such matters. Bail is now usually provided by relatives or friends of the defendant.

During the thirties and forties some lawyers handled only prostitution cases. Sometimes the lawyer received the equivalent of a retainer from a group of prostitutes. Typical was the arrangement in Oklahoma City, where one lawyer visited the bell captain of each hotel weekly at a specified time. Each bellboy gave the captain a percentage of his earnings from prostitution during the preceding week, and the captain shared his income with the lawyer. In exchange, the lawyer defended any of the women or bellboys who were arrested.

The small group of lawyers who used to specialize in prostitution cases has also been dwindling. Fairly typical of the change is the situation in New York City, where over half the prostitutes tried are represented by the Legal Aid Society. About a dozen lawyers in private practice specialize in prostitution cases and represent many of the women not served by Legal Aid.

In a few large cities a relatively few attorneys still dominate the representation of prostitutes in legal actions. In one city a single attorney handles four hundred cases of prostitution a year, and ten other attorneys represent most arrested prostitutes not referred to a public defender. Some police are said to work in collusion with criminal lawyers, and may suggest to a prostitute whom they arrest that a particular lawyer can help her.

PHYSICIANS

Physicians may be among the auxiliary personnel attendant on prostitution. The American Medical Association has explicitly denounced the medical examination and certification of prostitutes.[1] The Association regards a physician who examines prostitutes and gives them "certificates" as a collaborator in an unlawful racket. The AMA points out that the cooperating physician inferentially gives a feeling of security which is not warranted by medical realities. The average prostitute, the Association notes, must have several contacts per day even to pay her expenses. A thorough inspection of a prostitute would take several hours, and the results would not be available for a few days. During this time an infected prostitute might have contact with a substantial number of men. Even when prostitutes were inspected every two days it was not possible to identify cases of venereal disease before customers were infected.[2]

Physicians who work for brothels are usually careful in

what they say about their clients. They generally write on a prescription pad sheet that the patient has "blood test, negative," or "smear, negative." They seldom say that a woman is "free of venereal disease." Such statements are colloquially often called "health cards" or "health certificates." Many of the physicians who examine or treat prostitutes are quacks.[3]

The physician who works for prostitutes is not violating any law. No physicians have lost their licenses or been reprimanded officially because of cooperation with prostitution. Some physicians whose certifications have been used by prostitutes to attest to their freedom from venereal disease have, however, been embarrassed by public disclosure of their affiliations.

VI. WAYS OF PLYING THE TRADE

Many different ways of
bringing customer and prostitute together have flourished in
America. Most of these were adapted from other countries.
Some are still in use and others have had a relatively brief
life. The vast expansion of all business activity in America in
the 1920's was also reflected in the growth of prostitution.
New techniques for recruiting immigrant girls after the
hiatus in migration during Word War I, combined with the
popular credo of people like Polly Adler that "anything which
is economically right is morally right," encouraged new procedures for arranging meetings between customer and
prostitute.[1]

Perhaps the only approach never tried in the United States
is the enforced prostitution in wartime that has been reported in other countries. The diary of one of the women
forced into prostitution by the Nazis during World War II,
who ultimately committed suicide, is a graphic reminder of
the possible effects of such mandatory prostitution.[2] Nor has
the United States ever been occupied as a result of war, a
time when prostitution often increases as a means by which

women are able to obtain money or even assure survival itself.

RED LIGHT DISTRICT

Probably the best-known setting for prostitution in the post–World War I decades was the segregated, or "red light," district. The phrase "red light" seems to have had its origin in Western railroad construction camps, where prostitutes outnumbered other women by as many as fifty to one. A brakeman visiting a prostitute would hang his red signal lamp outside her tent so that a dispatcher looking for the men to make up a crew could easily find him. On a busy night, a number of such tents that were close together became known as a red light district.

New Orleans before World War I probably had more overt prostitution in its red light district than any community since classical Piraeus.[3] People mentioned in today's society columns might be surprised to learn that the first such listing in America was the *New Orleans Mascot's* weekly column dealing with prostitutes.[4] Called "Society," a typical item noted: "It is safe to say that Mrs. Thewer can brag of more innocent young girls having been ruined in her house than there were in any six houses in the city."

Originally, the Blue Book was not a listing of members of the upper class but the New Orleans directory of prostitutes, bound in blue and sold for twenty-five cents. It displayed the candid motto of the Order of the Garter, "Honi Soit Qui Mal Y Pense" ("Evil to Him Who Evil Thinks") and was revised periodically after its first appearance in 1902. The Blue Book was quite explicit about its purpose: "This Directory and Guide of the Sporting District has been before the people on many occasions. . . . It regulates the women so that they may live in one district to themselves instead of being scattered over the city and filling our thoroughfares with street walkers." The Blue Book listed the brothels in Storyville, the red light district in the thirty-six square blocks from Basin to

Robertson, between Iberville and St. Louis Streets. At its peak, Storyville had 230 brothels, thirty houses of assignation, and many thousands of prostitutes. Brothels featuring women from different ethnic backgrounds were grouped by street to make the customer's choice easier.

One of the city's former madams recently reminisced: "When I turned out, there were houses with ten . . . yes, as many as fifteen girls—real hustlers who knew how to make money for the landladies and for themselves even though the prices were only $5 in the best joints. . . . In the days of the red light district, we turned as many as 25 tricks a day. . . ." Today, parts of Bourbon and Canal Streets in New Orleans may create the impression that the city is still wide open, but according to another madam with four decades of experience, "It's tighter today than it has ever been in recent years." "When a landlady has one girl on call," she asks, "can you really call that a house?" The diminution in prostitution in New Orleans is typical of the change that has occurred in other large cities.

Almost as famous as New Orleans was San Francisco's Barbary Coast, where a red light district thrived until World War II. One former pimp observed, "Of course it's many years since the Barbary Coast has been broken up . . ." He explained that since the 1940's the city has become "tighter and tighter," except for streetwalkers, and today a man "hustler bound" has "to give her the office [start the conversation]. It isn't like the old days, when Pacific Street was called Terrific Street."

A cab driver recently said: "There isn't a 'house' running. Only a few cab drivers will deal out a call girl. Look the bars over . . . some may have a broad or two, but you got to 'hustle' them. . . . Bellboys won't handle the stuff. They'll say, 'Talk to the cab drivers. . . .' " Another driver recalled that less than twenty years ago he could stand on the corner of Market Street and look along O'Farrell, Ellis, Eddy, Turk, and Golden Gate, and spot "the joints a mile away. . . . You spot one, you spot them all. They had large translucent globes hanging over the sidewalk from the doorway. Each one had a big black number, the number of the house, painted on it." The globe as a mark of identification apparently had been used by brothel keepers in many Pacific Coast cities, from San Diego to Seattle.

Troy, New York, was a representative smaller city with a red light district that attracted customers from as far away as Portland, Maine. In the twenties and thirties Troy's brothels made regular contributions to the political campaigns of local, state, and national candidates. Physicians cooperated and frequently examined the inmates. The brothels charged as high as $5 a visit because of their medical expenses. The owners would send any man claiming to have contracted venereal disease at a house to a physician and pay all his bills. The houses were closed in 1942 as the result of pressure from the governor, who was outraged to learn of a poor family with three small children that had been dispossessed to make way for a brothel.

As in many other American cities, the pattern of prostitution in Washington, D.C., has changed radically in the years since World War I. Until the mid-1920's there was a large red light district, but with the building boom in the District of Columbia in the 1920's and 1930's the brothels were demolished and forced to disperse. Formerly there had been open solicitation by prostitutes from brothel windows and doorways. The site now occupied by the Department of Health, Education and Welfare, between 4th and 5th Streets on Independence, is the old location of several very well-known brothels.

Buffalo's red light district was on Oak, Elm, and North and South Division streets in the 1920's and 1930's. A number of brothels were operated under the guise of cigar stores and soft drink establishments. The principal madams in Buffalo were two sisters who had previously been active in New York and catered to the $2 trade.

Before Alaska's entrance into the Union, most of its cities had a red light district. Anchorage had eight brothels; a small

Alaskan community might have four. Customers generally were military personnel and construction workers. In Juneau, Ketchikan, and Sitka, fishermen and cannery workers were patrons during the halibut and salmon fishing seasons. It was common for fishermen not to walk out of a brothel until they had spent hundreds and sometimes thousands of dollars. In the 1950's Fairbanks' red light district of fifteen brothels remained open around the clock. "Panama Hattie's" was operated by a woman who had been a madam in Panama City. Most of her customers were servicemen from nearby Fort Richardson. Cab drivers would bring clients on a regular basis. Many of her inmates would return to the United States ("going outside") in the winter months because they could not stand the cold. Prostitutes in Alaska seldom charged less than $20. Many claimed that their chief competitors were the "klootches," Indian and Eskimo women and girls whose fondness for alcohol led them to exchange sex for drinks.

The red light districts were closed in Alaska when statehood came. Alma, one of the state's more notorious exmadams, recently interviewed in a bar where she spends her idle hours playing cards, admitted frankly that she no longer holds out hope for a renaissance of prostitution in Alaska. Not only is public opinion against commercialized prostitution, but "klootches" and their counterparts still take business away from "working girls."

One of the few cities in the United States which sustained an active red light district into the 1960's was Galveston, Texas. Galveston was run by racketeers who exercised power like that held by big-city gangster groups in the 1930's. Before 1964, when changes in public opinion enabled the Texas Rangers and a new city manager to eliminate the red light district, a group of racketeers ran the eighteen brothels and eleven bars which comprised the district in Galveston ever since World War II.

In some cities, programs for urban renewal have been largely responsible for the razing of many buildings formerly used for prostitution. The red light district on the east side of Kansas City, Missouri, from McGee to Troost Streets, has been cleared for low- and middle-income housing. From Twelfth Street to the Union Station on both sides of Main Street, there were once sixty hotels linked with prostitution. The area is now largely devoted to parking lots and automobile dealers.

A tenderloin is an area with very substantial incidence of brothel prostitution but in which the houses are more scattered than in a red light district. A decline in property values usually follows the establishment of a tenderloin. Home owners and apartment dwellers in the area are often reluctant to remain, and generally move as soon as they find adequate quarters. Once an area becomes known for its hospitality to prostitution, its reputation is difficult to change. An example of this situation was provided in the 1920's by Grand Circus Park in Detroit. When prostitution began to flourish in the area, many home owners sold their homes. The park area eventually contained more than two hundred houses of prostitution. From Grand Circus Park along the side streets east and west of Woodward Avenue literally hundreds of women would be looking out their windows to attract the passing trade. Three shifts of inmates worked around the clock. The area now consists largely of parking lots and automobile showrooms, and has experienced a great depreciation in real estate values.

St. Louis offers another example of the decline of property values as a result of a tenderloin. A number of areas in St. Louis are still blighted because of their once having been connected with prostitution. In the 1930's the city had two major types of "tap joints," so called because of inmates tapping on the window to get attention. One type of brothel was above a store with an entrance between two other stores. Another type was a small one-family building entirely devoted to prostitution, in the area from Twelfth Street to the Union Station, and also along Olive, Pine, Chestnut, and Market Streets, as far out as Grand Avenue.

America's acceptance of the tenderloin can be inferred from the prototypical one that flourished in Middletown during the 1920's. It was supported by various officials of the community and boasted more than fifty brothels. At election time there would be a period of "reform." In the mid-1930's one of the town's leading brothels was on a square opposite the courthouse. The citizens of Middletown seemed to accept this concentration of brothels with equanimity, like their countrymen elsewhere.[5]

THE BROTHEL

A brothel is a place that is exclusively used for the business of prostitution and where the inmates almost invariably share their earnings with the operator. The brothel probably derives its name from the public bath, which was brought to Europe by the Crusaders and was originally a locus for assignation. Many European rulers (for example, Queen Joanna of Avignon) established brothels in their communities and others (such as Henry II) issued regulations governing their conduct. Brothels in the United States have had much in common with those in Europe, as some American commentators noted when Alexander Kuprin's novel *Yama* was published in this country after World War I.[6] It gave a vivid picture of life in a brothel in a large southern Russian city.

Cathouse, whorehouse, parlor house, and resort are among the designations for a brothel, which today is likely to be called a "joint" or "house." "Bordello" is sometimes used in newspaper accounts.

Popular fantasies about the brothel were incorporated in the famous brothel scene in Joyce's *Ulysses*.[7] A graphic picture of the brothel in its prime is given in G. W. Pabst's film *Joyless Street* (1925), in which Greta Garbo and Asta Nielsen played girls driven into prostitution by adverse circumstances. The brothel scenes are probably the best representations of their kind in film. A similar milieu is presented in *Cannery Row*, John Steinbeck's novel concerned with a small-town California brothel[8] whose title derives from the name of a red light district in Monterey. The leading male character, a scientist, likes to visit the brothel and enjoys the warmth of its madam and inmates, all of whom have hearts of gold but have been unkindly treated by life. In *Pipe Dream*, the musical fashioned from *Cannery Row* by Rodgers and Hammerstein in 1955, the opera star Helen Traubel played the madam.

In the Southeast and along the Pacific Coast a popular method of advertising a brothel during the 1930's was a low-hanging awning over the premises, which sometimes concealed an inmate seated at a window tapping to attract men. The building's number would be conspicuously displayed on the transom, in order to insure that a prospective customer, perhaps while drunk, did not ring the bell of a nearby building that might be occupied by a competitor or a private family. Another reason for an awning was that it concealed customers from passersby. Many brothels were equipped with a three-sided "busybody" window mirror that made it possible to observe persons walking along the street from either direction and determine whether they were clients or policemen.

Brothels sometimes used prearranged signals with their customers to indicate whether it was safe for them to enter. Typical of these stratagems was a procedure originated in Sault Ste. Marie, Michigan. A woman sat at a brothel window wearing a red sweater to inform customers that the police were watching the building. If she wore a pink or white sweater, the customer was encouraged to enter. Another popular signal originated in East Providence, Rhode Island, and involved window shades. When the brothel's front shades were down, customers knew they could enter freely. A raised shade signaled trouble.

Some madams used to try to avoid the law by not locking the door on their place of business in order to avoid the charge of "receiving and admitting." When the police walked in, the madam would signal the inmates to return the customers' money. Sometimes the front door was never opened; clients and inmates went in and out via the side or back door.[9]

Brothels tried to maximize their customers' privacy so that "father and son won't meet in the same place," and because clients seldom wish to meet other clients. The hallway lights were usually dim. There were often side rooms where a customer could go temporarily in order to avoid embarrassment.

A report by a man visiting a typical pre–World War II brothel in Tennessee conveys the quality of the experience: "The large red house numerals on the transom made the resort easy to find. A maid promptly admitted me into the reception parlor and called, 'Company, girls!' Five inmates entered, all dressed in pajamas. The price was $3.00. One girl asked for a drink, and I bought a round for all of the girls. One said, 'Pick one of us, honey.' "[10]

The client usually could select any inmate. Reluctance to make a choice might place him under suspicion of not being a genuine customer. One client reported such an episode during the 1950's in Philadelphia. After looking over and chatting with five women whom the madam had brought before him, he decided against any of them. Before leaving, he said, "Well, I'm sorry I won't go with any of these girls, but maybe I'll come back tonight." As he was about to leave, two powerful-looking men came into the parlor and asked, "Why don't you take one of these girls?" The customer, slightly uneasy, said, "Well, maybe I'll come back tonight." One of the men said, "You're not coming back here tonight. Nobody leaves here without taking one of these girls. You've got to go with one of them." The customer, somewhat nervous by this time, said, "Well look, I don't really want one of these girls, but I'll give you some money, to calm you down." The men refused the money after the customer had satisfactorily identified himself, and later explained their fear that he might have been a representative of the police. If the visitor had actually been a policeman and had taken one of the prostitutes, the men could testify that he had done so and thus weaken his ability to testify against her.

Nearly all brothels had a maid who did the cleaning and helped identify customers. She often opened the door and welcomed the "trade." In a community where law enforcement was strict, the maid who did not recognize a potential customer would usually call the madam, who made the final decision on whether he could be admitted. The madam also often saw clients to the door and collected money, not only for sexual activity but for any damage or breakage. The madam's apartment was often furnished gaudily, with teddy bears, stuffed pink poodles, and Kewpie and long-legged dolls.

Another brothel employee was the towel girl, who was sometimes the same woman who functioned as maid and receptionist. The towel girl picked up towels and maintained a fresh supply in the prostitute's room. Although she received a regular salary, she also expected tips from the prostitute.

In the typical brothel the women, in a minimum of clothing, would assemble in the parlor and banter with a potential client. They might wear kimonos or shorts. Also popular was the "jockey suit," a chemise-type garment worn under a negligee. San Francisco was one of the few cities where women wore slacks while lounging with clients. At some places the women were completely nude. If law enforcement was strict, the women might wear street clothes in order to facilitate a hasty getaway.

Brothel inmates would generally speak quite directly to the client about the services they offered. A prostitute seeing her first customer for the day ("breaking luck") might tell him, "You have a maiden on your hands today." The customer presumably felt happy at the disclosure. Many a "maiden" might make the same remark to a number of men on any one day. Younger girls were often called "stock," and those under fifteen were "fresh stock."

Sometimes the frigidity of a brothel prostitute was legendary. Gertrude Livingston's brothel in New Orleans had an inmate called Josephine Icebox. Miss Livingston had a standing offer of $10 to any man who could get Miss Icebox emotionally involved in coitus. There is no record of any winners.

It was not uncommon for a brothel to have a specialist who worked with "difficult cases." Nell Kimball's brothel in New Orleans was typical: "I always kept a self-starter around, a girl who worked on shy johns, or adolescents down from college. She had to make the advances but not frighten them off. A house that got a rumor going against it as a place where shyness or impotence couldn't be brought round, lost a good part of its special trade."[11]

In some communities, brothels were also social centers. "Sightseers" were clients who bought some drinks, sat around and "snuggled" for a while, and left. No matter how much "sightseers" might pay for liquor, the income from some sexual contact was more lucrative. In Niagara Falls so many "sightseers" visited that they were charged $1 or $2 admission. Some houses required every visitor to buy a cigar for ten cents. On a Saturday night, through the 1930's, hundreds of cigars that had been purchased in brothels could be found along Buffalo Avenue in Niagara Falls.

The madam generally tried to keep drunks and policemen off the premises. Brothels located on a second floor often had an electric buzzer under a stairway step. Anyone walking up the stairs sounded a bell upstairs. The maid would come to the head of the stairs, inspect the new arrival, and decide whether to admit him. One feature of the San Francisco brothels was a rope running along the bannister to the first floor. Standing at the head of the stairs, the maid could unlatch the door by pulling the rope, and inspect the caller.

In spite of many jokes about the subject, relatively few pianists or other musicians played in brothels. Only expensive places had a pianist, who would usually sit in the parlor and play sentimental songs ("You Made Me What I Am Today," "Bird in a Gilded Cage"). New Orleans was an exception, and many of its brothels featured musicians who played background music all evening. The musician was generally not paid a salary but received tips from the patrons. Sometimes there was dancing to music, especially in brothels which had back parlors. The women might use the dancing to stimulate and provoke a potential customer and tell him about their services. Some brothels also had a phonograph or juke box in the parlor; the music helped to alleviate boredom while inmates waited for clients to appear.

Some brothels operated by reservation, and only men expected at a specific time were admitted. In other places a madam would tell a customer that he would have to wait because the specific woman he requested was not available or that all the women were busy. Such delays enabled the madam to sell a customer drinks while he was waiting, and often served further to arouse his desire. When the woman became available, his response would be more prompt and he would take a minimum of her time. In light of the traditional concept of romantic love, a man might be expected to have his desire quelled somewhat at the thought of another man engaging in sex with a woman just before he himself would do so. But waiting for another man to finish, or even hearing him, may also stimulate desire in many cases. Having a client wait also helped to convey the impression that a woman was a "star." Some brothels would have a preliminary "circus" in which women engaged in sexual activities with one another, often employing an artificial phallus ("dildo"). The "shows" were useful in arousing the appetites of some customers.

In order to minimize the possibility of extortion, some houses prohibited their women from asking a customer his last name or trying to find out anything about him. Even very recognizable politicians were known as Smith and Jones at brothels. Many houses prohibited women from touching a customer's clothes or pockets. Other houses encouraged their women to hang up the man's clothes, in order to check if he were carrying a badge or gun and if his clothing labels confirmed his identity.

Some prostitutes who met clients in brothels wanted to date them. If they could not get their telephone numbers, they would take their automobile license-plate numbers and then get the customer's name and address from motor vehicle records. Others would go through their clients' trousers in order to discover their identity and then try to contact them independently of the brothel.

Some madams used a peephole or one-way screen to check on prostitutes, especially if the madam felt that the prostitute was getting more money than she reported, or if the customer was paying extra on the side for a "perversion." Some houses had a rule prohibiting keys in the locks of the women's rooms, in order to permit the madam to maintain control in an emergency.

From the woman's point of view, working in a brothel represented the least demanding kind of prostitution. She did not have to engage in any sales activity and was not avoiding policemen or seeking clients on the street. Most prostitutes preferred to work in communities other than their own, in order to avoid recognition by people they knew. They would generally hear about the details of specific brothels from colleagues. Some might avoid a place where they already knew another prostitute, in much the same way that an ex-convict is afraid of meeting a former "college" chum.

The madam would interview and brief each potential prostitute about various practical matters. The candidate might learn that any bond and legal fees would be provided, and that she would get half of everything she earned from prostitution and liquor sales. She would usually be told that pimps were not permitted on the premises.

Some madams preferred to rotate their personnel so that clients would always have fresh "talent." Other prostitutes often became so well established that they remained in one brothel for a long time. Customers who visited the same brothel frequently would develop a relationship with one woman and ask for her. Unless she was occupied or otherwise unavailable, she would generally be assigned to the customer making such a request.

No doubt many prostitutes had feelings of considerable

loyalty toward a specific brothel and its madam. The more expensive and well-run the brothel, the more likely were the women to identify with it. Some women who thought the madam was making too much money might be eager to go to another brothel. Most did whatever the madam asked them to do, and had few aspirations beyond continuing to work in the house. Any who worked seven days a week had little time to do anything else, even if they wanted to.

Some madams had established procedures for punishing women who violated the brothel's rules. They might be fined. In some cases they were beaten, though not severely enough to be bruised or disfigured.

LOCATION

Brothels were often located near railroad stations, usually on the "wrong side" of the tracks or in a slum area, especially in small or medium-sized communities. Because some brothels that resembled hotels were located near railroad stations, girls arriving from out of town might unwittingly register and subsequently drift into prostitution when their funds ran low. Brothels were frequently located in slum areas because their neighbors were unlikely to complain to the police. Another preferred area was a secondary business district that was relatively uninhabited at night.[12]

Many brothels operated near factories or large industrial plants. When their existence was called to the attention of the factory owners, the latter would often complain to local authorities and help close them. Typical of such a situation were the ten brothels in Cicero, Illinois, which were geared to a clientele of employees of the nearby factories of the Western Electric Company during the 1920's. Workers would often come home with empty pay envelopes on payday, having previously stopped off at one of the establishments. After the company complained, local authorities eliminated the brothels. Many firms postponed building plants in communities that had open prostitution until the situation changed.

Thus in the 1930's an oil company that wanted to establish a refinery in the Baton Rouge area said that it would not do so until overt brothel prostitution was reduced. The company provided an impetus for the elimination of prostitution in the community.

SCHEDULES

In general, higher-priced brothels usually remained open until three or four o'clock in the morning, although go-betweens would not accept any drunken customers in the early morning hours. Cheaper houses in communities with some degree of law enforcement tended to close early in the evening, and expensive places shut down around ten. But even cities that were fairly close to one another might have different hours. In Buffalo, for example, midnight was closing time for the cheaper resorts, while in nearby Rochester they closed at 10 P.M.

The brothel prostitute of the 1920's and 1930's lived in a routine with established hours for work, eating, and relaxation, and specific rules about drinking. She usually worked seven days a week and might be on call twenty-four hours a day. In factory towns like Chester, Pennsylvania, there would be an 8 A.M. shift for factory workers on their way to work and another around 6 to 8 P.M. for the evening trade. The "three-platoon" system of three shifts a day prevailed in Detroit. The average prostitute would see fifteen to thirty men a day, and as many as fifty on payday. Weekends were much busier than weekdays for a brothel near a military installation. Monday was usually slow because many men spent their money over the weekend. To this day, Monday remains a relatively inactive day for prostitution.

Although many prostitutes would not work during a menstrual period, some did not wish to lose the income and continued on duty throughout it—but would not apprise the client of their situation. The use of cotton wool or various proprietary products was effective enough for many women to be able to work right through the several menstrual days.

The leisure of the prostitute might be spent in a "hen party" with other prostitutes, going to a movie with a pimp, or attending prize fights and other sports events. She sometimes went to a bar in a nearby community where there would be little danger of being recognized. Going to the movies, dancing, roller skating, swimming, sewing, picnics, reading, and playing with dolls were common avocations.

Brothel prostitutes took relatively few vacations. Since many vacation sites represented potential work areas, it might have been difficult for some women to go to such places for relaxation. Probably the most popular holiday for prostitutes was Christmas Week, when even regular customers were likely to be using their money for other purposes. The brothel often had a Christmas tree around which the women would assemble on Christmas morning to open their packages. Typical presents included teddy bears, silk stockings and other items of clothing, and perfume. Business usually picked up again after New Year's Day.

The average brothel in a smaller city through the 1930's had five prostitutes; a house in a larger city might have fifteen to twenty. The $1 and $2 houses in many large cities just before the depression usually had five to eight women. Prostitutes in small and medium-sized communities usually lived in the brothel, but few did so in large cities. Women who did not reside on the premises stayed in hotels, rooming houses, and apartments. Some lived at home with their families. Almost invariably, those who lived in the brothel also used their room for business purposes. There was a consistent and identifiable smell in the prostitutes' rooms, an amalgam of tobacco smoke, bath powder, perfume, and human secretions. One madam has vividly described the smell: "The house in the morning was still a bit strong. Body powder, Lysol, dead cigars, the woman smell of it always heavy, and spilled likker. After a while to me a house wasn't a good house unless it had that musk smell in the morning."[13]

The prostitute who lived in a brothel generally paid for

room and board, in addition to the half of her earnings that went to the madam. Meals were served on a regular schedule. If a client asked for a specific prostitute during meal-time, she would generally be excused from the communal meal. The cook also frequently doubled as the maid, and the madam might serve as cook.

Residents of the brothel were not permitted to have pimps stay in their rooms because the madam believed such an arrangement would interfere with business. But it was not unusual for pimps to drive their women to work. One prostitute naively pointed out that her pimp was quite considerate in driving her to work, but that he did not do so for the "girls" he had on the 8 A.M. to 4 P.M. shift.

EXPENSIVE BROTHELS

Some expensive brothels had facilities for customers who stayed overnight. They could shower, have their underclothes and shirts laundered while they were asleep, and get razors, toothbrushes, shaving creams, and lotions. Some establishments served a regular breakfast, and liquor and sandwiches might be free. In other houses, sandwiches were free if a customer bought liquor. In some expensive houses the sheets were changed after every customer. The frequency with which sheets were changed and laundered was a function of the price. At an expensive brothel the routine was fairly similar to that at cheaper houses. Among the special features of high-priced establishments was a supply of whips, canes, and similar materials for flagellation.

There have been many stories about brothels that were run for a limited clientele, as a kind of private club. It has been reported, for example, that a motel on the outskirts of Detroit was actually a brothel, with five prostitutes continually in residence to provide services for a group of distinguished citizens. The club allegedly had only fifty members, who were admitted by a special gold key.[14]

The growth of key clubs in the last decade has provided

another possible method of prostitution. A key club is a private club, admission to which is possible only if a person has taken out an annual membership. A private club is less subject to scrutiny from law enforcement officials than bars and other public places. Most of these clubs probably do not foster prostitution, but in some of the smaller private clubs there is reason to believe that some hostesses receive very little salary and are expected to be "nice" to men who visit, often in connection with business activities or conventions. Many hostesses at such clubs are all but forced to engage in prostitution.[15]

During the brothel's prime there was a demand for prostitutes to perform at stag parties, some of which remains today. Booking agents supplied prostitutes and sold admission tickets for such parties in farmhouses outside the city limits. Free beer would be served and the women would dance, strip, and mingle with the men. There were generally too many men present for the prostitutes to engage in sexual activity with all of them. Tickets for these parties were usually sold in taverns, at baseball games, and similar places. Somewhat similar is the stag party given for a prospective bridegroom at which a prostitute is hired for a "gang bang"— an event which has many of the characteristics of a primitive rite.

LIQUOR

Some impression of the importance of liquor to brothels can be gained from the experience of Cincinnati, when the city's brothels stopped serving liquor. Attendance was cut in half. Even before prohibition, "dry" cities often did not have much commercialized prostitution.[16] The sale of liquor at exorbitant prices and without benefit of a license was a part of brothel operations. Income from liquor was not usually shared by the prostitutes, but they nonetheless helped hustle it. During prohibition, bootleggers owned some brothels and were the exclusive purveyors of liquor to others. Prices for alcoholic beverages in brothels—fifty cents to a dollar a drink even before prohibition—were high. A bottle of beer usually cost $1, with everybody present receiving a drink in a small whisky glass. Some brothels had a separate room in which a cab driver could sit and drink beer while waiting for his passenger to finish his business.

FINANCES

Among the expenses in running a brothel were rent, payments to backers and politicians, breakage, repairs, upkeep, return of capital, "protection," medical examinations, maid, laundry, food, and wines and liquors. The furniture generally came from secondhand shops, with the exception of the madam's room, which often had expensive and gaudy trappings. Many brothels had tubular furniture which was chained to the floor to prevent drunken clients from throwing it. Madams seldom spent much money in furnishing a house because of the continuous threat of being raided and having to find another place.

The distribution of the prostitute's income was clearly established in many brothels.[17] For every dollar received by the prostitute, the madam got fifty cents, out of which she usually had to pay extortionists or officials. Of the prostitute's fifty cents, the pimp would receive twenty cents, the madam would get eight cents for room and board, and two cents would go to a physician for physical examinations. Some twenty cents would remain for the prostitute. Even busy prostitutes might be in financial difficulties much of the time because of their relatively small net income. Although prostitutes treated fees in a businesslike way, many handled money neurotically, squandering or giving it away. In as much as some customers tried to steal the prostitute's money, she often concealed it in a shoe, glove, or other hiding place, and kept relatively little in a purse or bank.

Many prostitutes who bought on credit payed outrageously high prices. Their uneasiness about the possibility of being apprehended may have led them to pay bills promptly. They seldom bargained. Perhaps for the same reason, brothel prostitutes often paid inflated prices to peddlers who kicked back part of their profit to the madam, who made additional money by selling the prostitutes clothes, toilet articles, and jewelry, much of which might have been stolen goods. Some madams deliberately sold merchandise to prostitutes in order to keep them in debt, so that they would not be tempted to leave: "When a girl owes me less than $25, I call the peddler."

The prostitutes would help each other apply cosmetics they had acquired from the madam or peddler. In some large cities a few beauty parlors were frequented by prostitutes, not only to prettify themselves but to obtain information about places of employment. The beauticians would discreetly ask the prostitutes if they were happy with their working conditions and then recommend a "better" place.

Some brothels had more than one kind of employee. Some houses with $5 prostitutes might also have others who charged as much as $15. Such arrangements involved more complications than if all prices were the same, because of jealousy among the women.

Prices for prostitution in all of its forms are based on those charged by the brothel. Prostitutes in bars, massage parlors, and hotels use the same price scale as the brothel but are able to cut prices. Brothel inmates must maintain the fees set by their employers. Around World War I, $1 or $2 was the standard price, which rose to $2 to $3 during the 1920's. Depression prices ranged from $1 to $3, with $5 the top price in exclusive establishments. By World War II, $5 became a new national average. A combination of the high postwar cost of living and police pressure led to the current average price of $10 in most communities. Today a "straight" is $10, "half and half" (oral stimulation before coitus) usually costs $15, and a "French" (fellatio) $20.

Prices for prostitution may vary by region but are usually consistent within any one community or section of the United

States. Prices are higher in large cities than in smaller communities, and white prostitutes charge more than nonwhites. A "short date" (ten or fifteen minutes) and a "long date" (one hour or more) differ in the amount of time that the woman spends with the man. The long date usually costs much more than the shorter period. The all-night date typically is $100. Bargaining may occur, even though there is an established asking price. On days other than payday, military personnel may get a reduced price.

Although the brothels in a community had a fairly standard rate scale, some provided services at a cut-rate price. One madam in Detroit consistently charged $5 when her competitors asked $10. As a result, the competitors would continually denounce her to the police.

Prostitution is a business almost entirely transacted with cash. The customer pays in advance ("up front" or "putting it on the line"). One reason for insistence on payment in advance is to underscore the businesslike nature of the transaction. Also, men who do not pay in advance may try to leave without paying.

In some establishments the maid collected the money from customers and gave it to the madam. Such houses assumed that it would irritate customers to pay a prostitute immediately before or after sexual activity. A rare few customers had charge accounts and paid their brothel bills on a regular monthly basis. In some brothels the customer paid his money in advance to the madam, who then punched a card for the woman assigned to him. At the end of the day the number of punch marks was counted and the prostitute credited with her share of the receipts.

There is no established tradition of giving a tip or gratuity to a prostitute, though a customer might say, "Here's an extra dollar." Some prostitutes have a baby bank or coffee pot conspicuously displayed in their room in the hope that the customer will drop some money into it. The prostitute may ask him directly to "give me some luck money." Even pennies and nickels are acceptable. A customer who does not give even a small tip is called a "skunk," and a prostitute will say of such a man that "he skunked me."

Where the customer seemed to be taking an extremely long time before reaching orgasm, the prostitute occasionally might return his money after fifteen minutes. Some few brothels even had a policy that a customer could get his money back if he was not satisfied. As one madam said, "I see to it that my clients always get a fair shake for their money. You can take that at least two ways."

Price is a recurring theme of jokes about prostitution. In one story that has been popular for thirty years, a famous tycoon has committed suicide by jumping out of his tower office. The police question every person surrounding the great man. In the background, weeping silently, is his attractive young secretary whom the police finally approach. "Miss Smith," they ask, "have you any idea why Mr. Jones should have done this?" She shakes her head. The investigator asks, "Did you notice anything strange, or did he do anything strange?" She replied: "Well, a week ago he asked me how much I would charge to walk around his desk without my dress on. I answered $50, and he said okay. Yesterday he asked me what I would charge to walk around with nothing on. I answered $100. He agreed, so I took off all my clothes." The investigator continued, "Anything else, Miss Smith?" The girl hesitated for a moment and resumed: "Well, today he called me in and said, 'Miss Smith, how much would you charge to let me?' and I answered, 'Why, $10, Mr. Jones, like I always charge,' and with that he jumps out of the window."

Exactly what service the prostitute is being paid for as well as the nature of the client-prostitute relationship are the latent themes in the story of the customer who is in bed with a prostitute when her doorbell rings. Although it is a cold winter night, he dashes in his underwear to the fire escape. The prostitute admits an old man who chats for two hours and gives her $100 without engaging in any sex. The prostitute goes to the window and lets in the original customer who asks: "Is the s-s-sucker gone yet?"

The extent to which folklore about prostitution prices adapts itself to current situations is one appeal of a story that was popular in the early 1960's. A madam had observed that clients were particularly fond of one of her prostitutes. Finally she asked one customer: "Why are you so eager to see Ruth when there are so many other attractive girls in my house?" The customer replied: "Oh, she is the one who gives Plaid Stamps."

THE PROHIBITION ERA

The brothel was still the pre-eminent locus of prostitution during prohibition, when a number of American films presented the practice in a relatively favorable light. *Honeymoon Flat, Husbands for Rent,* and *Breakfast at Sunrise* implied that women might try prostitution without harm. Some of the best-known films of Cecil B. DeMille and other prominent directors sympathetically presented the "high-class" prostitute: *Ladies Must Live, Pretty Ladies, Lilies of the Field, Ladies of Ease, Bought and Paid For, The Joy Girl,* and *Silk Legs* were typical of films which reflected the 1920's cynicism.

One of the period's most widely discussed films was G. W. Pabst's *Pandora's Box* (1929), a vice "spectacular" which starred Louise Brooks as Lulu in an adaptation of Frank Wedekind's play. The psychological and visual representation of the prostitute's life was conveyed with extraordinary sensitivity and nuance by Miss Brooks. Wedekind's play also served as the basis for Alban Berg's opera *Lulu,* once denounced in the United States for being sordid, but later performed (1963) to great acclaim.

While movies were exploring prostitution, Americans were developing some original approaches to bringing client and prostitute together. During the 1920's excursion boats of the Fall River Line, the Hudson River Night Line from New York to Albany, the Potomac cruise, the Old Dominion Line to Norfolk, Virginia, and the Moonlight Cruise near Pittsburgh were active sites for prostitution. Typically, bellboys would actively solicit men and bring them to the prostitute's cabin.

From 1919 to 1927 in Chicago, New York, San Francisco, and Los Angeles, the manicure parlor was a popular cover for prostitution. It generally consisted of one room in an office building. A man who was unaware of its real purpose might actually get a manicure, but the hostess derived her major income from services as a prostitute. One advantage to the customer was that he could visit a prostitute without leaving the building in which he worked. The last manicure parlor used for prostitution closed in Chicago in 1927.

Many of the speakeasies of the twenties that openly sponsored prostitution had rooms on the premises for the purpose. Speakeasy prostitution flourished in Boston, Los Angeles, New York, Philadelphia, Pittsburgh, and San Francisco, but disappeared with the repeal of prohibition in 1933.

One unexpected aspect of the development of the automobile as a low-priced means of transportation was its frequent use for prostitution. Some taxi drivers submitted a list of prostitutes to their customers and offered to drive them to any one on the list. In another procedure used in cities, a client would pick up a prostitute and rent a taxi. The client would direct the driver to an outlying area where the couple retired in the underbrush, for what came to be called a "grass sandwich." A number of the more prosperous prostitutes got automobiles of their own and cruised up and down the streets in search of trade. A roadhouse was often a lucrative adjunct, especially in cold weather.

The use of automobiles for prostitution presented many problems for law enforcement because the vehicles' elusiveness and mobility made them difficult for an ordinary police force to cope with. A series of state laws and municipal ordinances made it an offense to direct, take, or transport anyone for purposes of prostitution in an automobile. The use of automobiles by prostitutes also spurred many municipal and county police authorities to acquire motorcycles and automobiles. Probably the most effective measure against this traffic was the power of some municipal authorities to revoke the licenses of taxi drivers who took part in prostitution activities.

Some prostitutes with automobiles made a career of following the harvests. They would arrive in an area such as California's Imperial Valley just about the time the seasonal workers were being paid. After a concentrated period of work, they might move to Colorado and Utah, where the beet farmers were harvesting their crop, and then go to other harvest areas.

THE 1930's

The 1930's brought new methods for the organization of prostitution. So many prostitutes were available that the "syndicate" placed a ceiling on the amount that any one woman could earn. Women under mob control were permitted to work only three days a week in Chicago, providing enough income for them just to maintain themselves and sustain motivation for their work.

The thirties saw the advent on a fairly large scale of the "juke joint," a roadhouse in which prostitutes were available. Folk etymology suggests that the name derived from the Jukes, a mountain family which was presumably riddled with disease and pathology as a result of a Revolutionary War mating which led to "bad seed." Although modern students of eugenics ridicule this theory, it was very popular in the 1930's, and the name "juke" was said to have developed because many nitwits were said to go to such places. Women and girls who worked in juke joints were often itinerant. Some had been waitresses who were unable to find other work during the depression.

Many juke joints flourished in the southeastern United States from the thirties to the early forties. They were outside the city limits and could be reached only by automobile or taxi. The prostitutes sometimes doubled as waitresses and encouraged the customers to buy drinks and play the juke box or pinball machine. The girls would take their customers to cabins near the main building. One bizzare episode was reported by a taxi driver in Brunswick, Georgia, probably the birthplace of juke joints. The driver had taken a man "juking" one Saturday night and received instructions to pick him up again at a cabin the following morning. At 7 A.M. the driver appeared and was surprised when the passenger said he wanted to go to Jacksonville, Florida. While driving to Jacksonville, the passenger asked the cab driver what he would do if he found himself in bed with a dead person. The driver later returned to the cabin, where he found a dead woman in bed. Police were able to trace the customer and discovered that there had been no foul play; the woman had died of a combination of heavy drinking and an advanced case of syphilis.

A cover for prostitution to be found in Buffalo, Toledo, and other large cities during the 1930's was the cigar store or "soft drinkery." A madam stood behind the cigar counter and appraised the customers. If she knew a man who entered the shop, she sent him to the rear of the store where there were rooms for prostitution. If the customer was unknown or looked like a policeman, he was served a soft drink.

Burlesque provided another setting for prostitution in the thirties. The United States has always shown more enthusiasm for burlesque than any other country, and it reached a peak during the depression.[18] Attendance at burlesque was a potential prelude for contact with a prostitute because the performances involved so much sexual stimulation. Some burlesque houses had steerers waiting outside to direct men to prostitutes when the performance ended. It was fairly common to see men entering burlesque houses with large folded newspapers which they held over their genital area during and after the performance. Some men used large boxes of popcorn instead. Kinsey and his associates reported that 28 per cent of the men who had seen a burlesque show, questioned in the late 1930's and early 1940's, had a definite or frequent erotic response, while 34 per cent had some such response.[19] Burlesque has made a comeback in the last five years and there are now over sixty theaters devoted to it, but it no longer is connected with organized prostitution.

During the 1930's a number of traveling carnivals employed dancers with the understanding that they were free to engage in prostitution. The barker made his pitch in a provocative manner and implied that the dancers would be tantalizing. After the customer had paid his admission and watched the performance, the barker announced that an additional "special" program could be seen by paying another admission. The dancers at the second show were often prostitutes, and a customer could arrange to meet them after the performance.

Some California and New York prostitutes worked for escort services in the 1930's. The services were not legally responsible for the extracurricular activities of their female employees, who were generally rented out till midnight. What the girls did after midnight did not concern the employer, and many escorts would make their availability as prostitutes known to the clients.

Several enterprising "private" dance studios flourished in the West Seventies in New York and in other large cities from 1937 to 1940. The studios' respectable exterior made access easier for those customers who might be embarrassed or afraid to visit a prostitute in a more conspicuous setting. The customer pressed a translucent white button outside the building and was admitted by the "teacher." The studio's owner would sometimes sit in a nearby parked car where he could tell if a person were visiting the studio or going elsewhere in the building. When the button was pressed, a small bulb in the switch would light. The typical studio consisted of a sparsely furnished room on the first floor of a rooming house. The "instructor" would dance nude and provide either masturbation or coitus for a standard fee of $6. As many as ten studios might be found on a single block.

Also popular in the late thirties was the house of assignation, sometimes called a "riding academy." The client would meet his girl there and then take her to a hotel or furnished room. The house of assignation was pleasantly furnished and often had a private bar and restaurant. The girl would discuss the price while dining and drinking with the potential client. In some establishments the waiters never entered but passed drinks and food into the room through a wicket.

TODAY'S BROTHEL

In the last half-century, brothels reached the peak of their popularity in 1939. From 1941 through 1945 there was a steady decline in their number in communities near military installations or those frequented by service personnel. The anti-brothel programs that characterized World War II continued after the war, and the brothel never regained its former eminence. The discussion in the previous sections refers primarily to brothels from the turn of the century through the 1940's.

The typical brothel today is likely to be open from 10 A.M. to 6 P.M. A smaller number are open from approximately 6 P.M. to 10 or 11 P.M. Very few remain open as late as midnight, and practically none are open around the clock. Daylight hours are preferred because vice squads in many communities are not likely to be active during the day. Those brothels that do operate after dark generally have a "connection."

The average brothel today has two to four prostitutes, who display considerable discretion about showing themselves in abbreviated costume or explaining what they do. A customer today generally meets a "girl" in the parlor. They go to a bedroom and discuss the price and what she will do. Brothel residents no longer pay room and board, but they still give half their gross earnings to the madam. Brothels today seldom sell liquor, in order to avoid prosecution by state authorities for violation of liquor laws. Even if it were difficult to prosecute a madam on charges of prostitution, it would be relatively easy to do so for selling liquor without a license.

The contemporary brothel is relatively inconspicuous and unlikely to have its numbers on a red light, or awnings, or anything else that might call attention to its function. Its owners are continually developing tactics for evading law enforcement. An account by a recent visitor to a Nevada brothel gives an impression of how contemporary establishments work. When the visitor entered the establishment, the proprietor directed a girl to him. She said, "I'll sit with you. . . . Where are you from . . . ? I'm from Los Angeles. . . . Let's go to my room, so we can talk. . . ." In her room she continued: "I can give you a nice 'date.' . . . French for $15, or I can give you a 'straight' for $10. The price of a quickie is $5. For $20 and up, you could have a real good time. . . . You don't need to be afraid. . . . We get a smear examination once a week and a blood test once a month. . . . You won't have to worry—the doctor makes sure. . . . He checks us and we check everyone ourselves. . . . I have a certificate, but I keep it locked up." The woman would probably not have been so quick to offer her medical credentials if she had not sensed a lack of immediate response from the man. Otherwise, the experience of this man was relatively typical.

In a less open state than Nevada, the contemporary madam may try to avoid detection by having a cab driver take a potential client to a nearby bar. She picks up the client at the bar and takes him to the house, thus avoiding any concentration of cars parked in front of the establishment. Another way of circumventing the police is for the madam who receives a phone call from a person she doesn't know to tell him to go to a hotel lobby. She gives him a name for the occasion and tells him to respond when the name is paged in the hotel lobby. A cooperating taxi driver sizes up the potential customer. When convinced of his being "all right," he takes the customer to the brothel.

THE MASSAGE PARLOR

The massage parlor as a cover for prostitution has long been popular in the United States, yet there is no case on record of a legitimate massage parlor's becoming a locale for prostitution. The pseudo–massage parlor is so embarrassing to legitimate masseurs that they seldom acknowledge its existence, even for the purpose of complaining about it. Probably the only community in which legitimate masseurs objected was Atlanta, although illegal massage parlors in many cities have clouded the legitimate activities of the profession.

In a number of cities and states it is illegal for a masseur of one sex to treat a client of another sex, except by doctor's prescription. Some parlors deal with such laws by having pads of pre-signed prescriptions that are obtained from a cooperating doctor. Clients seeking a prostitute often get information about specific services from the manner in which the parlors phrase advertisements in sex tabloids, newspaper personal columns, or in the yellow pages of the telephone book. A number of establishments have names like the A-1 or AA Massage Parlor. Their proprietors reason that a newcomer seeking a prostitute will telephone the parlors in the telephone book in the order in which they are listed. Some parlors convey their business by indicating that they have "new operators, just arrived from abroad," "an operator just in from Paris," "foreign specialists," and similar phrases.

The massage parlor is used for prostitution today primarily in the Southwest, Midwest, and in Alaska. Once found only in large cities, massage parlors are also found in smaller communities today. Some of them offer a "magnetic" treatment in which the operator uses the tips of her fingers and touches the hairs of the client's body in order to simulate an electrical effect and lead to orgasm. Many parlors provide "local treatment" or masturbation as well as sexual intercourse and "perversions." Among communities with a substantial number of massage parlors are Honolulu and Las Vegas, where several advertise in newspapers and classified telephone directories. Anchorage has steam baths, massage parlors, and even sauna baths that are covers for prostitution.

In the years before World War II some massage parlors enjoyed international reputations. The Marble Slab in St. Louis was a notorious parlor. America's best-known parlor was Anna Swift's on West 70th Street in New York City. Miss Swift's fame as a masseuse was so great that a potential customer of another massage parlor would use her name as a password. The response of the masseuse to Anna Swift's name told the man whether he was in a legitimate massage parlor or one that offered prostitution. One Buffalo parlor for many years advertised that flagellation was available for improving circulation of the blood. "Masseuses" almost invariably are older and relatively unattractive women. They usually wear white uniforms and represent themselves to be registered nurses or graduates of some nonexistent massage school.

One recent development has been the establishment of a number of massage parlors providing homosexual activity. A typical newspaper classified advertisement for such a place reads, "Uptight? Cool it, man. Climax your day with a mind-blowing massage by Pierre, by appointment. Your home or my studio."

THE TAXI-DANCE HALL

Relatively few taxi-dance hostesses today are prostitutes, but many used to be during the 1930's. Many communities with taxi-dance halls now prohibit hostesses from sitting side by side with their clients and require them to sit facing each other. Hostesses may keep a customer dancing with them all evening because they promise a subsequent "date." Some men go to taxi-dance halls for close bodily contact with a "sock-it-in" hostess. Proprietors often try to meet the needs of such clients by dim lighting in corners of the hall. At some dance halls almost all the couples are in the dark crowded corners rather than in the middle of the floor where there is open space as well as bright light.

Most taxi-dance halls have a live band. A light on the bandstand is likely to be connected to a button in the cashier's office. When someone who looks like a policeman enters, the cashier presses the button which turns on the bandstand light. This signal warns the bandleader who abruptly terminates whatever he is playing and begins a prearranged alert number, usually "Meet Me Tonight in Dreamland." As soon as the girls hear the alert music, they push their partners away. When the police enter, the couples are dancing sedately. Sensual dancing is resumed when the police leave.

At some dance halls, "brush boys" in the lavatories sell condoms to the men, so that they will not stain their trousers while dancing. At a number of dance halls it is expected that the hostess will bring her partner to orgasm in the three minutes allotted for each dance. A recent visitor to a taxidance hall struck up a conversation with one hostess who said, "You couldn't get a better deal in bed. If you buy six dollars' worth of tickets, I'll give you a real sex rub. . . ."

THE CRIB

Approximately four by six feet, the crib was very similar to the corncrib from which its name derives. It had just enough space for a cot, chair, and washstand. Cribs were very popular in the 1930's. The last cribs in the United States were closed in Reno in 1941 and in Casper, Wyoming, in 1942.

The Reno cribs were in a hoseshoe-shaped concrete building known as the bullpen. As the Southern Pacific train entered Reno, many passengers would eagerly go to the windows to look at the bullpen. Very few of Reno's sixty-six cribs were ever unoccupied.

Prostitutes did not live in the cribs; they rented them at $5 for each of the three eight-hour shifts. The tenants paid almost $750,000 annual rent to the men whose total cost for building the cribs had been less than $20,000. At the entrance to the bullpen, a policeman checked the prostitutes' "health cards." Another policeman watched the entire area to maintain order. Prostitutes were not permitted to beckon to a man or to "steal" customers from each other. Although the sale of liquor was forbidden, many kept liquor which they sold by the drink to clients. A cafeteria on the premises provided lunch.

New Orleans had an extensive series of cribs which were owned by a major city official who rented them to prostitutes for $10 a day. From 1939 to 1941 the situation was quite flagrant, but the cribs disappeared by 1942. Cribs also characterized much of the prostitution in Phenix City, Alabama, where one woman owned most of them in the thirties. Her clients would select a girl and take her to the crib, which had a mattress on the floor. The madam would charge fifty cents for rental of the mattress, in addition to the fee of $5. A maid would knock on the door in fifteen minutes and remind the client that his time was up. The cribs closed when the community was cleaned up.

WORLD'S FAIRS

The many men who attend an international exposition or world's fair make such situations of potential interest to prostitutes. The notoriety of San Francisco as a recruiting center from which women were sent all over the West Coast was strengthened by the substantial incidence of prostitution when the city was host to the Panama-Pacific Exposition of 1915 and the Pan American Exhibition in 1939. The Century of Progress Exposition in Chicago in 1933 spurred considerable prostitution activity.

When the New York World's Fair opened in 1939, a special staff under the direction of former New York deputy police commissioner Henrietta Additon successfully minimized prostitution. Policewomen, some of whom wore civilian clothing, patrolled the fair and were on the alert for prostitutes and sexual molesters.

Nowadays some prostitutes feel that the men going to fairs are no longer potential customers. A Portland prostitute who had decided not to "work" the Seattle World's Fair said, "Conventions, yes . . . fairs, no. The guys who go to fairs don't go for 'girls.'" There seems to have been little prostitution in connection with the New York World's Fair of 1964–1965. The trend in fairs is away from "girlie" features and toward more educational, scientific, and artistic exhibits.

STREETWALKING

Streetwalking is almost a universal method of getting customers. A streetwalker typically walks the same route, especially if it is relatively free of police. During the twenties and thirties a streetwalker often paid the local policeman for the privilege of walking her beat. Now as then, she tends to use a fairly standardized method of soliciting. It begins with her smiling pleasantly but weakly at a potential client. She usually continues on her way and does not turn to see if he is following, but may glance into a store window to observe him while keeping a few steps ahead. She will be alert for a place to stop and chat unobtrusively with the potential client.

If they go into a hallway or a store front, she will probably greet him cautiously: "Hello," "Lonesome?" "How are you today?" "What direction are you going?" or "Are you a stranger in the city?" If the man responds, she will suggest where they might go. Both streetwalker and client rely on established verbal cues. A customer or a streetwalker may ask the other, "How would you like to do something?" The other will reply "Okay," and both will understand that they have made an arrangement for sexual activity for pay.

Although prices are fairly standard, an experienced prostitute can often evaluate the appearance of a client and guess how much he is willing to pay. As one streetwalker said, "I don't mean how much he earns—I mean what he'll pay me." She may have a flexible price scale and rely on her impression of the customer's ability to pay to evaluate whether a client is "a live one," a "deadhead," or a "sightseer" who will not buy.

A streetwalker who is new in a community will walk around, size up the streets, and inquire about where she might be able to take her trade. She will often approach a cab driver to get such information. Many beginning streetwalkers have the address of a cooperating landlady, provided by another prostitute.

Streetwalkers generally wear clothes that are flamboyant. When aware of strict law enforcement, they are exceedingly circumspect in their efforts to attract trade, and try to make their first approach appear to be a flirtation. They may postpone their proposition until after the prospect has bought them something to eat or drink, knowing that an arrest under such circumstances would probably be dismissed by the court as entrapment.

One occasional disadvantage of streetwalking from the prostitute's point of view is that two women may disagree over which of them has seen a customer first. An advantage for some is that they can service a client in a doorway or alley, which some prefer "because you don't have to do it regular." Many a prostitute has found that if she keeps her legs together the customer does not penetrate her but is unaware that he has not done so.

Some streetwalkers pretend to be pickups who are so eager for sex that they want the man to "do it" on the street. The woman takes the man into a doorway and embraces him while maintaining a steady stream of endearing comments. After locating his wallet, she may complain that his belt is hurting her and unbuckle it with one hand while removing the money from his wallet with the other hand. She returns the wallet to his pocket and continues to stimulate the man. The woman terminates the contact as quickly as possible, often urging the man to register at a nearby hotel where she will join him "in a few minutes."

In the past a prostitute generally worked on specific streets, and she or her pimp would likely cause trouble for a competitor who sought to work the same streets. Some prostitutes used to pay the incumbent prostitute for the right to seek customers on particular streets, and sometimes bought the right to work a locale from a woman who had previously been established there, in a manner similar to that in which a physician buys a practice. With the advent of the automobile, however, prostitutes became less dependent on a specific area to pick up customers.

Automobiles are still used by prostitutes in a method perhaps best described as streetwalking on wheels. Two women in an attractive sports car recently stopped two businessmen who were walking along a New York City street around midnight. They asked, "Are we going north?" One of the men replied, "Yes, you're going north. Just keep going." One of the girls asked, "Where is ———?" naming a prominent nightclub. She added, "We're going there—do you want to go with us?" The man said, "Well, I don't know." The girl said, "It will be 'half a C' for both of you." The man said, "Well, you didn't really want to go to that nightclub, did you?" The girl said, "No. That was just a gag." Many prostitutes use this kind of approach by automobile as an effective way to attract customers.

Many streetwalkers walk in twos and threes, especially in large cities. This provides safety in numbers from muggers. One woman might spot a policeman who is not known to the others. And there is a certain legitimacy about a group of women walking together.

In a large city, streetwalkers must go to areas of high customer incidence, which now tend to be located in theatrical areas. Thus in New York City streetwalkers concentrate in the area from 42nd to 57th Street, between Lexington and Eighth Avenues. Perhaps the most active single block is 49th

Street, between Sixth and Seventh Avenues, which includes seventeen bars, thirteen restaurants, seven hotels, a liquor store, and a "skin" movie. Racial segregation and physical decay in large cities have led to a concentration of streetwalkers in such entertainment sections because white customers are afraid to go into ghetto areas such as Fillmore in San Francisco or Harlem in New York.

A big-city variant of streetwalking is provided by some women who walk expensive dogs. The dogs give them an excuse to be outside at almost any hour of the day or night. A relatively unusual dog may provide an opportunity for conversation with a man who may be outside with his own dog. If the man does not strike up a conversation with the woman, she can take the initiative by praising his dog. A man without a dog may discuss the appearance and pedigree of her pet. She can communicate her availability in slow stages, by saying something innocuous such as "Let's go somewhere and have coffee." If it is inappropriate to make her proposition directly, she will have avoided the risk of an embarrassing situation. If she thinks it feasible to do so, she can give the price and other details.

Streetwalking is definitely on the decline. The concentration of streetwalkers in one area of a community makes them very conspicuous. They are found today, in any quantity, in only six cities: New York, Chicago, San Francisco, Los Angeles, Detroit, and Minneapolis. In New York, streetwalkers are active not only in the evening but also during the day. Sightseeing buses often stop at West 49th Street to show tourists the women loitering on the street. Daytime streetwalkers tend to be relatively young because customers can detect the signs of age fairly easily in daylight.

HOTELS

In some hotels the management condones prostitution and expects bellboys to derive most of their income from it. Other hotels frown on it. Cheaper hotels are more likely to be hospitable to prostitutes than more expensive establishments. A desk clerk often charges a prostitute more than the listed price of a room and pockets the difference. In return, the woman can bring back to her room as many clients as she can get in an evening.

Some prostitutes walk into a hotel carrying stolen or duplicate room keys or burglar's tools. They bang on a door and enter if nobody answers. If a man answers they ask, "Do you want a girl?" Some hotel industry sources have estimated that 90 per cent of all crimes in hotels can be attributed to prostitutes and their cohorts.

The mezzanine floor in some hotels is called "the racetrack." It is usually fairly narrow and has tables at which guests can sit and write letters. Women come in from the street and walk up and down soliciting trade. Many prostitutes who work in hotels try to rent rooms on the mezzanine or first floor just above the lobby, so that they and their customers can walk to the room without being seen by room clerks or elevator operators. A prostitute who meets a client on the street often tells him to walk to the hotel via a route other than the one she takes, in order to deceive any police who may be watching them.

Naturally, bellboys and porters operate very cautiously when they know the local vice squad is on the alert. In some cities a known "john" is usually escorted into a room and asked to disrobe. A regular customer is not likely to mind; an unfamiliar customer is told that if the prostitute appears and does not find him naked, she will immediately leave the room. If the unknown man is a law enforcement officer, the prostitute can claim in court that the officer had immoral relations with her. A witness will testify that he saw the officer nude in bed. Under such circumstances, the case against the prostitute and the go-between is usually dismissed.

Some prostitutes frequent hotels because of the continual supply of men from other communities, which minimizes embarrassment in possibly seeing the person again under awkward circumstances. One man asked a prostitute in the lobby of a large hotel to come to his apartment, as his wife was out of town. The woman indignantly said that she would not do so because "that's not my kind of trick." She explained that she worked only in hotels. It may be that the impersonality and ephemeral nature of a hotel contact make the woman feel safe.[20] A related example of selectivity was provided by a woman who recently struck up a conversation with a businessman in the lobby of a luxurious Chicago hotel. She told him that "another guy whose wife is out of town wanted me to go to his apartment tonight. But I wouldn't do that—I'm not that kind of girl." She went on to say that she sensed he was not married and that she would be very happy to have a date with him.

In some hotels, ingenious approaches to customers are used. In the lobby of a fine New York City hotel, an attractive and well-dressed woman of about thirty-five approached an executive. She said, "Bon jour, Monsieur Jackson." The executive, whose name was not Jackson, looked quizzically at the woman. In excellent English, but with a definite French accent, she reminded the man of their meeting recently in Dallas. When he explained that there must be a misunderstanding, she seemed embarrassed. They walked out together, and continued chatting while walking. Soon she paused before a modern apartment building. She explained she had an apartment there and would like to invite him up for a drink, but she did not think it was right because her daughter was not home. She did not want to invite a strange man to her home without someone else being present.

The executive liked the woman and called her a few days later. She agreed to have dinner with him and he met her sixteen-year-old daughter. They had a pleasant and expensive dinner at a fashionable restaurant. Back at her apartment she explained that a financial emergency had made it imperative for her to raise $200 almost immediately, and invited the executive to spend the night with her if he could help in her financial emergency.

During the winter season, prostitution in Miami Beach

hotels is not uncommon. At the height of the season there are approximately five women for every man. A few of the hotels tacitly cooperate in the prostitution trade. One leading hotel has a set of rooms on its ground floor arranged so that prostitutes do not have to go through the lobby and risk being seen. A Miami hotel bartender recently said, "In our place the prices for the girls are practically on the menu." Some enterprising prostitutes rent a poolside cabana where they receive phone calls for assignments. A clue to the atmosphere can be obtained from the experience of a stenographer who accompanied her husband on a Miami Beach vacation. A woman approached her husband and asked him to dance. When he declined, she asked him if he would like to "date" her. He replied, "No, I'm here with my wife." The girl snorted, "Bringing a wife to Miami Beach is like bringing a ham sandwich to a banquet."

In the South, hotels are used quite frequently by prostitutes. Knoxville, Atlanta, Little Rock, and Fort Smith have a high incidence of hotel prostitution. Kansas City still has one flagrantly conducted brothel in the guise of a hotel, in which a porter, by nodding his head to a potential customer who looks into the lobby, communicates the availability of a prostitute. But Kansas City's Twelfth Street, from Baltimore to Broadway, once lined with hotels catering to prostitutes, no longer has them. Another community that formerly had a great deal of hotel prostitution was St. Louis, where many hotels on Market Street near the Union Station were almost wholly devoted to the practice. Porters would stand outside and attempt to attract the attention of young girls who appeared to be from out of town. The porters would urge them to stay at the hotel and then introduce them to prostitutes, who encouraged them to enter "the life."

For many years Las Vegas hotels encouraged prostitution. Approximately five hundred prostitutes used to patrol the Strip hotels, though they became less aggressive after Howard Hughes moved into Las Vegas and began buying up hotels in 1967.

The general decline in hotel prostitution can in large part be attributed to the rise of the motel in America. A motel can be used by a prostitute with greater facility than a hotel. The ease with which she and her client can get a motel room has been a boon to the prostitute.

BARS

The presence of prostitutes helps to attract some customers to bars, taverns, and nightclubs. Bars may employ or provide a convenient setting for prostitutes or for B-girls who encourage men to buy drinks. The prostitute who works out of a bar is likely to meet men who prefer a free pickup to paid sex. An experienced customer in a bar can generally identify the prostitute. She may be looking uneasily at her watch, over a period of time. The customer often asks the bartender to tell such a woman that he would like to buy her a drink. Her response to his proposal and the subsequent conversation enable him to determine if she is a prostitute. A prostitute often spends considerable time in a bar before a man finally leaves with her.

A B-girl (also called a "come-on" or "percentage girl" or "drink rustler") often spends six to seven hours in a bar every evening. She usually has an arrangement with the bartender whereby he will serve her "downs," or diluted drinks with a minimum of alcohol. "Downs" enable her to give the customer the impression that she is drinking with him. The customer is charged for "downs" at an exorbitant rate. Many B-girls ask for "sloe gin," which is a signal to the bartender that they want some colored water ("belly wash") or tea. The bartender keeps track of the number of drinks a B-girl's customers buy. He may have a row of glasses, one for each girl, along the cash register. A small check is dropped into her glass for each drink credited. In other bars a girl saves the stirring sticks that she gets with each drink.

Some B-girls start as employees whose only work is to get men to buy liquor. Many bar proprietors do not want their

B-girls to be prostitutes because they prefer the customer to spend his money on liquor. But sometimes a bar owner feels almost forced to hire prostitutes to meet the competition of other bars. Perhaps typical is the story of one owner who changed his bar into a honky-tonk: "I opened this spot as a legitimate tavern. I have a big investment and catered to a respectable element, so I wanted to run a respectable place." He explained that his tavern was on a street on which honky-tonks later opened, and he was sandwiched between two taverns which employed prostitutes. He added: "These spots were always crowded. My place was deserted. Respectable people bypassed it. I was about to go out of business, and that's how I got into the racket."

Some B-girls become interested in the opportunities for greater income in prostitution. They may become prostitutes working at another bar, or continue at the same bar and drift into prostitution. Prostitutes who work in collusion with bars often are at the same table every night and develop standardized procedures for dealing with customers. At a well-known New York City bar, one prostitute sits every evening with a fresh crossword puzzle. She asks each man who approaches, "What will you pay?" and hands him the crossword puzzle. If he fills two spaces with XX, she adds V.

Some bar prostitutes try to get a client at any price he can pay. One woman approached a man in a bar and said, "I can give you a good time for $10. That would include some half and half . . ." When the man indicated that he didn't have $10, she said, "The lowest is $5, but that's a fast one. . . . Why not now? You have enough money for a quick one. Then get more later . . ." Another technique is this approach used in a bar: "We can get together for a nice date, but I have to work here until 3 A.M. So you'll have to wait here until then. Don't worry about the price—just buy drinks. I have my own room we can go to. Will you buy us another drink?" One reason for the prostitute's encouraging her customer to buy drinks is that she may look better to him after four or five drinks.

Some bar prostitutes are quite candid. One recently told a customer, "My old man is on the nut [out of work] and I can't get any other job except looking at the ceiling [prostitution] in a hook shop [brothel]. I came here as a dancer, but I really make my money by hustling. How about it?'

Prostitutes who seek customers in other places may go to a bar if their usual "beat" does not yield customers. Women who work out of hotels and who have not found a "date" by fairly late in the evening often go to a bar about an hour before closing time to see if they can find a "sleeper" or unexpected customer.

One kind of bar prostitute is the "roller." She is less interested in fees than in "rolling" her client and taking his wallet after he is drunk. She may put soporifics ("Mickey Finn") into the customer's drink so that he will fall asleep by the time they arrive at her room. If she takes the customer to a cooperating hotel, by the time he wakes up she is gone and the hotel management denies any knowledge of the woman.

During the 1930's and 1940's, Harlem in New York City became a "roll" center. Calumet City, outside of Chicago, was also well known for the frequency with which its bar prostitutes tried to "roll." They got the customer to take them to a dark street and engaged in sexual intercourse while going through his pockets. Many "rollers" offered "perversions" to a customer so that they could go through his pockets more easily.

Boston has long been a center for bar prostitution because it is a big military and port city with a substantial transient population. Until recently Boston permitted policemen to work in uniform when off duty. A number of policemen worked as bouncers at taverns frequented by prostitutes and added an air of legitimacy. A sailor commented: "The town is loaded with hustlers. They hang out in the drink spots. There are also lots of 'sea gulls' [semi-amateurs, who follow the fleet from port to port] in the bars. Just go into the right bars and you'll be hustled. The same spots have been running for years."

Another center for prostitution is Philadelphia, long famous also for its "chippies," or women who "give it away." Even the notoriety received by several high municipal officials in the 1930's for their cooperation with prostitution had little effect on the practice. Philadelphia has always had many bars with prostitutes as well as private clubs that remain open all night.

In Baltimore, on four blocks of East Baltimore Street, is The Strip or The Block, which is studded with bars in which there are B-girls, strippers, and a large number of prostitutes. Many bars have dark booths in the rear, and a girl may approach a customer and say, "Let's go to the back of the room so I can really love you up." Some clubs permit sexual intercourse in the booths. In other clubs the dances and other performances are overtly sexual. One Baltimore club has a staff of thirty-five prostitutes. The Baltimore clubs have an established price scale for every service. At one typical club the women dance on the floor just in front of the man and offer themselves. For $1 a man may put the woman's breast in his mouth. For $2 he can put his finger in her vagina. For $8 he has intercourse at the table and for $10 in a room upstairs.

Open bar prostitution can bring convention trade to a city. The Block is known to be a major attraction to groups planning conventions in Baltimore or nearby cities. Atlantic City is another convention city with bars known to be hospitable to prostitutes. Local authorities seem to avoid arresting prostitutes who are involved with convention-goers.

Anchorage, Alaska, has much bar prostitution. As one resident recently told an interviewer, "Just stagger into the night and you'll be hustled." At one typical bar seven women sharply eyed each man who entered and one or another would accost him. One of the women sat next to a patron and asked, "Mind if I join you? Will you buy me a drink? The bartender knows what I like. . . . Would you be interested in a date with me tonight? I'm glad I got to you first before any of the other girls. . . . We're all working girls here. . . ."

Puerto Rico's many bars are filled with prostitutes soliciting drinks and openly plying their trade. The average bar in Puerto Rico has ten prostitutes. Cab drivers will often take miltiary personnel to the "right" bar. Most of the prostitutes are quite young and many appear to be pregnant. Nearly all have pimps nearby, not only for protection in case of trouble but also to check on the number of customers. The role of pimps in Puerto Rico today bears a close resemblance to that of pre–World War II pimps in many cities in the United States.

Bar prostitutes in Puerto Rico take their clients to nearby small hotels, where they charge from $5 to $7. When the fleet is in, the number of prostitutes on duty doubles. Many servicemen prefer the quieter spots but others are attracted to the "tubs of blood," which derive their name from the frequency of fights and blood-letting. It is not unusual for bouncers to hurl difficult customers down the stairs or into the street. The prostitutes are as rough as their customers. One recently offered to crush a beer can with her fist if given fifty cents. In one deft stroke she bent the can into a U.

THE CALL HOUSE AND CALL GIRL

The call house is an established arrangement for prostitution, probably more popular in the West than in other parts of the country. Call houses are of three types. In one type, the madam asks the client for a description of what he wants, and arranges for a meeting at another location which she selects. In the second type, the madam directs the woman to the customer, who is responsible for selecting a place of assignation. The third type is a combination service in which the madam either provides a room or sends the woman to the client, depending on the circumstances. In all call arrangements, the madam receives half the customer's payment. The prostitute generally uses taxis and the client pays her taxi fare both ways.

A call girl or "pony girl" is a prostitute who keeps individual dates with her clients at a place selected by mutual consent; arrangements are made for each date, usually by phone or some other procedure, or by a person outside the immediate client-prostitute relationship. Women who work through a call house are call girls. They have always been around, but the increase in their number since World War II is largely the result of the decline of the brothel. The call girl has flourished more widely in the United States than elsewhere. The attractive, well-dressed companion who charges high fees meets the demands of convention-goers who used to visit brothels and were willing to pay more for additional services. Most call girls use a telephone answering service in order not to miss any calls.

The call girl, for the extra payment she receives as compared with other kinds of prostitutes, is expected to be pleasant and friendly in greeting customers, and to be able to identify them by name. She is also likely to be aware of specific preferences, for example, whether a customer likes a certain kind of liquor or uses a pillow. Her demeanor during sexual intercourse itself is likely to be a polite and encouraging friendliness.[21]

The call girl will probably not show signs of recognizing a customer when she sees him in public, or steal from him, or permit him to overpay her when he is drunk. She will make every effort to satisfy a client. She does not reveal the inadequacies of any one man to another. There is a *noblesse oblige* attitude among some call girls who feel that it is indelicate and otherwise inappropriate to see more than three customers in a single day.

One of the call girl's major concerns is to develop a substantial clientele. The average call girl sees perhaps sixty men a month. Many call girls find that by developing a large clientele they can earn a substantial income by acting as a referral source for colleagues, who will pay 50 per cent of their fee. A call girl often has to be a part-time madam because a customer may ask her to bring a friend for another man, and she must know women who are available on relatively short notice. A woman recruited for a double date usually kicks back half the fee.

Call girls usually get new clients by references from existing clients. Just as commercial organizations sell mailing lists to potential purchasers of products or services, madams may sell telephone numbers of established customers to call girls. A girl may purchase such numbers as a precaution against a decline in the number of her own clients.

The call girl occasionally phones clients to solicit business. Many call girls develop great skill in making telephone appeals. They telephone the client with a story about an economic emergency, and hope to get the man to suggest a date. Some clients, of course, enjoy thinking that the date is a result of factors other than money. Such men often arrange to meet the girl at some public place, dine at a fashionable restaurant, and then attempt to "talk" the girl into going home with them. She may mildly resist the man's overtures. Such clients are of sufficient importance to some madams that they have arrangements with restaurants, which are expected to pay the madam a percentage of what they earn on the business. The clients may discreetly place the fee in a drawer, or "lose" it in a game of cards.

A marathon is a date that includes a full evening of activity, usually dinner and visits to several nightclubs before sex. A marathon usually costs $100 and generally involves at least three hours. An ordinary call girl date requires only ten or fifteen minutes and brings a minimum of $20 and an average of $50, so that the dinner date is much less productive financially.

Call girls may gross as much as $40,000 a year. But a substantial portion goes for pimps, madams, bribes, medical expenses, clothing, rent, and beauty parlor bills. The call girl is often overcharged and seldom saves money for the future.

Some call girls explicitly state their fee. Others make it a practice not to discuss money with a client but to collect it unobtrusively after the date. Many a call girl has found that she makes more money by not specifying any price to a client. If she conveys enthusiasm for him, he may feel that the call girl is enjoying his personality and charm and give her more than she ordinarily gets. Some clients prefer to put the money in an envelope, perhaps because seeing the bills reminds them of the nature of the transaction. One reason for the call girl's ability to charge substantial fees may be that her "refined" appearance helps to assuage any guilt the client may feel.

Call girls have interested writers and mass media because of their "glamor" as the elite of their craft who service influential and important men. John O'Hara has dealt extensively with the call girl and her clients. In *Butterfield 8*, O'Hara's major character is a high-priced model and call girl in the speakeasy era.[22] She is a ruthless but sympathetic person who has the hard, brittle qualities of O'Hara's Pal Joey. In 1959 Edward R. Murrow narrated a radio program on "The Business of Sex" over the Columbia Broadcasting System. His discussion of the use of call girls by big business aroused much interest. In some competitive business situations in which the products are not fundamentally different, there have been rumors of call girls being used to influence buying decisions. A manufacturer usually knows if a buyer wants a girl and can arrange for her to visit his hotel room. Such an arrangement may help the manufacturer to cement a personal relationship with the buyer. There is no way of knowing how widespread this practice is.[23] The alertness of call girls to modern business trends can be seen in the 1963 indictment of a madam by a federal grand jury in Chicago. She was a pioneer in "play now, pay later" prostitution. Business firms which were alleged to have sent her clients were billed at the end of the month.

Related to the call girl is the prostitute who works as a receptionist or a model but is expected to be available for clients or other businessmen whom her employer suggests.

The garment industry has traditionally been the locus of this kind of prostitute, who is often called a "party girl." She may begin dating her employer and then go out with some buyers. Such leads provide a ready source of customers, and the girl can still maintain her other job.[24] "We used to have a receptionist-model on the payroll to entertain the buyers from out of town," a man in the garment industry noted recently. "She got $100 a week, which was $50 more than she was worth. When business was slow, the boss would accommodate himself."

Another call girl or a pimp is primarily responsible for the novice call girl's learning the details of her trade.[25] The average period of training seems to be from two to three months, and generally involves an experienced call girl, rather than a pimp, living in an apartment with a trainee. The pimp faces severe penalties if he is apprehended living with a trainee prostitute. He also usually wants to be sure of the prostitute's loyalty before moving in with her.

The apprenticeship consists of learning the values and mechanics of the call girl life, as well as a series of "dos" and "don'ts" of relationships with other colleagues, pimps, and customers. Instruction may include information on how to drink alcohol, how to broach the amount of the fee and how to take it, what to discuss with customers, and hygiene. Sometimes, call girl instruction includes the trainee's bringing a customer to her apartment. The trainer eavesdrops on what happens and discusses it later with her.

The trainer may also be the person who recruited the call girl. One Cleveland call girl mused: "I got into the racket through a man I met at a bar. I had been working as a secretary. One night a man called Bob, very handsome, began talking to me. We talked for about an hour. He told me that he liked me and wanted to meet me at his hotel, that he was only in town for the day and would ordinarily have taken me to a nice dinner and show. The dinner and show would come to $100 or so and he'd rather give me the money. Bob actually slipped the bill across the table to me and said he'd wait outside for me for a few minutes. I could keep the money whether or not I joined him.

"I did join him and we spent a great night together. A few weeks later he called and said he'd like me to date a friend of his and there might be some money in it. I said okay, and after I had seen the friend, Bob called again and told me he was a recruiter and that he had tried me out and that I could make lots of money if I worked with him. Bob would take care of getting the dates for me. I'd only be dealing with him. He'd get me an apartment and teach me the ropes. He did, and it has worked out fine for me. I never have to hustle for johns, and the cops have never bothered me."

One Chicago call girl reminisced: "The things you have to learn in this business! I learned never to break wind unless the john does it first. Some johns want you to have warm water or oil of wintergreen in your mouth—it gives them a zippy feeling when I French them. I had to learn to control my throat muscles so I wouldn't gag after Frenching the john. He doesn't want you to pull your head away after he comes, so you have to hold it till you can get to the bathroom and spit it out and use a mouthwash to rinse your mouth and prevent VD.

"I also got to know which creams are best for lubrication in anal intercourse. It doesn't matter how *long* the man's penis is, but it could be too thick for comfort.

"I learned that some things johns ask for, like 'a trip around the world,' don't mean any one thing—you have to find out what he wants. A lot of johns have eyes bigger than their stomachs, and most of them can't make it more than once. If they come too quickly, I say something like, 'You did that because I'm an exciting woman—let's relax and see what happens.' But very few of them can do it again, unless I use a vibrator, the kind you strap to the back of your hand."

Restrictions on wiretapping make call girls more difficult to arrest than other prostitutes. Many have verified lists of customers, will not see someone whom they do not know, and are very guarded on the telephone. Call girls generally make it a practice not to be explicit about money or sexual activity during a telephone conversation. Code designations are used instead. Paintings may represent one code, so that a "picture of Grant" means a contact that will cost $50 and a "picture of Franklin" one for $100. "Will show you a French painting in a lovely black frame at ten tomorrow morning" might mean that a brunette will call at the client's room at 10 A.M. and expect to engage in fellatio.

Another code is based on the vocabulary of the insurance business. The woman pretends that the customer is an insurance salesman; their discussion of premiums is actually a clarification of prices. A discussion of appointments in the salesman's office deals with a time when the customer will come to the prostitute's place of business. Another approach is to discuss the number of bottles of liquor that will be required for a party or social event. The number of bottles of liquor—for example, bourbon—would represent the number of prostitutes involved. If the liquor is said to be $10 a bottle, the price per prostitute would be $100. Still another code for cover stories is that of a dry cleaning establishment. A customer says he wants to be sure there will be a specific number of items of clothing available for him to pick up. The madam can then respond by telling him, "I am sure we'll have all four of your trousers ready," meaning that she will have four women available.

Call girls appear to be familiar with but do not personally endorse traditional or stereotypical aspects of prostitutes' attitudes, that customers should be exploited, for example, or that prostitution is not immoral and should not be stigmatized. Their mobility or unwillingness to identify with such occupational perspectives may reflect the relatively isolated nature of their work, the occupation's lack of cohesiveness, its comparative glamor, its absence of stigma, and similar factors.[26] The attitudes of call girls may be overrepresented in studies of prostitution because they are more accessible and verbal than other women whose ideology may be more central.[27] Just as they fascinate novelists, they may also have attracted the comparatively few recent students of prostitution to a disproportionately high degree.

PART-TIME PROSTITUTES

Part-time workers began to be a significant element in prostitution during the depression of the 1930's, when many women found their ordinary sources of income to be inadequate. Brothels in various communities provided several different kinds of part-time workers for their clients. Brothels in St. Louis featured women who were said to be college students. In Shreveport, Louisiana, a number of houses featured "sitters," married women who worked from 1 to 4 P.M. and were able to arrive home in time to prepare dinner for their husbands. They were usually older than the brothel inmates.

Some of the more expensive brothels in New Orleans also employed "sitters." An extra fee accompanied their services, which were usually identified by the madam as "something private." "Sitters" seldom worked every day of the week, and some only saw clients with whom they had a regular appointment.

In the last ten years there has been a decidedly large increase in the number of part-time prostitutes. One reason for this, cited by a number of such women, is the continuing upward spiral of prices. Many women seek to obtain extra luxuries and consumer goods by selling sex.

The call girl's ability to control her work schedule makes it especially easy for her to work part time. Some call girls work only afternoons. They see executives and others who are able to leave their place of work for an hour or two. In general, customers are more available in the afternoon than morning, perhaps because of psychological problems in contemplating sex in the morning and difficulties in taking morning time from work. Edward Albee's play *Everything in the Garden* (1967) and Luis Buñuel's film *Belle de Jour* (1968) are concerned with wives who work afternoons as prostitutes and get home in time to have dinner with their husbands.

The development of so many active fields for sexual encounter has broadened the range of part-time prostitutes and made it easier for them to avoid police detection. Most observers would agree that there are several times as many part-time as full-time prostitutes. The part-time or demi-prostitute can work at sporting events, fairs, conventions, hotels, bars, and as a car-prowler as well as a call girl. Expansion of prostitution in this country in the future will likely result from the recruitment of more demi-prostitutes.

SOME UNUSUAL SETTINGS

American ingenuity, famous in many other ways, has also manifested itself in some of the peculiar arrangements Americans have developed for prostitution. The taxi-dance hall and the dance studio were first developed in the United States as covers for prostitution and have been copied in other countries. One unusual setting for prostitution in America is the private yacht. As one madam noted, when the yachts go out to sea they have "not only to be manned, they also have to be girled." This is an expensive procedure but has the appeal of the exotic and of relative immunity from police harassment.

World War II saw the first regular use of the trailer for prostitution. Women would travel by trailer from one community to the other, wherever there were customers. The trailer would park in some location convenient to access by customers. This approach to bringing customer and prostitute together has largely lost its wartime popularity. A related approach could be seen in Phenix City, Alabama, after law enforcement became stricter. A prostitute meeting a potential client would tell him to go to a street corner or some other rendezvous. A one-ton truck with covered sides would pick him up at the designated place and take him to the outskirts of the community. Meanwhile, the prostitute would be driven there in a truck which had a mattress in the rear. Prostitute and client would engage in sexual activity in the rear of the truck and later be driven back to town.

In recent years various body-painting studios have become prostitution centers. Many large cities have studios where a client pays an average of $20 an hour in order to paint on the body of a nude model. He withdraws with the model to a private room and can make his own arrangement with the girl for whatever sexual services he requires. The studios seem to attract customers who regard themselves as sophisticated, because of the "swinging" connotations of body painting.

For many years there have been recurrent rumors of brothels with male inmates which had female clients. These rumors have never been substantiated. The "stud" who expects to earn a livelihood by finding women who will pay him for sexual access is likely to be as disappointed as was Joe Buck in the film *Midnight Cowboy* (1969). A curious version of the good-hearted prostitute, Joe Buck comes to New York from Houston expecting to get money from women for being a "stud." Instead, Joe is so innocent that he ends up paying the women while his vicious and corrupt clients exploit him. Like the prototypical literary prostitute, Joe keeps giving his body because he can only establish contact with other people by offering it. Like generations of literary prostitutes, Joe is sensitive and lives for the pleasure he can give others. Joe's difficulties in finding clients accurately reflect the near impossibility of a "stud" earning a livelihood from prostitution.

VII. THE CLIENT

Writings about prostitutes have not shown much interest in their clients. Typical of the general lack of interest in clients is the generally enlightened Wolfenden Report, which attracted much attention in both England and America and which neglects the client almost completely.[1] Yet it would seem obvious that any systematic consideration of prostitution as a social problem can hardly ignore the client.

As of the late forties, Kinsey and his associates reported that some two-thirds of American men had at least one contact with a prostitute, and perhaps 15 to 20 per cent had such relations more than a few times a year. Four per cent had sexual relations exclusively with prostitutes, and from 3.5 to 4 per cent of the total number of sexual contacts in this country occurred with prostitutes. Higher education is negatively correlated with contact with prostitutes, so that 74 per cent of those who did not graduate from high school had some experience with a prostitute, but 54 per cent of graduates and only 28 per cent of college men.[2]

Probably roughly the same proportion of men visit prostitutes today as thirty years ago, but the number of contacts per man has dropped somewhat. One reason for the decline is the decrease in the number of brothels. It was once relatively easy for a customer to go to a brothel. With prostitution more a matter of individual entrepreneurship today, a customer has more difficulty in sustaining contacts.

There is a difference in age between the representative customer today and the customer of the past. When most cities had brothels, their clients included many single young adults and men in their late twenties. Today more customers are married men in their thirties, forties, and fifties, and the number of younger clients appears to have declined, which is perhaps explained by the loosening of sexual mores among the young that is said to be part of the so-called "sexual revolution."

Frequency of sexual intercourse with a prostitute varies greatly among customer groups. Some men may see a prostitute only as part of travel or other change in their routines. For other customers a visit to a prostitute seems to be a regularly scheduled activity. Such men are relatively easy for the woman to handle because the customer plans a certain amount of time for the encounter and the sexual activity is routinized.

There has been only one large-scale study of the attitudes of men toward prostitution, and it was conducted in the 1920's.[3] Roughly one-third of the ten thousand men interviewed would brave a variety of obstacles to get to a prostitute, about one-third would take or leave it in accordance with its accessibility, and one-third did not wish to bother. The decreased accessibility of prostitutes would probably lead to different results if this survey were to be taken today.

When law enforcement in a community makes it difficult for prostitution to survive, clients must decide what to do. Some will travel a considerable distance to find a prostitute. After law enforcement improved in New York City, many clients began driving to Scranton, Bethlehem, and Easton in Pennsylvania, and to Hudson in New York. When prostitutes left San Antonio, Texas, groups of five or six men would share expenses and rent a taxi to Nuevo Laredo, Mexico, 175 miles away. In some situations seeing a prostitute involves considerable planning because the prostitute may be at some distance from the customer. In such cases customers may seek information about the availability of women and then combine a visit to a prostitute with a business trip.

Some men use considerable ingenuity in planning their meetings with prostitutes. One middle-aged man in a large city would walk out of his home every Wednesday in slippers. He would tell his wife that he was going to the corner in order to wait for the truck delivering morning papers. He would actually go to a brothel and meet with a prostitute with whom he had a permanent date. If she were not available, he would not see anyone else and would go home carrying the morning newspaper.

Many jokes and stories deal with the substantial proportion of customers who are married. The equation of marital sex with that available from the prostitute is the theme of one Oedipal story that deals with a teen-age boy who meets his father in a brothel. He upbraids his father for coming to such a place. "Well," the father says, "it's only a few dollars. Why should I bother your mother for a few dollars?"

The reactions of clients to the circumstances under which they see a prostitute vary greatly. Some resent the speed with which they must accomplish their sex and are bitter about the "rush act." Others don't care that they have such a short time or that the surroundings are relatively unpleasant. Some customers might actually be uneasy if the prostitute were in an attractive setting and responded to them. Some men are so pleased about having a "good time" that they are practically oblivious to the surroundings.

Many customers give fictitious names, especially those who visit the same prostitutes regularly. The names are chiefly of the one-syllable variety, like Mack, Jones, and Smith. The reason for the pseudonym is that many prostitutes record customers' names, and there is fear of blackmail. Most customers also know that police making a raid are likely to look for the address books kept by madams and prostitutes.

PROCEDURES

The clothing removed by a customer when with a prostitute varies from one situation to another. With prostitutes who are very busy, the customer is likely to take off an absolute minimum of clothing. In situations in which the customer does not remove his shoes, there is usually a folded blanket at the foot of the bed so that he will not dirty the bed sheets. Some men prefer to remove all their clothing but for an undershirt; others do not even remove their shirt and tie.

The great range in the time that it takes men to complete their business with the prostitute has led to some descriptive slang. When 78 rpm phonograph records began to receive competition in the late 1940's from the long-playing 33 rpm record, the contrast between the two provided one classification of customers. A customer who worked quickly was called a "78" and one with a slower response was a "33."

A "lover" is a customer who is determined to arouse the prostitute or to get her to respond to him. Such customers often squeeze and pinch the woman in a manner that seems to be suggested by various manuals. One former call girl commented, "I am still looking for the marriage manual they all must have read which advises grabbing little handfuls of flesh and twisting, wringing the neck while kissing, a stroking motion and patting of the flanks, similar to the way a farmer caresses a beloved cow, and spitting in the ears."[4] "Put some life into it," some men occasionally say, but such comments are relatively infrequent.

Among the customer types is the man who may drink a little, talk quite a bit, engage in sexual intercourse, but visit the establishment primarily because his relationship with his wife is unpleasant or uncomfortable. Another type comes to the brothel either drunk or intending to get drunk. He is often loud and argumentative and engages in practical jokes. Another kind of client has a condescending attitude toward the woman and is eager to discover the details of her career: "I hope you don't mind my asking, dear, but how did an attractive girl like you get into this kind of work?"

Some prostitutes feel that one of their occupational hazards is the need to listen to customers' conversation. Although there has been a great deal of speculation about the conversation of prostitutes, less thought has been given to the comments of customers. Some men talk about the attractiveness of the woman's body and make some remark about seeing her in the future. One popular subject for conversation among customers is their family situation: wives, children, and difficulties being experienced with them. Many a prostitute feels that she needs to be half psychoanalyst to cope with the neurotic and rejected men she sees.

Many men try to make careless and flip conversation. One prostitute's most effective ploy with such clients was to ask, "Do you eat lettuce?" When her customer replied that he did, she would say, "You must be a jackrabbit." Prostitutes frequently use such ambiguous "riddles" to interrupt the tedium of clients' musings. One way of ending such conversations and chastening a customer who talks a great deal is to show him a picture of her "baby," or to display a baby bank which contains coins and dollar bills. Many prostitutes use pictures of themselves when they were children as "baby" pictures. Prostitutes and their associates often call the client a "john." He may also be called a "sucker" or "meatball," and occasionally a "patron." In the Midwest he is often called a "beef buyer" or a "piper."

YOUNGER CLIENTS

A young man's sexual initiation by a prostitute ("copping a cherry") was once more frequent than it is today. Although between 20 and 25 per cent of male American college students first experienced coitus with a prostitute during the 1940's and early 1950's, only 2 to 7 per cent of a comparable sample did so in 1967.[5] What are the implications of the belief that it is good for a young man to visit a prostitute before marriage in order to gain experience?[6] Such a man may come to believe that the function of a woman is to gratify his whim, without any reciprocity on his part. A later attitude of contempt may cause difficulties in relationships with other women or with a wife, especially in an America in which romantic love is still the basis for many marriages.

Men have always speculated that contact with prostitutes may have deleterious effects on personality. The alleged failure of Brahms to achieve certain goals as a composer has been attributed to his having played as a boy at an inn where prostitutes worked.[7] Prostitutes would sing obscene songs to his accompaniment, take the lad on their laps, and awaken sexual feelings in him. Such experiences may have first attracted and later repelled young Brahms, who was never subsequently able to integrate tender love and sexual love.

Visiting a prostitute as an important mode of sexual initiation has had such fascination for writers that it is difficult to tell whether its popularity in drama and fiction mirrors its actual incidence. Innumerable plots hinge on the complications of a young man's being taken by a relative—often an uncle—to a brothel. The traditional novel of personal development in European and American fiction often has an episode in which a sensitive young man reacts to a brothel. *One Hundred Dollar Misunderstanding* deals with the relationship between a stuffy and self-righteous undergraduate and a fourteen-year-old prostitute called Kitten.[8] The young man comes to the brothel posing as a successful burglar who has $100 for a weekend of sport. The girl detects the prospect of a permanent arrangement, while the undergraduate convinces himself that her attentiveness is proof of respect for him. The teen-ager who goes to a prostitute in order to prove his manhood is a hero of the movie *Tea and Sympathy* (1956), made from the successful play by Robert Anderson (1953). A prep school student has been accused of being too close to the physical education teacher at a school and goes to a brothel in town in order to prove the charge false. The prostitute who laughs at the young man is presented as a heartless person, and the young man runs away from her.

An experience with a prostitute can evoke a tremendous range of reactions in the customer, from extreme depression through elation. The spectrum of response undoubtedly includes several dimensions of status and ego satisfaction. Some customers say they do not enjoy the experience as one way of counterbalancing feelings of guilt about it.

Since the prostitute is usually working in her own establishment, the customer is often embarrassed and at a considerable disadvantage. The generally direct behavior and conversation of the woman may also help the customer feel he is participating in an impersonal process. One way of overcoming embarrassment is for younger customers to visit the prostitute in the company of friends.[9] Some boys may be challenged by the group excitement. Others derive prestige from their knowledgeability about prostitutes, or from the mere fact of their visit. Some young men are motivated to visit prostitutes after a long discussion of sexual behavior, which can act as a direct stimulus.

When a group of young men visits a prostitute, they are often candid with one another in later describing their experiences. But when talking to others they are likely to make it sound more attractive than it actually was. The precautions in which the prostitute may engage are seldom discussed. Many young men are somewhat confused when the prostitute uses soap to wash their sex organs. This routine precautionary procedure strikes some young clients as being too businesslike. Her washing of his genitals may make a customer uneasy because it reminds him of his mother's bathing him as a child.

Many customers visiting a prostitute for the first time have problems in performing the sexual act, usually in having an erection. One difficulty in obtaining accurate information about the experience is that it may be awkward for young men to report failure. Many are so apprehensive about a visit to a prostitute that their mood makes it almost impossible to engage in sexual activity.

One Buffalo madam commented that her most "interesting" customer was a twenty-year-old who was so nervous that he missed the chair when he sat down in her parlor. When she asked him what happened, he said, "You seemed so tense, I wanted to break the tension." Some customers manifest tics or display tension by drumming with their fingers or tapping with their shoes.

Young customers in groups may be offensive because of concern about what their friends will say about their not being "experienced." They may request "deviant" sex and use jargon to show that they are truly "sophisticated." It is not uncommon for young men to engage in considerable drinking before visiting a prostitute. Being drunk or near-drunk seems to take away some of the responsibility, shame, or distress they may feel. The drinking is not necessarily related to a desire for a prostitute, but some young men may be responding to the same inner need by drinking and visiting a prostitute in the company of others. We have no way of knowing whether the drinking-prostitution combination is typical of only our society, but there is reason to doubt that it is, for James Boswell has graphically described how he got drunk on the frequent occasions when he visited a prostitute: "We drank a good deal until I was so intoxicated that instead of going home, I went in a low house . . . and like a brute that I was, I lay all night with her."[10] American customers frequently seek to minimize their responsibility by saying they were drunk when they went to a prostitute.

A substantial proportion of the sexual companions of one group of male students studied were prostitutes.[11] In an analysis of the personal histories of two hundred male college students, the reactions of those who had been in contact with prostitutes varied from "most disgusting" to "delightfully charming."[12] After one or more unsatisfactory experiences with prostitutes, some students seemed to relinquish hope of a better experience with any other woman and talked as if they were ready to become homosexuals. Others reported very pleasant encounters with prostitutes. One student who had his first contact with a prostitute overseas at sixteen, later felt more at ease with a prostitute than with a "normal girl," suggesting the great importance which the student placed on his first sexual experience. A girl's first experience of lovemaking is traditionally believed to be crucial; it is rarely assumed that males are equally sensitive or as strongly influenced by their first sexual experience.

REASONS FOR VISITS

Why do men visit prostitutes? Among the main reasons are: drunkenness, curiosity, restlessness, bravado, interest in "perversions" not otherwise obtainable, revival of waning manhood, or what the man perceives as simple biological necessity. Prostitutes meet needs for lonely or deviant men not otherwise able to find a sexual outlet.[13] Some prostitutes have a strong curiosity value to customers.

Among the reasons for married men's going to prostitutes are a desire for variety, sexual deprivation in the marriage, anxiety and shame, no need to worry about pregnancy, avoidance of a wife's requests, and possible attachment to prostitutes, not to mention various neurotic reasons.[14]

Some married customers want a prostitute who is the exact opposite of their wives. The customer with a tall blonde wife may want a prostitute who is short and dark. Such men may enjoy a woman vastly different from their wives in order to minimize guilt. Other customers prefer prostitutes who resemble teachers, nursemaids, mothers, sisters, aunts, and other women with whom they formerly had a significant relationship.

Los Angeles was one of several cities that had a "House of All Nations," so named after the famous Parisian brothel. It had women from different backgrounds, including Orientals, quadroons, and mulattos. A number of customers prefer such types and similar women outside their regular social circles who were unlikely to remind them of wives or mothers. Some customers believe that nonwhite women are more "primitive" and sexy than American women. With such "different" women it may also be easier for the customer to feel relaxed about engaging in petty deceptions like exceeding the agreed-upon time.

Men who visit a prostitute may pride themselves that while they may not be getting a pretty face, at least the woman is likely to have an attractive body. Given a choice between the two, many men would select the body. The men may, of course, be rationalizing a situation in which they essentially have no choice. It may also be part of our folklore that prostitutes have attractive bodies.

A classification of customers that was developed in England may have some relevance to the United States.[15] Some respondents went only with prostitutes, were inhibited with other women, and often had an ambivalent relationship with their mothers. A second group consisted of men with roving occupations, like sailors, who showed passivity in their relationships with women. A third and more impulsive group consorted not only with prostitutes but also with pickups and girl friends. They sought out girls in dance halls and cafés, but their relationships remained superficial. Such men often came from a home with an inadequate father, where the mother provoked resentment in the son by being the source of both discipline and control.

Some of the men who had venereal disease seemed to experience guilt for the "sin." Their feeling of injury about the sexual apparatus may have awakened previous castration fears and injuries to self-esteem. There was also fear of infecting the wife and concern about impotence and sterility. Those men who experienced very shallow relationships generally projected blame for the venereal disease onto the prostitute. A third of the men did not actually have venereal disease but were anxious about getting it. In some patients the venereal disease phobia acted as a defense against the risk of marriage.

The extent of potential guilt in the customer-prostitute relationship is suggested by Karl Menninger, who cites cases of customers who ostensibly contracted gonorrhea from women although the women's serological tests yielded negative results.[16] Perhaps because the men felt guilty, they may have unconsciously wanted to get venereal disease as punishment for being with a prostitute. There may also have been feminine identification, with the gonorrhea discharge equated with menstrual flow. The client might have a masochistic tendency and an unconscious wish to give the prostitute venereal disease, both of which might be reciprocated by the prostitute. Some men may consort with prostitutes because they unconsciously expect to get venereal disease.[17] Others consciously wish to infect a prostitute, and they urinate before visiting her so that inspection of their penis will not show any discharge.

A sample of 732 customers in America was interviewed in order to establish how the customer in this country perceives himself and the prostitute.[18] The men's ages ranged from eighteen to sixty-one, and averaged forty-four. There were 574 married and 158 single men. Each respondent was asked about his most recent visit to a prostitute: "Would it be possible for you to tell me about her?" When the respondent had said all he could on this subject, he was asked, "Would it be possible for you to tell me how you felt at the time of your visit?"

The comments made by the clients could be summarized as follows:

Gives me what I want (73 per cent). Most of these men wanted someone other than the person with whom they ordinarily had sexual relations.

Colorful, interesting (71 per cent). These clients responded to the deviant nature of the prostitute's job rather than her specific sexual activities.

Negative mother image (63 per cent). Such men saw the prostitute as a woman who could take but not give and who was like their mother, and perhaps their wife. In the relationship with the prostitute they found confirmation for their belief that a woman could not give emotional closeness.

Money goes to pimps (56 per cent). These men were aware of the pimp and his role.

Prostitutes in mass media (54 per cent). These clients were attracted by the idea of prostitutes as portrayed in the mass media.

You can recognize them (49 per cent). These men felt able to identify a prostitute by her appearance.

Might fall in love with me (47 per cent). This was seen as a possibility by these men.

Might change her life (46 per cent). Such men appeared to hope that the prostitute might give up her work.

Compare with wife (41 per cent). The comparison of the prostitute with the wife was generally to the latter's disadvantage.

Should be legal (37 per cent). Their feeling that prostitution should be legal may have reflected some guilt.

Harmless (35 per cent). These respondents may have expressed a reaction against the harmfulness of prostitution.

Convention activity (32 per cent). Such clients made contact with a prostitute in connection with a convention.

Madam (30 per cent). These clients made some comment on the madam.

Cheaper (29 per cent). Some men saw a prostitute as a cheaper way of having sex than "going out on a date." Other reasons cited were: *no responsibility* (27 per cent); *impotent with other women* (17 per cent); *like to tell stories about them* (16 per cent).

Different themes in the respondents' perception of themselves were drawn from the above answers and were quite diverse:

Gives me something different (78 per cent). These men felt they were getting something different from the prostitute.

Empathy with prostitute (74 per cent). Such clients made some identification with the woman.

Identification with the pimp (71 per cent). For these men an identification with a pimp was significant.

Other customers (70 per cent). These clients were aware of the prostitute's other clients.

Falling in love (66 per cent). The possibility that they could fall in love with the prostitute existed for these men.

Got name from friends (64 per cent). Getting a prostitute's name from a friend enhanced the situation.

Refurbished battered ego (61 per cent). The prostitute helped to alleviate these clients' feelings of inadequacy.

Doing something illegal (55 per cent). Such men responded to the illegality of visiting a prostitute.

Expensive (37 per cent). These men commented on the cost of visiting the prostitute.

Hostility to wife (34 per cent). Some men said they thought of their wives when they visited a prostitute.

Wife unavailable (31 per cent). These men visited a prostitute when their wives were unavailable, for whatever reason.

Birth control (23 per cent). These respondents felt their wives or girl friends did not use appropriate birth-control measures.

Among the other reasons were: *avoid contaminating wife-mother* (22 per cent); *would like to go more often* (19 per cent); *learn about sex* (17 per cent); and *imitate the wealthy* (12 per cent).

Visiting a prostitute seems to serve a wide variety of functions, and any one visit to a prostitute is likely to have a number of reasons. Emotional, fantasy, cultural, or symbolic overtones of the situation may be more important to the clients than their desire for sex. The customer's relationship to a prostitute is far more complex than has traditionally been believed.

Some homosexual components in visiting a prostitute can be inferred from comments about her. The homosexual component was suggested by Boswell: "My lively imagination often represents her former lovers in actual enjoyment with her." One homosexual practice that is not uncommon is for two men to visit a brothel and have intercourse with different women. Each man then has intercourse with the woman who had previously seen his friend.

An example of the complex functions served by a visit to a prostitute is provided by a young man who suffered from erotic depression after a disappointing love affair.[19] His girl friend's preference for a younger and sexually more aggressive friend revived problems centering around rivalry with a young and precocious brother who had been preferred by their mother. After his disappointment in love, the man roamed the streets, seeking a prostitute, but would usually freeze at the moment of orgasm. He had wet his bed as a child, and bed-wetting, like orgasm with a prostitute, was frightening. He could revenge himself on both sweetheart and mother by going to a prostitute.

CUSTOMER GROUPS

Ecological considerations may be important contributors to the decision of some men to pay for sex. Prostitutes represented a major sexual outlet in Chicago's Hobohemia, where homeless men led anonymous lives. Although living in the most crowded parts of the city, the men were extremely isolated and unable to obtain an economic foothold in society. Without any opportunity for a normal married life, their sexual activities were limited to prostitutes and homosexuals.

The location of some cities seems to make it easier for men to become customers. Up to the early 1940's Ogden, Utah, was a popular locale for prostitution because it was a rail junction. Men could visit a brothel between trains, and indeed might plan their travel to permit a layover in Ogden. Some natives would enjoy driving their cars to Ogden's 25th Street on Saturday night to watch the prostitutes and their clients. As the geographic focus of a substantial cattle area, Kansas

City drew many men who had been working on the cattle ranches and stopped over for "fun."

The many beautiful women around Hollywood provide opportunities and challenges for prostitution. In years past a bevy of prostitutes was generally on hand after a premiere to service actors and executives. A movie executive or actor who was accompanied by his wife would twist a forefinger around his left ear as a signal that he would be unable to meet with the prostitute.

Hollywood was noted for high-priced prostitution. The difficulties encountered by movie officials who had encouraged potential actresses to cohabit with them became so well known that a number of the officials helped to organize expensive brothels, the women of which had no interest in movie careers. The Hollywood houses were especially proud of their new girls, and word would spread rapidly when a new "fresh pink" had arrived.

Some prostitutes prefer "rough trade": steel and cattle workers, miners and unskilled laborers. Prostitute folklore holds that "rough trade" is easy to handle. Once they have accomplished sexual intercourse, such clients seldom "hang around" but tend to leave promptly. They are also likely to visit a prostitute on payday and to be relatively free with money.

An occupation that requires a man to engage in considerable traveling, like sales work, may allow him greater exposure to prostitutes. The transient, or fleeting, nature of hotels can help to encourage his interest in contact with a prostitute. Some men enjoy sexual intercourse in a hotel because it has connotations of the illicit.

A content analysis of a large number of jokes about prostitution reveals that there are practically none that deal with the client's vocation or social status other than the many stories about clergymen as customers.[20] One ancient story deals with Pat and Mike, who were standing in front of a brothel when a minister walked into it. Pat says to Mike,

"Humph, just like those Protestant hypocrites." A little later, a rabbi also entered the brothel. "Aah," exclaims Mike, "Wouldn't you know, a Jew." A short time afterward, a Catholic priest knocked on the door. "Begorrah," Pat exclaims, "someone is sure sick in there." One prostitute has said that a number of her clients were sanctimonious clergymen whose overcoats were turned up in order to hide their collars. One clergyman tried to convert her to his religion with one hand while he made love with the other. Another begged her to go to church the next day.

During the 1930's many of the young men in the Civilian Conservation Corps were customers of prostitutes. Military men who have a permanent station and visit the same woman or brothel may be among the very few clients who can establish credit for as long as a month; they are expected to pay after payday. Servicemen and especially sailors seem to be more likely than other clients to want the same woman. Some sailors prefer the same woman because they got "good treatment" from her. The higher the rank or grade of a serviceman, the more welcome he is likely to be as a client. The higher ranks have more money and are likely to make fewer demands than younger clients.

Prostitutes often prefer sailors, perhaps because a sailor who comes into port is likely to have saved a considerable sum. As one San Francisco prostitute said, "I'll take a sailor every time. He goes for all the money he's got." The relative popularity of the sailor client can be seen in folk songs like "Venezuela," which deals with a sailor who spent much time with a prostitute:

> He gave her a silken sash of blue,
> A silken sash of blue,
> Because he thought that she would do,
> With all the things she knew, she knew,
> To pass away the time in Venezuela.

The importance of sailor business was the theme of the 1954 musical *House of Flowers*, with book by Truman Capote and music by Harold Arlen. The plot deals with a dispute between Madam Fleur and Madam Tango over whose brothel should get the business from a visiting battleship. The name of the brothel that gives the play its title derives from each prostitute's being called after a flower, such as Poppy.

French and English sailors also are found among American prostitutes' clientele. One New York City woman who has been a prostitute since World War I and has had extensive experience with such clients, summed up the views of many of her colleagues in saying, "I don't like those Limey or Frog sailors. They're much more tight-fisted than the American sailor boys." Many American and foreign merchant seamen, especially during the thirties and forties, were regular clients and would traditionally look for the nearest bar and available women in port. A more subdued type of merchant seaman now seems to be the rule.

Places suspected of being associated with prostitution may be placed "Off Limits" for military personnel. Such signs were relatively effective during World War II, when military personnel were required to wear uniforms at all times. Peacetime personnel have been authorized to wear civilian clothes when off duty, and many servicemen in mufti feel free to visit "Off Limits" premises. Military Police and Shore Patrol are often alert to recognize military personnel by their haircuts, shoes, and socks, even though the rest of their costume may be civilian.

The proportion of American servicemen who visit prostitutes has declined since the end of World War II. Military income has not kept pace with the increase in prostitutes' prices. The pressure of American military commitments overseas has also cut down the length of time that troops spend in the United States.

Ethnic differences in customers are the subject of some folklore among prostitutes. A number of prostitutes in New York and Los Angeles have observed that Jewish men are their most generous customers, often display guilt and embarrassment, and do not hesitate to pay whatever they are asked. In Pacific Coast cities the brothels that once catered to Orientals have largely disappeared. But one prostitute in Salinas, California, recently refused to accept a white customer, telling him that "I only see Orientals." Prostitute lore holds that Oriental customers are businesslike and considerate, do not "hang around" or "chatter," and are likely to bring little presents. They are also said to volunteer to do odd jobs around the establishment.

Prostitutes usually feel uneasy about customers of different racial backgrounds meeting one another in a waiting room or a hallway. A Negro or Oriental customer leaving a brothel may be spirited out discreetly, the assumption being that a white client who saw a Negro client leaving might himself leave. One reason for the general rule that pimps are discouraged from being in a brothel is that a customer might mistake a Negro pimp for a customer. In the 1920's and 1930's white customers who saw a Negro customer consorting with a white prostitute might rip the place apart or even set fire to it. There appear to be few brothels with Negro women that are exclusively for Negro customers, although brothels with white women sometimes cater only to Negro clients.

PSYCHOLOGICAL SATISFACTIONS

Psychoanalysts have developed the concept of the split between the tender and sensual components of the erotic impulse that leads some men to prefer prostitutes. Many men can achieve high sexual capacity with a woman whom they regard as inferior but not with one whom they love. A related function the prostitute serves for the man, on a symbolic level, is to provide an example of "bad" women, so that he can more readily believe in the existence of "good" women. Other men may reinforce their feelings of "disgust" toward women by visiting a prostitute.[21]

Men's fantasies about prostitution may involve a woman with real or supposed inferiority. They may also deal with leading the prostitute to a better way of life. Prostitution

fantasies sometimes occur in men who cannot allow themselves fantasy relations with wives or girl friends without
guilt.[22]

The male fantasy of helping the prostitute to a happier life
is combined with ambivalence toward the woman in one popular story. A businessman observed that the chambermaid in
his hotel was attractive but had a speech defect. He asked
her if she would have intercourse with him. She replied,
"Yes, for a quarter." He gave her the coin and they engaged
in coitus. Afterward, he noted, "You're pretty, maybe I can
help you get that speech defect fixed." The woman replied,
"That's no defect, that's where I keep my money"—and a
cascade of quarters emerged from her mouth.

Some customers' fear of the prostitute may be found in a
famous folk song, "Charlotte the Harlot, the Cowpuncher's
Whore," the lyrics of which provide an example of the fantasy
of *vagina dentata*. A snake enters Charlotte's vagina and she
finally dies as a result of its sting, perhaps as a concession to
male chauvinism. Another popular fantasy in folk song is the
preacher's daughter who bargains for the price to be paid for
her services.

Agoraphobia is not uncommon in clients. For one man
whose prostitute was a sister in fantasy, the concepts of
street, sister, and prostitute were interchangeable in his unconscious.[23] The prostitute may be identified with the street
itself, as in the French colloquialism *La Rue*. Nuns may represent prostitutes in fantasy because they are called "sisters."
One man had a fantasy of a brothel in which the parlor was
furnished like a chapel, the girls dressed as nuns, and the
madam called "mother superior." As a displacement from a
mother in an Oedipus complex, the sister represents a de-
based mother.[24]

One customer, a devout Catholic, went to a different prostitute every Monday so that he had almost a week to repent
before Communion and could truthfully promise the priest
on Sunday that he would never see the woman again. A similar attitude toward women might be expected in a man with

authoritarian personality characteristics.[25] Such a person tends to show both excessive moralism and promiscuity. His sex relations often are isolated, depersonalized, and not integrated with the ego. The more extreme the man's authoritarian tendency, the more likely is his orientation toward women to be externalized and contemptuous. Many jokes reflect the trivialization of sex occurring between customer and client, as the customer sees it. One such story became popular after the 1954 Supreme Court desegregation decision, and dealt with a salesman who checked into a Southern hotel and told the bellboy, "I would like a girl for tonight." The bellboy answered, "Yes, sir, but she will be a Negro." The man said, "Okay. I don't want to go to school with her, I only want to have intercourse with her." This story also reflects the hostility toward minority groups that is surely part of many men's attitudes toward prostitution.

Voyeurism is an important component of men's interest in prostitution, judging from the large number of jokes with voyeuristic themes. In one famous story a drunk was walking outside a New Orleans brothel which had a series of balconies. A prostitute and her client were having sexual intercourse on a second-story balcony; not realizing they were teetering on the railing, they fell to the ground in the middle of the act. The drunk saw them fall and knocked on the door of the brothel. The madam opened the door and said, "You're drunk. Go away." She slammed the door in his face, but he knocked once more. When she irritably again began to close the door, he said, "Look lady, I just wanted to tell you that your sign fell down."

Peeping at the sex life of famous men is the theme of a story that is a long-time staple, even though the identity of its hero changes regularly. It deals with a prostitute who recognizes her client as a famous actor, just after they have engaged in intercourse. She says, "You're ———." "Yes," he replies modestly. She rushes to the telephone, still nude, and dials a number. "Mother," she excitedly shouts, "guess who I just laid! ———, the actor!" This story is told as a "true" story about whatever actor is most popular at the moment. It gives the listener a voyeuristic thrill, while the sexual transaction is made to seem silly. The heroine is not doing anything she is afraid to discuss with her mother, and indeed feels that the incident would actually please mother. There is reinforcement of the fantasy about the celebrity as customer and of the woman as "devouring Medusa," who uses an active rather than a passive verb to describe her work.

Another voyeurism story that has been very popular for the last fifteen years deals with a man who goes to a brothel one evening. Soft music is playing when he enters, and the madam greets him enthusiastically. A nude waitress serves dinner and later fetches a cigar and after-dinner liqueur. The man is even more pleased when the madam encourages him to take any one of several beautiful girls. He spends the night with one and is almost beside himself with pleasure. Before he leaves in the morning the madam serves him a delicious breakfast. Finally, with some trepidation, he asks how much he owes her. She smiles and says, "Nothing at all." All day long he can barely wait to return in the evening. He dashes back excitedly at 7 P.M. and the door is opened by the madam —dour and unpleasant. She asks for "$15 in advance" and calls over her shoulder, "Here's another john for a trick." An ugly slattern appears and says, "Okay, buddy, this way." The man is completely confused and turns to the madam, saying, "I don't understand this. Last night I got such a good deal here, and today it's all different." The madam says, "Oh, last night was Thursday. Thursday we're on television."

Voyeurism was surely also a factor in the great popularity of stories about the Profumo case in England in 1963. The relationships of prostitute Christine Keeler with some high officials of the British government attracted international attention.[26] It was said, for example, that Miss Keeler's mother was writing a book, *My Daughter, The Cabinet-Maker*. Miss Keeler was also reported to be writing her own autobiography called *Life Under the Tories*. When asked what she read during the week, she allegedly replied that she read one

Daily Mail, two *Mirrors,* and as many *Times* as possible. Other Keeler stories express delight in catching prominent notables "with their pants down."

The case also gave rise to many limericks. Referring to the wide publicity given the belief that Minister Profumo's mistake was not in his consorting with Miss Keeler but in lying to the House of Commons about the liaison, the following limerick became very popular in both England and America:

> *What have I done, said Christine,*
> *I've ruined the party machine.*
> *To lie in the nude*
> *Is not very rude*
> *But to lie in the House is obscene.*

One aspect of male fantasies about prostitution comes through in the large number of stories about the client's extraordinary sexual organs. A story that has survived several decades deals with a man without arms or legs who appears at a brothel's front door. When the madam responds to the doorbell, the man asks for a girl. The madam inquires, "What could you do with one of my girls in your condition?" The man replies, "I rang your bell, didn't I?"

The fantasy of the prostitute's falling in love with a customer has a long history in literature and folklore. One version of this theme was the most successful single stage attraction in Europe during the 1950's, *Irma La Douce.* It is the story of a prostitute whose boy friend decides to find out whether she can love one of her customers. He disguises himself as a customer and tries to develop a romance with her. The plot deals with the ambivalence of the boy friend as the prostitute actually begins to fall in love with her "client."

SERVICES REQUESTED

Coitus was the staple service offered by prostitutes before World War II, but it has since become a minority preference. Through the 1930's one woman in every brothel would usually provide "perversions" and had the least status among the prostitutes. Today the single most requested service is fellatio ("French" or "derby"). Anal intercourse ("Greek") is popular, as is cunnilingus ("going below 14th Street") and fellatio before coitus ("half and half"). A "flat-backer" who offers only coitus ("old-fashioned" or "straight") is likely to lose customers.

Increasingly, and especially in the last decade, prostitutes and madams report substantially more customers who are seeking oral satisfaction ("muff diver" or "face man"). Annual surveys conducted by the American Social Health Association suggest that as many as nine out of ten customers now want some form of oral satisfaction in contrast to the 10 per cent requesting it in the 1930's. The trend toward orality has been continuous, with a substantial increase after World War II.

We can only speculate on the reasons for the tremendous increase in oral sex. One possibility is that it reflects a general increase in passivity. Another likelihood is that it mirrors an increase in orality in nonprostitute sex. Another explanation is that "straight" sex is more available today outside of prostitution than it was thirty or forty years ago, so that the prostitute's customer is paying for a more specialized sexual diet. A remoter possibility is some customers' belief that fellatio makes them less likely to contact venereal disease.

From the woman's point of view, fellatio makes venereal disease less likely and is less fatiguing than coitus. She may find that fellatio makes it less necessary to simulate affection. The customer usually has his orgasm more rapidly and leaves the premises quickly. There is also often a higher fee for oral activity. Many prostitutes favor "half and half" because it often results in an orgasm for the customer without his fully penetrating the woman.

A substantial proportion of prostitutes today are addicts, many of whom presumably have oral-passive personalities and may favor oral sex. Women entering prostitution today may be more passive than was the case several decades ago, when their predecessors had a more limited vocational choice.

There are regional differences in the services offered by prostitutes and in what men want from them. In the South, with the exception of New Orleans, there appears to be a smaller proportion of women who engage in "perversions." The areas with the greatest interest in "perversions" are the Southwest, the West Coast, and New York City, where practically every prostitute will offer several "perversions." One way in which a number of prostitutes seek to preserve a minimum integrity is to have at least one activity they will refuse to do. There are many obscene jokes about specific services that a prostitute will refuse a client, even though she may be perfectly willing to do others that appear to be at least as demanding or humiliating.

Up to World War II one of the most popular jokes told by American men dealt with the naive immigrant who visited a brothel with some chums. When he went with the prostitute into her room, she asked him what he wanted to do. He didn't know what to answer, so he said, "Anything you like, I don't care." She engaged in fellatio. His friends later asked him what happened. When he told them, they said, "That's terrible, you'll go crazy from that." He visited the same brothel the following week. When his friends later asked him what he had done, he explained that he had engaged in cunnilingus. "Let *her* go crazy," he said. This story is not told at all today, suggesting the greater acceptance and routine nature of such previously frowned upon and feared oragenital activity. Simultaneously there has been a decline in the use of vulgar epithets for persons who engage in oragenital activity.

An active prostitute may be exposed to a wide range of "perversions." Some clients asking for unusual services are diffident and apologetic, but others are forceful. Some customers like to cry or wear makeup. Others enjoy sexual intercourse with a prostitute while she is tied to a bed or chair. Still others attach a collar and leash to a prostitute and have her walk around the floor on all fours. Some customers engage in sexual intercourse with a prostitute *a tergo*, while she is eating from a dish or lapping up milk from the floor.

There are many stocking fetishists who prefer a prostitute who wears only stockings. Other men will masturbate while she removes her stockings. Some clients simulate strangling a prostitute with one stocking. Some brothels had a small funeral chamber in which the prostitute would be laid out as if she were about to be buried, complete with recorded funeral music and candles at either end of the casket. The prostitute would be instructed not to move while the customer had intercourse with her.

Some clients ask the woman to whip them, or want to whip her. They may wish to be tied up, or to tie her. Others bring specific items of clothing, often lingerie, for the woman to wear. Feathers, often ostrich feathers, and clothing made of red or black velvet are other items to adorn the woman. Some clients enjoy a woman nude except for furs, while others want her to wear nothing but long black gloves, or slippers. Biting, scratching, clawing, and punching are among the special requirements of some customers. The women who meet such specialized requirements are likely to get extra pay. Among the most enthusiastic clients are sadists and masochists, who are likely to be older than the general clientele. Many customers prefer a prostitute who will resist them.

Some customers want the prostitute to talk to them in a specific way. One man was potent with a prostitute only if she used obscenities. He received the additional gratification of degrading the woman because he paid her with his mother's money. A man who requires a nonprostitute sex partner to use obscene words may be trying to degrade her to the level of a prostitute.[27]

VIII. THE LAW

Most of the enforcement
activity to suppress prostitution is under state laws, among
which the injunction and abatement laws represent important legal weapons. The first complete injunction and abatement law in the United States was passed in Iowa in 1909. It
declared brothels to be public nuisances and gave any citizen
or county attorney the right to apply to a court for an injunction restraining the operator of such a nuisance from maintaining it. If the judge was satisfied that the nuisance existed,
he granted a temporary injunction. If a trial established the
existence of a nuisance, the court issued a permanent injunction. The court could also issue an abatement order, under
which the personal property used in the house could be sold
and the premises closed for one year. Every state now has
such a law, with the landlord held legally responsible even
if he claims not to know the use being made of his premises.

Nine states provide that law enforcement officials *must*
(rather than may) initiate actions to enjoin and abate prostitution. The injunction and abatement laws have generally
been upheld in higher courts. In some states, passage of the

law was a signal for legal and executive action to close the red light districts. The possibility of citizen action under the injunction and abatement laws also led to other procedures against prostitution by previously unwilling or indifferent officials.

In 1919 the American Social Health Association drafted a model vice-repression act, which was subsequently enacted into law in nineteen states. It defined prostitution to include the giving or receiving of the body in sexual intercourse for hire and penalized the customer as well as the prostitute. Since the 1920's, laws against keeping and maintaining a house of prostitution have been passed in every state, but the public interest that helped to bring about the laws has not extended to their enforcement. This apathy continued during the 1930's, a decade in which no significant anti-prostitution laws were passed.

In most jurisdictions, engaging in or offering to commit an act of prostitution is a misdemeanor, while pimping and pandering are felonies. The pimp and pander are regarded harshly by the law because they are third persons who profit from the prostitute's activity. The prostitute receives a lesser sentence because the law assumes that she may have been an innocent who was led into prostitution without being aware of the consequences.

Legislation dealing with prostitution has become increasingly stringent in the last twenty years. Its enforcement, however, varies as the result of differences in community attitudes and in changing administrations. Some communities prefer to invoke local ordinances which are usually milder than state laws, while others prosecute prostitutes for vagrancy because conviction is more likely under this charge. Some communities prefer to levy fines; others are more likely to require a convicted prostitute to serve a prison sentence.

Streetwalkers, because of their visibility, are likely to be arrested more frequently than any other type of prostitute.

Women who work in bars and hotels are less subject to police activity. The brothel inmate enjoys some immunity from arrest because she does not seek customers in public places. Law enforcement officers have considerable difficulty obtaining evidence against call girls.

Medium-sized or large cities usually have morals or vice squads to deal with prostitution. In communities where the vice squad membership remains constant, madams sometimes go to court and make notes on the appearance of policemen who testify against prostitutes. The personnel of some vice squads are frequently changed in order to avoid their becoming easily identified. A relatively small vice squad is handicapped because its members quickly become known to prostitutes. Such a squad may be augmented by men from neighboring towns—for example, Lynchburg, Virginia, has borrowed policemen from neighboring Petersburg for this purpose. Vice squads often work on the basis of complaints from disgruntled customers, neighbors, or policewomen who penetrate prostitute groups.

On the basis of a study of representative cities, it would appear that only 11 per cent of the complaints made about prostitution to police are verifiable. Most police do not have enough time to conduct investigations on their own and must rely on complaints. Police activities are generally as effective as public opinion will permit them to be. During the 1930's, when public opinion in the Southeast, Southwest, and on the Pacific Coast was generally apathetic about prostitution, police activity was not vigorous; its tempo increased with World War II and public concern about "our boys in uniform."

It has been widely alleged that police officers on some vice squads have an informal quota of arrests. A policeman who does not make "enough" arrests may be regarded by his superiors as taking graft or not doing his job. Completion of the quota for a particular week could mean that he will not make any more arrests for the week. Police officials, however, have consistently denied that there are arrest quotas.

There are only a few recent situations in which police have been apprehended taking "oil" or payoff money from a prostitute. Some idea of the extent of police graft just before and after World War I can be obtained from the derivation of "tenderloin," a word supposedly first used by a police official who was assigned to a New York City area which had many brothels. He allegedly said, "I used to eat chuck steak, but now that I'm working in this district I have tenderloin every day."

For some years people involved in prostitution spoke of handing out "hats" to police. A "hat" was named, perhaps apocryphally, in honor of former New York City Police Commissioner William P. O'Brien's comments to his staff around Christmas time. Although police did not accept bribes, O'Brien noted that ". . . if you happen to hold out your hat and somebody happens to put . . . something in it . . . that's different." It is next to impossible to find anyone who admits receiving or giving a "hat," but it currently means a $20 bill given to a police officer.

Related to the "hat," some police exploited madams in the 1930's by encouraging them to move into a neighborhood with the promise that there would be no difficulties with law enforcement. The police would later "roust" or harass the madams and seek protection money, threatening arrest or eviction if the madam did not cooperate.

Most prostitutes learn to identify a law enforcement officer posing as a client. To make it more difficult for prostitutes to use this skill, police have developed techniques to conceal their identity. Most official cars are small and inexpensive, so the police may borrow a large car when seeking to arrest prostitutes. Since few police normally wear spectacles, vice squad personnel may wear them. They may limp, slump in order to look shorter, or exhibit other characterisitcs a policeman is unlikely to have.

A vice squad member trying to make an arrest ("heat") would typically pick up a woman and follow her suggestion that they go to a room. The officer often tries to get the woman to strip, so that he may note identifying marks on her body. Once the woman has made an offer to engage in sexual activity the policeman shows his badge and places her under arrest. Many critics feel that such police are being forced to function dishonestly. Police who combat prostitution are often said to be doing work that is degrading; they depend on informers for information, raid premises illegally, and engage in entrapment by concealing their true identity in posing as customers.

One representative city of approximately 400,000 has a vice squad that uses informers and decoys.[1] The policemen occasionally park near a vacant lot, from which they can survey prostitution activities with binoculars. They watch the woman contact a customer, and if she enters his car they will try to make an arrest while the couple is engaging in intercourse. Arrests are also made by using informers who will telephone to report that a prostitute has brought a man to a hotel room. In the decoy method, police or "special employees" pick up a prostitute. "Special employees" are paid $5 by the police for each arrested prostitute. Decoys account for 56 per cent of this community's prostitution arrests.

Prostitutes sometimes try to determine if a customer is a decoy by kissing him on the lips. Many police avoid kissing because they are uneasy about their decoy role and the possibility of being accused of sex play with the prostitute. The decoy technique is responsible for many of the more than four thousand cases handled annually by New York City's courts in recent years. In a typical case a policeman testified that a woman smiled at him and asked him if he wanted to "have some fun." In most cases the women were convicted, even though they swore that the policeman spoke to them first and that there was no mention of a sexual act. One New York policeman posed as an advertising jingle writer. He aroused suspicions in one prostitute who asked him for a sample of his work. He wrote:

It's been quite a party, girls;
We've pulled out all the stops,
But we're not the guys you think we are
We're just a pair of cops.

In any community the prostitute's behavior after arrest is related to the manner of the arresting policeman. If he condemns her, he is likely to arouse her hostility. When treated with impersonality, the prostitute often reacts with equal detachment. By being solicitous toward her, the officer may minimize her hostility.

Bail is sometimes set fairly high in order to assure the appearance of the prostitute at her trial. It may or may not be effective in doing so, for the cash outlay required for $250 bail is only about $15 less than is needed for $500 bail. A court may decide to establish high bail for all prostitutes; Judge Joseph Grillo in Los Angeles requires $500 bail from women accused of prostitution. In some cases a prostitute will pay the bail and then leave the community.

One aspect of law enforcement that has attracted considerable attention is the use of addict-prostitutes as informers, with the understanding that they will receive special consideration in sentencing. In New York City a judge recently admitted, "Certainly we parole the women for this purpose. It is not a nice business." The practice seems questionable in many ways. A drug user who has been arrested for prostitution is likely to be friendless and harassed. When she needs some hope of rehabilitation she is offered help—but only on the condition that she become an informer and contribute to the arrest of her friends and former associates. Such a woman is hardly likely to gain much respect for herself or for society.

Nonwhites, as mentioned earlier, tend to be overrepresented in arrests of prostitutes. Nationally, Negroes account for 11 per cent of the population but 53 per cent of all urban arrests for prostitution. In Los Angeles 33 per cent of the prostitutes arrested are Negroes, although they comprise only 9 per cent of the population. Such imbalance may be due to the relative instability of Negro families, the availability of more migrant Negro women in Los Angeles, police prejudice, or to some combination of such factors. The rate of arrest for prostitution among Negroes parallels their rate of arrest for other crimes, suggesting that similar factors may operate in other law enforcement. On the other hand, the country's awakened interest in civil rights may make it more difficult for police departments to make arrests of Negro women suspected of engaging in prostitution. In a number of cities, like Detroit, police no longer arrest persons who may be loitering on the streets and are suspected of prostitution activities. Detroit civil rights groups asked the police to change this procedure, and they were upheld by the courts.

In some communities police still arrest suspected streetwalkers and detain them overnight before releasing them the following morning.[2] The arrests are not preludes to prosecution but are part of a program of harassment, intended to get the women off the street. Such an arrest, for being a "disorderly person," seldom meets the conventional criteria of probable guilt, according to which the woman must accost a man, propose a specific sexual act, and name a fee.

A prostitute over twenty-one may be charged with loitering, disorderly conduct, prostitution, or vagrancy, depending on the circumstances of her arrest. Loitering statutes are now used relatively infrequently because some appellate courts have held that a law which prohibits people from congregating unless they can give a "reasonable account" of themselves violates the Fifth Amendment guarantee against self-incrimination. Dayton, Ohio, has developed an effective unlawful-assembly ordinance which enables police to arrest known prostitutes who congregate in places known as prostitute hangouts and where previous prostitution arrests have been made.

In many communities the woman is examined for venereal disease after her arrest. If she has it, she often remains in custody until cured or rendered noninfectious. In 1965 two

San Francisco prostitutes claimed that their constitutional rights were being violated when they were held in the city prison for venereal disease quarantine after arrest. Attorneys for the prostitutes successfully used writs of habeas corpus to get their clients out on bail without an examination for venereal disease or a penicillin treatment. In 1967 New York City eliminated its requirement that women charged with prostitution receive compulsory examinations and medical treatment for venereal disease.

When arrested for the first time the woman is likely to experience an initial tremor and be embarrassed, but her subsequent reaction is often that of a Los Angeles prostitute who shrugged, "Damn, what lousy luck." First offenders are often given a suspended sentence; women with a considerable record may be incarcerated for up to six months. In New York State the maximum sentence for prostitution was reduced to fifteen days in 1967, in frank recognition of the token nature of a jail sentence. The maximum sentence was increased to ninety days in 1969. The woman seeking probation may claim that she plans to leave the field. She often says almost anything to shorten her stay in jail, but an experienced probation officer can usually distinguish sincere from spurious promises.

Prostitutes are often more concerned about the sentence and fine they will receive than about the arrest itself. If the fine is high and frequently applied, the woman usually leaves the area. Some women feel that a relatively low fine is almost a license. A prostitute who may be willing to pay a $10 fine might reconsider if she had to pay $100 or more. In communities like New Haven and Hartford, where the usual fine for a first offense is high, it appears to have a deterrent effect.

Judges vary radically in their attitudes toward prostitution and in their feelings about what constitutes appropriate penalties.[3] Consequently, defense attorneys often try to have cases held over until a specific judge is sitting, so that they get a more lenient sentence. In some communities judges appear to be lenient; for example, there were only two convictions for every hundred arrests for prostitution on the Strip in Las Vegas during recent years.

In addition to a judge's bias, there are other reasons for many communities' relative nonenforcement of laws against prostitutes and their associates. The changes effected by elections may bring into office a group of political leaders who encourage prostitution to flourish. Even in communities with organized prostitution, it usually disappears in the few weeks preceding election day, because the prostitution leaders do not wish to embarrass political incumbents whose associates may be accepting "protection" money. If a candidate could publicly identify a prostitution locale before an election and embarrass the party in power, investigation of the place would be unproductive because it would have closed for the pre-election period. Prostitution activity generally resumes its established level immediately after election in those communities which condone the "racket."

Another reason for nonenforcement of the laws in some jurisdictions is that judges may be oriented toward rehabilitation rather than punishment. Even if the police department arrests a substantial number of prostitutes, judges may dismiss many cases because they feel that nothing will be accomplished by putting the women in jail except contact with more experienced prostitutes. Few communities have adequate rehabilitation procedures, so a judge may even dismiss the charge rather than send the woman to jail. In New York City, for example, over half the women arrested for prostitution in a typical recent year were discharged. Such a high proportion of nonconvictions may result from inadequate evidence or an energetic and effective legal defense as well as the reluctance of judges to remand prostitutes to a merely custodial situation. Some judges sentence prostitutes to prison to get them out of the vocation, at least temporarily. Others will send a prostitute to prison to discourage a pimp from preying on her. Some judges may have emotional attitudes toward prostitution that interfere with their functioning on the bench.

A major factor in the development of a community's attitude toward prostitution is the general absence of public complaint about prostitution. Clients are unlikely to come forward, and their very involvement in the situation would probably make their observations suspect. A client who has contracted a venereal disease may feel reluctant to identify the prostitute who infected him. Customers may also be silent because they feel that some prostitutes work for criminal groups which may not hesitate to use violence. There is no case on record of groups of former customers getting together to stamp out prostitution in a community.

Although customers are inactive in campaigning against prostitution, citizens' committees have developed public opinion on the issue.[4] In New York City the Committee of Fourteen functioned very effectively for more than two decades before and after World War I. Volunteer anti-prostitution committees usually were designated by the number of members, so that Utica had a Committee of Sixteen and Chicago a Committee of Fifteen. Such euphemisms were used because it was believed they gave the cause greater public appeal.

Yet the most earnest and persuasive official report on prostitution by an official body may achieve nothing. Reports which contain extensive recommendations may even have an undesired effect on their readers, who may think the recommendations have already been implemented. Most communities that took substantial action against prostitution did so because of either grand juries or citizens' committees which pursued the problem until something was done about it.

Law enforcement may be helped or hindered by telephone companies and answering services. Some telephone companies will remove the phone from an establishment devoted to prostitution if they discover its use, but many companies do not care how a phone is being used. Recent court decisions have made it difficult for police to subpoena the records of telephone answering services. In many large cities the services are used by streetwalkers and call girls. A client, bellboy, porter, or cab driver who phones is usually asked to furnish the operator with his name, telephone number, or address. The operator advises the caller that "Miss ——— will get in touch with you as soon as possible." Prostitutes often ask clients who telephone to call them by their last names so that the messages appear to be legitimate business transactions. Some try to use telephone answering services associated with physicians in order to minimize suspicion. Others set up their own service on a cooperative basis.

NEVADA'S "LEGAL" PROSTITUTION

Nevada provides the most unusual legal arrangements for prostitution in America. In Nevada, houses of prostitution may be established or maintained so long as they are not on principal business streets or within four hundred yards of a schoolhouse or church, or do not disturb the peace of the neighborhood. Power is also given to incorporated cities and unincorporated towns and cities to regulate, prohibit, license, tax, and suppress houses of prostitution. The power to regulate makes it possible to authorize the operation of brothels under specified conditions.[5] There is, however, one legal barrier against the establishment and operation of houses of prostitution in Nevada. In the 1949 case of *Cunningham v. Washoe County,* the county brought an injunction against Mae Cunningham who ran a house in Reno. Although the house was not within four hundred yards of a school or church, or on a principal thoroughfare, and was not run in such a manner that the neighborhood was disturbed, the Nevada Supreme Court held that a house of prostitution is a common-law nuisance and could be abated by appropriate action. The court stated: "The nuisance resulting from the operation of a house of prostitution is aggravated by its location within 400 yards of a school or church for which the Legislature imposed an additional and criminal liability without limiting the right to the initiation of abatement proceedings. . . ."[6] This case has not been overruled, so that houses of prostitution are subject to civil injunction proceedings.

The operators of houses of prostitution in Nevada are, moreover, individually subject to many provisions of the criminal code. The sections of the Nevada criminal law relating to pandering, prostitution, and disorderly houses are broad enough to commit every operator of a house of prostitution in the state.[7]

Obviously, the maintenance of a house of prostitution in Nevada is of doubtful legality if it is subject to abatement through injunction proceedings. Yet prostitution flourishes in fifteen of the state's seventeen counties. Only Washoe (Reno) and Clark (Las Vegas) counties have enacted ordinances which make it illegal. Although Reno has no brothels, only ten minutes away, off Interstate Route 80 in Stokey County, is the Mustang Bridge Ranch, a twenty-four-hour-a-day brothel with a dozen women on duty at all times. Mustang Air Service provides scheduled daily flights to such communities as Lida Junction, where the only business is a brothel. Nearly all Nevada's large towns have brothels.

Although fifteen million tourists visit Las Vegas each year, it has no brothels. There is no doubt that some men visitors seem interested in paying for a sexual experience, the established price for which is $100. But women from out of town who are attracted to Las Vegas by the prospect of making a lot of money in a short time in prostitution are not likely to be successful. Their outsider status can be inferred from the story of the two prostitutes from Los Angeles who had arrived for the weekend and picked up two clients in a casino. All four went upstairs, and each woman received four chips with the number 25 on them as payment. The women were delighted, knowing that the sophisticated way to pay for anything in Las Vegas was with chips. They later returned to the casino and cashed in their chips, only to learn that each chip was worth only twenty-five cents.

In Nevada brothel prostitutes are fingerprinted and carry

cards, obtained from police or district attorneys, which identify them as prostitutes. The communities generally require the women to have weekly medical examinations. Prostitutes are usually not permitted to leave the house and mingle with other residents of the community.

Perhaps typical is the situation in Winnemucca, a town of three thousand. It has five brothels with an average of five women each. They sit in the windows of the brothels and smile at male passersby. The brothels are open from 4 P.M. to 5 A.M. Police drive by every half-hour in case any customers get rowdy. The brothels generally refuse to admit servicemen in uniform in order to avoid possible trouble. One Winnemucca minister lost his job because he spoke out against prostitutes. Such is the general attitude toward prostitution that in a nearby community a school and brothel were in adjacent buildings. A local paper editorialized, "Don't move the brothel—move the school." The school was moved.

WHEN LEGALIZED PROSTITUTION CEASES

Clues to the effects of ending legalized prostitution can be found in the experiences of Honolulu and Terre Haute, Indiana. Military police in Honolulu had established a system of regulated prostitution in 1920, and the police department took it over in 1932. Seven brothels were situated in close proximity to the city's main business area. Each averaged fifteen women. On payday, long lines of military personnel waited to enter the establishments. Military authorities took over the brothels early in World War II.

The system was described in a novel about Mamie Stover, a blonde prostitute, by William Bradford Huie.[8] Miss Stover's brothel featured the slogan "$3 for 3 minutes." She would service four beds at once, slipping from one to the other, after each serviceman-client had been appropriately prepared by an assistant. By the end of the book she was earning $20,000 a month. In the movie made from the novel in 1956, Jane Russell plays Miss Stover. Although she leaves Hawaii triumphantly at the end of the novel, in the film she is forced to leave the island.

On September 21, 1944, Governor Ingram M. Stainback closed Hawaii's houses of prostitution. Many citizens and civic leaders expected that the venereal disease rate would skyrocket and that rape would increase. Instead there was a sharp reduction in the number of venereal disease cases. In the eleven months before the brothels closed there were 1,072 cases of gonorrhea and fifty-seven cases of syphilis. In the eleven months immediately after the closing there were 671 cases of gonorrhea and thirty-two cases of syphilis.[9]

Another concern of those worried about closing the Hawaiian houses was that rape and sex crimes would increase. In the eleven months before they closed there were twenty-nine rapes and 559 other sex crimes. In the eleven months after the closing there were twenty-two rapes and 404 other sex crimes. Analysis of the arrests suggests that different kinds of men are involved in sex crimes than visit prostitutes. There was also a decline in juvenile delinquency after the houses closed. Although such changes cannot be directly attributed to the houses' closing, they had some relation to it. On the basis of such criteria the cessation of official prostitution appears to have been advantageous. Law enforcement in Hawaii is currently strict, and indices of social pathology have remained at a low level.

Similar effects were reported as a result of the closing of the fifty-four brothels in Terre Haute's "West End" in 1942.[10] In the year before the closing, forty-eight robberies occurred in Terre Haute. There were thirteen robberies in 1943, the first year after the closing. Aggravated assaults dropped from thirty-six in 1942 to fourteen in 1943. Decreases in murder, robbery, aggravated assault, burglary, larceny of $50 value or more, and auto theft averaged 31 per cent. In 1942 crimes against the person in Terre Haute were 30.8 per cent of the national average in cities of comparable size; in the following four years the city's average was 66 per cent below the national average, though there was an increase in the national average for other such crimes in other cities. In the years after the closing of the brothels, traffic deaths went 54 per cent below the national average for cities in the same class. In terms of every important index of anti-social behavior or community problems, Terre Haute was a healthier and safer city after the brothels closed, and there is reason to believe that elimination of the red light district had a good deal to do with the change.

Probably the most direct evidence of the effect of a reduction in prostitution on the general crime rate and on anti-social behavior could be obtained during World War II, when it was relatively easy to maintain records of both the military and civilian population. In general, every community with a decline in prostitution had a parallel reduction in rates for accidents, arrests for drunkenness, and such military infractions as being absent without leave.

When prostitution declines, so do other crimes. Contrariwise, a decline in the incidence of crime in a community seems to be related to a decline in the incidence of prostitution. When the general observance of the laws is on a superior level, enforcement of the prostitution laws is also likely to be fairly rigorous. One reason for the interrelationship of prostitution with the incidence of other crime is that prostitutes are often narcotics addicts, and bring other addicts and "pushers" into an area. When a male addict needs money, he may turn to robberies, burglaries, and muggings. Prostitution is also related to many other kinds of anti-social activity.[11]

DECLINE OF PROSTITUTION IN VARIOUS CITIES

Vigorous law enforcement has led to a decrease in the incidence of prostitution in a large number of cities. Around and just after World War I, for example, New York City was estimated to have a minimum of fifteen thousand full-time brothel prostitutes, each entertaining an average of ten men a day. Now, "New York has the name but not the game," as a veteran New York madam put it. Brothels are very difficult to find. Few bellboys and cab drivers offer to provide prostitutes. The few panders insist on seeing identification by the potential customer as proof they are not dealing with a law enforcement official. Such precautions are very different from conditions in New York in earlier days.[12]

During World War II, when the city played host to thousands of servicemen, many bars and taverns in the Times Square area were hangouts for prostitutes. The vice squad and armed services police conducted intense drives against bar owners and prostitutes, resulting in many convictions and cancellations of liquor licenses. Several "sock-it-in" taxi-dance halls were eliminated. In recent years go-betweens are more difficult to find, few bars are identified with prostitution, and only a limited number of hotels cater to the trade.

The effect of relatively mild penalties on the incidence of prostitution in New York could be seen in the late 1960's. In 1967 the state penal code reduced prostitution from a misdemeanor to a violation with a fifteen-day maximum sentence. Prostitutes flocked to the city from across the country, and the 8,045 arrests for 1968 represented a 27 per cent rise over 1967 and a 70 per cent increase over 1966. Some observers estimated that New York City had more than 25,000 full-time prostitutes during 1968.

In 1969 New York ended its two-year experiment with a lenient prostitution law. Policemen began picking up suspected or known prostitutes on sight. As one vice squad member said, "The best we can do is to harass them." Most such arrests were thrown out of court for insufficient evidence. Some prostitutes would clear up several charges with a single plea of guilty and a token fine. As Criminal Court Judge Jack Rosenberg said, when the maximum penalty was increased from fifteen to ninety days on September 1, 1969, "The prostitutes have no respect for the court. They come in here like it is a supermarket."

As one result of vigorous law enforcement, prostitution in Philadelphia has declined in spite of a large population of servicemen. There are a few temporary brothels, in which a madam and a few women work in conjunction with taxi drivers. Although part of the former red light district of Philadelphia on both the north and south sides of the city still stands, prostitutes have left the area, which has become a slum. When a veteran pimp was recently asked about the availability of prostitutes in Philadelphia, he said, "I couldn't put my finger on a decent hustler. Only fools would take a chance today."

The only current reminder of Philadelphia's earlier fame as a prostitution center is Locust Street from 11th to 17th Streets ("Swing Street"). Its several bars and "private clubs" have a substantial number of prostitutes. Membership in the "clubs" can be obtained on the spot for $1 or $2, which is credited against the price of drinks. The clubs remain open later than bars, which must close at 2 A.M. One large bar has a basement club with B-girls; another room has a number of homosexual prostitutes in regular attendance; a third room has a large staff of prostitutes.

One of the most active prostitution centers in the United States used to be Calumet City, Illinois, where three blocks ("The Strip") were lined with "showplaces." Doormen stood in the entrances, invited passersby to enter, and did not hesitate to mention the availability of prostitution. These shows consisted of "showgirls" completely in the nude. At a typical show one performer appeared in a bathtub, and fondled and vigorously scrubbed her body. She shouted obscene remarks as she pointed to various parts of herself. Some of the patrons were literally dragged to the bar by B-girls and forced to buy drinks. A number of clubs had dimly lit booths to which some girls took their customers for intercourse. The dancers circulated among the patrons asking for drinks, their hands wandering over the customers' trousers.

One of the most dramatic changes in the history of prostitution in America occurred in Calumet City. When Joseph Nowak was elected mayor in 1961 he set himself the task of eliminating prostitution. The suburban community of home owners supported the mayor in his efforts. Today the bars once identified with prostitution are unoccupied, and the glitter and glare of former times are scenes of peeling paint and shattered windows. The community seeks to attract industry and to sustain the momentum that was generated during the attack on commercialized prostitution. Although many previous attempts to clean up the situation in Calumet City had failed, the population explosion which reached the southern part of Cook County and engulfed Calumet City was primarily responsible for providing the support that enabled Mayor Nowak to eliminate the disreputable bars and strip-tease joints.

San Antonio, similarly, was once a wide-open city. During the 1920's and 1930's a number of prostitutes there used one-room shacks that belonged to poor families. The prostitute would say to the family, "I'd like to use this shack every day from four until twelve, and I'll give you $3 for letting me use it." The family members absented themselves in order to earn what for them was a substantial amount of money. Today prostitution in San Antonio is minimal. The former red light district ("Spic Town") on the city's west side is a shambles. Many of the shacks that housed prostitutes have been razed and others are now the living quarters of Mexican families. The singsong "Come on in, honey" of the prostitutes is no longer heard, and the corner beer joint juke boxes no longer play "You Are My Sunshine." The Mexican ("Tex-Mex") B-girls who hustled "two-bit" bottles of beer or glasses of wine have disappeared.

Cab drivers have recently said they do not know of a "spot" anywhere in San Antonio, and some added that if they did they would not "hustle johns" to it. One declared: "I've been pulling this cab for years. I knew every joint—Mexican, colored, and white. I supplied Allie, Maggie, and Florence, and all the others with customers. They're all gone. There ain't a spot running, that's for sure. . . . There's no stuff around except some pig that a guy might run into in a beer joint." A

serviceman said, "I've been at Fort Sam Houston a long while
. . . come to town often . . . can't seem to score. . . ."

A longtime Seattle brothel-keeper, interviewed recently
about prostitution in her city, said, "Just before World War II
there were more than a hundred houses here. Now I doubt
there's one." The houses in Seattle were run under the guise
of small hotels. Some of the madams from Anchorage, Alaska,
moved to Seattle in 1949 and 1950 to try to re-establish themselves, but were unable to do so because of strict law enforcement. Derelicts still roam and loiter south of Yesler Way,
Seattle's skid row, where $1 and $2 brothels were once located. Some former brothels have been razed or converted
into flophouses, and commercial buildings have gone up on
the sites of others. One bartender said: "You're bound to run
on to a hustler in some of the spots if you look hard enough
and cover the waterfront. But you can take it from me, for
a seaport town Seattle is tight. . . ."

To the casual observer, Portland, Oregon's skid row has
remained unchanged for years. But while panhandlers and
derelicts continue to gather in their favorite haunts, the
brothels in the same area have disappeared along with the
prostitutes who frequented the drink spots. The administration of Mayor Dorothy McCullough Lee, from 1949 through
1952, was largely responsible for the decrease in prostitution.
In taverns, as one tavern owner noted, "Nowadays, the girls
play it cool. They got to know you before they'll take you
on. . . ."

Flagrant prostitution activities have been entirely eliminated in Los Angeles. Prostitutes can be found in some bars
but will not proposition anyone unfamiliar to them. The notorious "joints" on Main Street have been razed, their sites
converted into parking lots. One cab driver recently said,
"Anyone who would peddle 'girls' these days is out of his
mind. . . . The days of making a fast buck are over." Another
Angeleno remarked: "A few years ago you could stand here
in front of the hotel and get solicited by swell-looking num-

bers. . . . That Caddy there is mine. I specialize in sightseeing. Years ago my business was mainly 'liners.' Today I wouldn't touch a 'liner' with a ten-foot pole. Put a $50 bill in my hand and as much as I like money I couldn't and wouldn't put you on to one broad. . . ."

Prostitutes once solicited openly in Phenix City, Alabama. Servicemen from nearby Fort Benning were their main targets. Men in uniform were often robbed and beaten by prostitutes and their cohorts, but protests against these conditions fell on deaf ears, especially since members of the city council were involved in the rackets. A. L. Patterson, the crusading state attorney general, swore when he took office in 1951 that he would clean up the community. Patterson had scarcely begun when he was warned he would be killed. The underworld made good its threat, and the murder aroused public indignation throughout the state. Martial law was declared by Governor Gordon Patterson, the late attorney general's son, and law and order were ultimately established. The new attorney general secured 741 indictments. The men indicted for the murder of Patterson included a former state attorney general, the state solicitor, and a deputy sheriff. Today Phenix City has no rackets and stands as an example of what can be accomplished when citizens finally become aroused.

In the last ten years vigorous police action and new building have have combined to discourage prostitution in Washington, D.C. Even though Washington ranks high in other indices of social pathology, it is difficult to find a prostitute openly plying her trade in the city. The former slum area on G Street between 4th and 5th, which had a nest of bars with prostitutes semi-permanently attached, has been razed to make way for new buildings.

VICE SATELLITES

Frustrated within the city itself, entrepreneurs in many large urban areas have developed satellite communities with substantial concentrations of prostitution. These vice satellites were set up because they were not subject to the more energetic law enforcement of the city or other larger community.

Suburban vice satellites are close enough to the larger community to be able to draw a large clientele. Collinsville was a satellite of East St. Louis, Illinois, until its brothels, operated and owned by racketeers, were closed in 1942. Taxi drivers in Cincinnati would tell their customers that they could find some "action" over the river in Newport, Kentucky. Brothels in Scranton, Easton, and Bethlehem in Pennsylvania drew many customers from New York City. A red light district with prostitutes soliciting from brothel windows in Hudson, New York, used to attract clients from as far away as New Hampshire, Vermont, and Massachusetts. Four out of every five cars parked on Hudson's Columbia Street had out-of-town license plates. The red light district in Hudson was cleaned up in 1940, reopened in 1943, and finally closed before the end of World War II. When the brothels in Portland, Oregon, were closed a number of them moved to nearby Coos Bay early in World War II.

A man who asked a taxi driver in New Orleans for advice on where to find a prostitute was told, "You ain't going to find anything here. You might as well go home. But come back tomorrow morning and see our antique shops." He also advised the potential client to visit Jefferson Parish, outside of New Orleans, where brothels and bar prostitutes flourish.

Perhaps the most successful recent vice satellite was Gary, Indiana, which drew customers from Chicago. Boys of eight and ten would accost and take men to Adams and Jefferson streets, where waiting women stood in doorways or sat in windows. An amenable Gary mayor could average a personal income of $1 million a year merely by doing nothing about prostitution. This steel community once had many migrants and workers living in furnished rooms and other relatively anomic circumstances. Its prostitution had been organized by the Capone mob. In March 1949 the community's women became sufficiently incensed about prostitution to lead a march on city hall. As a result of such pressure the city was temporarily cleaned up, but prostitution soon became overt again. On a later occasion the community's schoolteachers protested the situation and one was accidentally shot and killed. The reform Democratic administration which came into office after the November 1967 election largely made good on its campaign pledge to clean up prostitution.

PROSTITUTION AND ORGANIZED CRIME

Prostitution was once closely linked to organized crime in many communities. The scandal occasioned by the famous Herman Rosenthal murder in New York City before World War I, and the charges of being an accessory to the murder brought against police Lieutenant Charles Becker, exposed the relationships among prostitution, organized crime, and police protection.

Rosenthal, a gambler, was murdered by four men just before he was to file a complaint with the district attorney against Lieutenant Becker, who was head of the vice squad. A man called Jack Rose confessed that he had been hired by Becker to arrange the murder. Becker was afraid that Rosenthal would report to the district attorney that Becker was receiving "protection" payments from brothels and gamblers. Becker was tried, convicted, and executed for being an accessory to the murder. When it appeared likely that chief procurer Motke Goldberg would be murdered because he could testify about graft payments, he went to Argentina, re-established himself as a white slaver, and flourished into the 1920's.

The most visible link between crime and prostitution was provided by the Chicago crime syndicate during prohibition.[13] The largest syndicate of brothels in the United States was run by a group of Chicago gangsters generally believed to be headed by Al Capone. Brothels operated under the guise of hotels in Chicago, Minneapolis, Fargo, Bismarck, Butte, Walla Walla, Spokane, and Seattle. A prostitute, accompa-

nied by her pimp, would start in Chicago and work her way
west, spending two weeks in each place. At any one time the
average brothel in the chain had six prostitutes. The brothels'
"new faces" were very popular with customers.

Chicago in the late twenties and in the thirties was unique
because the brothel proprietor was a man rather than a
woman. A man could handle relationships with racketeers
and other criminals more easily than a woman. Perhaps the
only other male proprietor in America was "Blind Joe," who
in the 1930's ran a brothel in the Diamond Hill area of Paw-
tucket, Rhode Island, and who had a police dog advance on
any customer whose voice he did not recognize.

The Capone mob was said to be in complete control of
most prostitution in Chicago. During the 1930's there were
many stories of prostitutes whose faces were badly cut and
who were then thrown into a scalding shower as punishment
for not turning a share of their earnings over to the mob.
Capone was believed to own the Speedway Inn in the Chicago suburb of Burnham, where business was so brisk that
turnstiles regulated the traffic. Each prostitute's efficiency
was regularly evaluated and less productive women were dismissed. As he went through the turnstile, each customer was
handed a towel and soap. The customer would go up one side
of the staircase, be assigned to a prostitute, and leave the
premises by going down another flight of stairs. The Speedway Inn was the largest brothel in the United States. It had
fifty women whose prices ranged from $2 to $5, depending on
the services offered. The Inn was a large, pavilion-like building with a bar and cigar store on the ground floor. The prostitutes worked in small rooms on the upper floors. License
plates from many states could be seen on cars parked nearby.
The Inn flourished during prohibition and closed in 1934;
other kinds of gang-run prostitution also existed in Chicago
in the prohibition years.

Gangsters and other underworld elements dominated prostitution in other cities. Up to World War II Buffalo was
known in underworld circles as a wide-open community. A

prominent pimp (Big Aleck) was the most active figure in the Buffalo prostitution underworld. Aleck was so large that he used to walk sideways through doors. His brothels would open for business only when the vice squad was off duty.

Los Angeles in the 1930's was another community in the grip of organized crime which controlled prostitution. The syndicate did not permit any brothel to operate without payment for protection. One man who had just opened a brothel said: "Just as soon as the syndicate heard about it they sent over a couple of strong-arms. They told me to quit, saying 'You can't tell what will happen.' They said that if I didn't pay they would send the vice squad in to see me so often that I couldn't stay in business. The syndicate paid off for every joint they had."

Peoria, Illinois, had organized prostitution from 1941 through 1953. During the next five years it emerged from gang rule and lost most of its prostitution activity. Ironically, the mayor of Peoria during its worst period was the father-in-law of Eliot Ness, the distinguished public official and crusader against vice. Prostitution returned in the early 1960's, and the city currently has nine overt brothels and four hotels that encourage prostitution.

Until the 1930's New York City had a very well-organized prostitution racket. Racketeers did not exactly solicit competition, but they did not eliminate it. After the Rosenthal murder and the investigations that it engendered, many of the leading New York madams left New York and prospered in other communities. Mrs. Lax and Anna Banks resettled in Buffalo, and Lena Hyman moved to Toledo. During the 1930's there is some reason to believe that organized racketeers in New York City were not running brothels but were engaged in blackmail and extortion related to them. Both patrons and employees were victimized.[14] A gangster might come to a brothel and say, "You've got a good thing here; if you don't want trouble, I want $300 a month." A madam was hardly likely to complain to the police about the extortion attempt, and generally paid in order to keep her business going.

In some communities the underworld figures who ran gambling also controlled prostitution, as in Phenix City, Alabama; Galveston, Texas; and Newport, Kentucky. Prostitution has been associated with horse racing in Southern communities. Lexington, Kentucky, was a center for racing which was especially attractive to prostitutes. In front of Lexington's leading hotel for several decades stood a cab driven by a well-known steerer. A customer who approached him and asked, "What's going on in town?" was inviting the driver to take him "down the line." The driver would say, "Same old tale, but it's good tail," and take him to the red light district. The Agua Caliente race track was a popular place for prostitutes to get customers. The gambling rooms associated with the tracks were often used for rendezvous with prostitutes. The traditional association of prostitution with horse racing was illustrated when a ring of housewife prostitutes was broken up in 1964 by police in New York's Nassau County. The women had been doing a large part of their business during the Roosevelt Raceway season.

Sexual activity and gambling offer similar enticements even on a physiological level. Both involve tension, extended anticipatory activity, and a rapid climactic interaction. In as much as gambling and prostitution often seem to be closely related, some personality factors may be common to clients of both activities. Proprietors of gambling casinos are presumably unaware of such psychodynamic factors but have been making money on the basis of connections between the two fields. It has been estimated that in recent years some 10 per cent of the 65,000 population of Las Vegas engaged in prostitution or various auxiliary activities.[15] Many wine and cigarette girls, cocktail waitresses, change girls, cashiers, and other employees of gambling establishments in Las Vegas were known to be part-time prostitutes.

Criminals not only have controlled some brothels but occasionally have sought refuge in them. For many years there were cities in which brothels were used as criminal hideouts. A criminal could expect to disappear into the red light district in such communities and remain hidden for extended periods of time. The underworld called these cities—such as St. Paul and Toledo—"holy cities." John Dillinger hid in St. Paul brothels during the 1930's.

Armed robbery of brothels was common. The large number of brothel robberies in New York was one reason for the development of a "protection" racket. In exchange for regular payments from brothels, the protectors guaranteed that there would be no robberies. Although there were a few robberies in Chicago after World War I, the mob that dominated Chicago prostitution in the 1920's largely eliminated them. In Buffalo rival gangs occasionally held up each other's brothels.

Some thieves sought to capitalize on the prostitute's fear of the law by posing as police officers and allegedly "raiding" a brothel or "arresting" a prostitute. They would then seek a bribe from the madam or prostitute in order to "forget" the alleged violation. Sometimes the bogus police would be easily identified by the women. On other occasions the women would gladly pay in order to avoid what they expected to be certain arrest.

Today only a relatively few communities have syndicates that control both prostitution and gambling. For the most part these syndicates were dissolved as a result of several interrelated factors: improved law enforcement, bickering among the syndicate members, and the availability of new illegal activities with a rapid rate of return and reimbursement—such as the vast expansion of narcotics traffic since the late 1940's. There has also been a continuing trend toward criminal syndicates' investing the money they get from illegal activities in legitimate business.

LAWS AGAINST CLIENTS

Various laws have been designed to provide that prostitutes' clients be subject to penalty. As long ago as 1922, the United States' Assistant Surgeon General Claude Connor Pierce said, "It is recognized by the Public Health Service and all other agencies aiming at the elimination of prostitution that the male partner is equally guilty. Equal treatment for men and women apprehended in prostitution is now demanded by public opinion." Such public opinion, however, has been slow in expressing itself.

In New York the bill to penalize clients became known as the Customer Amendment. Much legal discussion of the amendment stemmed from the 1923 Breitung case in New York, in which one woman was charged with permitting her apartment to be used for prostitution and two others with offering to engage in prostitution with a Mr. Breitung. The woman who made her apartment available received a thirty-day sentence, one of the other women was placed on probation, and the third was committed to a hospital because of venereal disease. Mr. Breitung, though called as a witness by the defense, declined to testify. The facts were not disputed and the argument dealt solely with interpretation of the vagrancy law of New York State. Magistrate Moses R. Ryttenberg held that "a man cannot participate in an act of prostitution . . . because prostitution is a practice of women only, a man participating therein could not be held to be a principal. . . . On the authority of 203 N.Y. 73, one cannot be said to participate in unlawful acts unless he profits therefrom."

The Breitung decision was widely quoted by opponents of the Customer Amendment, who also claimed that a successful prosecution would be impossible if prostitute and client were co-defendants, because a co-defendant cannot be convicted on the basis of the unsupported testimony of the other. Its opponents also claimed that the amendment was an attempt to make people moral by law and would create additional opportunities for blackmail. The law was finally passed in New York in 1965 as part of a revision of the state penal code.

The twenty-one states that currently penalize customers' activities are Connecticut, Delaware, Illinois, Indiana, Kentucky, Maine, Maryland, Michigan, New Hampshire, New Jersey, New Mexico, New York, North Carolina, North Dakota, Ohio, Oklahoma, Rhode Island, Tennessee, Texas, Vermont, and Wyoming. There may be an increase in the number of such laws in the future, for the American Law Institute included a customer amendment in the model penal code which it adopted in 1961.

What happens when a law directed against customers is in force? The experience of Indiana, whose statute dates from 1905, provides some clues. In recent years about one hundred customers have been arrested annually. Patrons are arrested only if apprehended during a raid and when there is clear evidence of their actually having used the services of a prostitute. About a third of the patrons are convicted, with the usual penalty a fine of not more than $100. Jail sentences of up to sixty days have been given occasionally. Publicity is generally avoided, but newspaper reporters may get the patrons' names from the police blotter and publish them. One effect of the law is that arrested patrons are generally very cooperative in providing information about prostitutes. In general, communities have been reluctant to implement customer amendments because punishment would remove many men from their daily activities.

In 1961 Illinois passed a law which makes a patron found guilty of frequenting a prostitute subject to a fine of up to $200 and/or not more than six months in jail. Although a number of patrons have been arrested in the state during the last several years, there appear to have been no convictions. As in Indiana, the law has proved helpful in obtaining detailed information about prostitutes from patrons who responded to the threat of a fine or jail sentence. No information on patrons is made available to newspapers.

The ability of the client to avoid prosecution despite the customer amendment has led to some bizarre results. In New York City a client who testified against a prostitute might go into considerable detail about a birthmark on her body which positively identified her as the woman with whom he had been apprehended. Such a man was often effusively thanked by the judge for his "public-spirited" testimony, and then dismissed, though he provided the evidence that convicted the woman.

County Judge Martin Schenck of Albany, New York, in December 1959 reversed a police court conviction of an alleged prostitute because the man whose testimony jailed her was not identified. The judge maintained that if "Mr. X" couldn't be seen, his testimony shouldn't be heard. Since most clients are permitted to appear as "Mr. X" or "John Doe," Judge Schenck's reversal struck at an important aspect of the law. Few appellate jurisdictions have upheld this view, perhaps because few prostitutes have the money or time to carry appeals to higher courts.

Customers detained in connection with the arrest of a prostitute are usually asked to post so small a bond that its forfeiture will not be difficult if they do not appear in court. One of the curious features of our current procedures is that married customers admit to adultery when they testify to activities with a prostitute, yet there are practically no cases in which a customer has been charged with adultery.

Our ambiguous treatment of customers has not been completely unnoticed by prostitutes. Hattie Smith and Jeanette Macdonald, convicted of soliciting in Oakland, California, in January 1966, claimed they were denied equal protection of the law because their male companions went free. Their attorney argued that they were discriminated against because of their sex and that there was mutual solicitation of both men and women. The women have appealed their convictions.

One difficulty in prosecuting customers is that signing a false name in a hotel register is not a violation of the law in many states. Massachusetts is one of the few with a "true-name law," which prohibits signing a name other than one's own on a hotel register. Most hotels merely require a guest to have baggage in order to register for a room. If a hotel establishes that a "man and wife" have baggage when they register, it cannot be accused of having "guilty knowledge" of possible prostitution. Some prostitutes have a suitcase containing a few telephone books, which they check at a locker. When a client appears, they remove the luggage and use it when registering for a room. Most men registering at a hotel with a prostitute use a common name like "Smith" or "Jones." A popular name is "W. R. Knottman," which is written W R Knottman. A curlicue at the end of the initial "W" is actually the small letter "e," so that the name means "We are not man and wife." Many hotel desk clerks know the name as a code for a man with a prostitute.

In some communities police harass potential customers with considerable persistence. They may use a flash-gun camera to photograph a man being accosted by a prostitute. Such a customer often becomes uneasy and is not likely to continue his discussions with the prostitute. In other communities the police may accuse a potential customer who is in an automobile of blocking traffic or a similar charge, as one way of discouraging him from staying in an area where prostitutes are looking for customers.

On balance, customer amendments are, like many other procedures for coping with prostitution, ethically sound but essentially unworkable. A prostitute is unlikely to testify against a client or a client against a prostitute. In July 1969, of 486 arrests for prostitution in New York City, only eleven men were arrested on charges of patronizing a prostitute and none was convicted. One additional practical argument against the customer amendment is that a police officer would be violating the statute every time he offered money in exchange for sexual access. Vice squads would be severely handicapped by the statute, unless the courts ignored such behavior by police.

BACKERS AND "CONNECTIONS"

In the period between the two World Wars, at least one man in each city was the power behind a number of its brothels. He tried to be inconspicuous, and handled the details of lease or purchase of the premises and the establishment of a "front." The lease might be made with the tacit understanding that in the event of a dispossess, a new lease would be available to the same tenant under a different name.

The man behind the brothel was often called "the big shot," and during World War II the military phrase "VIP" (very important person) was widely used. VIP was also used subsequent to World War II for the "fixer" who had the ear of local law enforcement officials, took care of payoffs, and was alerted when token raids were planned. In Buffalo a police captain owned the city's highest-priced establishment. Oklahoma City's protector of brothels was a lawyer, and in Portland, Oregon, ward politicians were behind the scenes.

Prostitution racketeers in Philadelphia used to have extremely effective "connections" with personnel at the office of the mayor and police commissioner in Philadelphia. During the late 1920's the Marine hero General Smedley Butler was the city's police commissioner and announced that he was going to clean up prostitution. When the commissioner would go out to see what was happening along "the line," by the time he had turned the corner away from his office someone in police headquarters had telephoned ahead and alerted the prostitutes.

One of the most prominent episodes in the involvement of public officials with prostitution occurred in Pittsburgh in the 1930's when the mayor received money from brothels. Madam Nettie Gordon was "bag" woman for the mayor and collected the tribute which other madams and exploiters had to pay. Both she and the mayor were ultimately convicted.

New Orleans was once notorious for the involvement of its public officials in prostitution. One of the more unusual features in Louisiana prostitution during the late 1930's was the unofficial requirement that every brothel had to subscribe to a weekly newspaper published by a prominent state official. The paper had few other readers. A brothel that did not subscribe usually received a visit from the police. One easy way of identifying brothels was to take a stroll on Thursday morning when the paper was delivered and observe the buildings which had the newspaper on its steps. When another state official told the publisher-official to clamp down on prostitution, he merely relocated the brothels from the French Quarter to an area south of Canal Street.

A New Orleans madam recently reminisced: "I had connections. Sure I had 'em. If I didn't I couldn't operate. Remember, I was the only one who had a joint on Royal Street in the Vieux Carré. You had to stand in to run there. . . ." She then mentioned Huey Long, Governor O. K. Allen, and their cohorts, and declared: "When they disappeared from political life, that was the beginning of our end. . . . In the past the law, the D.A.'s, the courts, all had larceny in their veins." Speaking of the police, she said, "With few exceptions they're not hungry for the fast buck today." In 1945 New Orleans had sixteen brothels with a total of 145 women. They gradually closed in 1946 and 1947, but many reopened around 1949. More recently there appear to be five brothels operating in the city.

Prostitution was rampant in Memphis for many years but disappeared almost overnight. It is generally believed that a prominent political leader who experienced a personal tragedy in his family became remorseful about having permitted prostitution to flourish. He is said to have decided to stop it before World War II, and to have done so promptly. Much the same thing occurred in Kansas City when another major political figure decided to clean up prostitution. In both communities crusading newspapers had spent much time and energy denouncing prostitution, but little was done about their recommendations until the politicians changed their views. One of the curious features of prostitution in Memphis was an insurance company, set up with the support of a politician, to write insurance on the lives of prostitutes. This insurance was quite widely purchased by prostitutes, who ordinarily might not have been able to obtain coverage from established companies. The company bore a name and

trademark very similar to those of a nationally well-estab-
lished firm. Kansas City was one of the most corrupt communities in the United States in terms of the protection provided by officials. Today such protection is no longer available, and the expensive brothels that lined Wyandotte and
Passeo Streets have closed.

IX. PROSTITUTION AND THE MILITARY

The two World Wars are benchmarks in the history of prostitution in the United States. Although modern opinion polls were unknown in 1914, there can be few doubts about attitudes toward prostitution just before World War I. Most communities had segregated red light districts, and many cities also had houses of prostitution in business and residential areas that were within easy access of the downtown area. Streetwalking was common, and the back rooms of saloons were openly used by prostitutes. Accosting was frequently done in full view of police officers.

Some idea of the level of acceptance of prostitution before World War I is conveyed by Upton Sinclair's report that his contemporaries would play "brothel" at the age of five in the same way that other children played dolls—and quarrel about who would be madam.[1]

The United States' entry into World War I provided an opportunity to evaluate the effects of a national appeal for continence on the issue of prostitution as a virtue comparable to patriotism. Expansion of the army from fifty thousand to five million occasioned much concern about the welfare of the men in uniform. In order to keep military personnel fit to fight, government authorities felt that conditions inimical to their health and welfare had to be removed; moral hazards like the segregated prostitution districts had to be minimized. As a result, the United States became a vast sociological laboratory for testing social hygiene measures.

The usual increase in prostitution during war is a reflection of many charges in social life. Lack of the restraints of living at home and a desire to emulate peers may lead many men in uniform into contact with prostitutes. Being thrown together with a number of other men in a situation that stresses manliness, and a search for relaxation after the rigors of bivouac, combat, or a sea voyage, are among the factors related to servicemen's interest in prostitution.

The imminent possibility of death seems to lead many participants in a war to feel that they ought to enjoy themselves while they can. Nell Kimball, the New Orleans madam, has commented on the sexual excitement generated by war: "Every man and boy wanted to have one last fling before the real war got him . . . one shot at it in a real house before he went off and maybe was killed. I've noticed it before, the way the idea of war and dying makes a man raunchy, and wanting to have at it as much as he could. It wasn't really pleasure at times but a kind of nervous breakdown that could only be treated with a girl and a set-to."[2]

During a war, prostitutes also concentrate on industrial personnel working at defense plants. Such workers usually earn good money and many may be alert to opportunities for sexual activity. In 1917 these factors were all the more potentially explosive because prostitution was already quite flagrant.

During 1917–1918 many young girls, sometimes called "charity girls" or "victory girls," had "khaki fever" and were eager to do something patriotic. Many went to training camp areas with no idea of how they would maintain themselves, and gradually drifted into prostitution. Other women in communities in which large numbers of men were drained off by military service also drifted into prostitution. Among the reasons for their doing so were boredom, a feeling that the present ought to be enjoyed, and a desire to "take care" of military personnel.

In May 1917 President Wilson was authorized by Congress to regulate conditions in or near military camps, and the Secretary of War was empowered to do everything necessary to suppress prostitution in any area related to the war effort. The Training Camp Activities Commission was established in April 1917. Commission director Raymond B. Fosdick had been Commissioner of Accounts of New York City, a staff member of the Bureau of Social Hygiene, and had also conducted a major study of European police systems.[3] How effectively Fosdick did his job could be seen in the extent to which the procedures he developed were later used in World War II. The commission had nine members, with a section on women and girls under the staff direction of Mrs. Jane Deeter Rippin.[4] Fosdick noted: "Our first line of defense lies in the positive recreational facilities which we are providing for the men. It is not enough merely to erect *Verboten* signs along the way; that does not necessarily mean progress. We must *compete* with the forces that we are trying to put out of business . . . and our second line lies in the police method which has been adopted to keep prostitutes of all classes away from the camp."

The commission's plan for combating vice and venereal disease in the military service had four major elements: (1) measures to occupy the soldiers' leisure time with interesting and wholesome activities; (2) educational procedures to inform military personnel about prostitution and venereal disease; (3) protective and law enforcement activities directed against the third parties in prostitution; and (4) medical techniques to cope with venereal disease.[5]

The commission developed an ambitious program of athletics. Military units developed their own teams which competed with each other—squad against squad, regiment against regiment, and division against division. This program was later widely used in World War II. Military installations worked with neighboring communities to help the community provide amusement and recreation for men on leave. This program later was described in *Survey*, the professional social workers' journal, as "the most stupendous piece of social work in modern times." It is surely one of the most successful attempts at social engineering ever undertaken. Many military personnel developed new interests and were helped in coping with the problems of being away from home. The men were encouraged to do things for themselves: organizing their own theatrical performances and amateur orchestras, participating in various study groups, and teaching one another painting and music. A public fund-raising effort just before the Armistice raised $200 million for the program.

In 1917 the commission developed recreational resources for military personnel on leave, through the War Camp Community Service, which operated over five hundred clubhouses. More than 2.5 million men used this service in 1918 and over twenty million relatives and friends were accommodated. A number of clubhouses arranged for local families to invite a soldier or sailor home to dinner. A typical annual budget of $42,000 for a city included maintenance of the clubhouse, entertainment, music, athletic supplies, singing, and an information bureau.

The commission ran a tremendous campaign of public information on prostitution and venereal disease, emphasizing the fact that this disease constituted the greatest single cause of absence of men from active duty. All government buildings displayed cards and posters. Volunteers gave lecture courses and films and used other audio-visual procedures. The slogan "Smash the Line" was borrowed from the fighting front and applied to campaigns for eliminating the red light district's line of brothels. Congress created the United States Interdepartmental Social Hygiene Board and established the Division of Venereal Diseases as a part of the Public Health Service in 1918.

The Training Camp Activities Commission established a

Law Enforcement Division in September 1917. Supervisors were stationed at central points in each of ten districts and cooperated with the Department of Justice, the agency responsible for enforcing federal laws. Agents of the division did not apprehend or prosecute offenders but secured information about local prostitution conditions. If the agents were unable to convince prostitutes and their associates of the undesirability of their activities, the full force of various government agencies was brought to bear.

Later in 1917 a committee was established by the commission to do preventive work with "good girls" and thus to lighten the task of law enforcement officials. After a few months it became apparent that the problem was less the amateur than the prostitute. The duties of the committee were accordingly enlarged and transferred to the division of law enforcement, which created a section on women and girls.

Houses of detention and reformation were established to treat and rehabilitate girls and women who were engaging in prostitution with military personnel. During 1918, 28,000 such women came to the attention of the commission staff. Mental and physical examinations as well as treatment of venereal disease were provided. A typical program included isolated hospital facilities and an industrial farm with separate units for women and girls.

The program was sometimes complicated by the entanglement of police, court, health, and probation jurisdictions in a case. Venereal disease was occasionally used as evidence of guilt of prostitution rather than as a reason for appropriate rehabilitative measures. The treatment program was transferred in 1919 to the Interdepartmental Social Hygiene Board and gradually shifted to state and local officials and voluntary agencies.

Other anti-prostitution programs in American communities grew out of Section 17 of the Draft Act, which prohibited prostitution near training camps. By the middle of 1917 the commission sought additional investigation of prostitution. New agents were recruited by Dr. William F. Snow to check on promises by city officials to eliminate prostitution. One example of the new agents' work could be seen in Douglas, Arizona, which had a flourishing red light district. When commission agents presented evidence on the district to the commanding general of the nearby military post, the general requested that the district be closed. The city repealed its ordinance licensing the red light district.

The change in attitude was perhaps most striking in New Orleans, where the brothels were so protected by local politicians that the commission was assured the situation could not be changed. The district was finally closed in November 1917, but only after pressure from Congress, the Secretary of the Navy, and the governor. Another successful example of community cooperation occurred in June 1917 in San Francisco, which had long been headquarters for the Pacific Coast underworld. When local officials decided that the red light district should go, it was closed. New York City was cleaned up by assigning a large number of military policemen to patrol the city. They were able to get local businessmen to cooperate in keeping New York "safe for the doughboy." Every important red light district in the United States was closed by the end of 1917.

The armed forces were especially concerned about soldiers who would be incapacitated as a result of venereal disease contracted from a prostitute. The army educated soldiers about venereal disease, provided prophylactic measures, and gave medical care to those infected. Any soldier or sailor with infectious venereal disease was not permitted a leave or furlough.

The army venereal disease rate per 1000 per annum fell from 108 in 1917 to 60 in 1919. It continued declining for several years after the war until it reached 50 per 1000 in 1922. The navy rates were slightly higher because of shore leave in foreign ports where commercialized vice districts still flourished. Civilian venereal disease rates declined along with the military rates.

Special plans were developed for the American Expeditionary Forces in Europe. The prevailing attitude of many European governments was favorable to prostitution, and it was not possible to establish separate zones under the protection of American commanders. Short leaves and furloughs, so important for morale reasons, brought the men into contact with prostitutes. When American troops embarked in France there were no administrative procedures to cope with prostitution. French brothels were not put off limits to troops until alternative attempts had been made to deal with the rising rate of venereal disease.

General Pershing was concerned that military personnel who had been in the mud and grime of the front should have an opportunity of seeing the more attractive aspects of French civilization, and encouraged unit commanders to grant leaves and furloughs to Paris. When it became clear that venereal disease would be a considerable problem in France, Raymond B. Fosdick requested Bascom Johnson of the commission's Law Enforcement Division to send fifteen agents to France. On the basis of their report, Fosdick recommended to General Pershing that the brothels there be placed off limits. Accordingly, on December 18, 1917, General Order #77 placed houses of prostitution off limits. French Commander General Foch cooperated by placing neighboring zones under military control and increasing the number of police assigned to these zones. Early in 1918 the British War Office placed licensed houses of prostitution out of bounds to members of the British expeditionary forces.

Facetiously, it was said that every one of the American military police stationed in front of the Parisian brothels went home rich because it was easy to identify a brothel by the military police in front of it. A soldier or sailor entering the house might pay the guard ten francs to look the other way. Some French officials wanted to provide "legal" prostitutes for American military personnel, but the American military leadership refused.

The commission tried to combat the problem by using some

of the same techniques it had applied successfully on the home front. Automobiles and trucks brought motion picture equipment to the front. The soldiers' newspaper, the *Stars and Stripes*, was taken daily to men in the trenches, and the Salvation Army made doughnuts and hot coffee easily available. The Librarian of Congress, Dr. Herbert Putnam, organized a staff which delivered current books to the men.

When the war emergency was formally ended in March 1921, the Draft Act became inoperative and the army and navy ceased to have any control over civil conditions. When the peace treaty with Germany was signed on August 25, 1921, retrenchment of appropriations on behalf of military personnel included the program against prostitution. The Training Camp Activities Commission developed an elaborate program during the post-armistice period. Sending men for a week or two to selected places of interest in Europe proved to be a popular procedure. A series of vocational and academic courses was set up and soldiers were offered the opportunity of going to universities in France or England with a guarantee of at least six months of studies in residence. Similar services were provided by other voluntary agencies.

The transfer of law enforcement activities from the commission to the Interdepartmental Social Hygiene Board was accomplished in 1919. The board continued its activities through 1922, when congressional retrenchment practically eliminated it. Many of its activities were transferred to state and local groups and voluntary agencies which continued its work during the 1920's.[6]

WORLD WAR II AND ITS AFTERMATH

The techniques and procedures developed during and after World War I proved relevant to the problems posed by World War II. Commercialized prostitution flourished during the early mobilization period between 1939 and 1941. Military establishments were rapidly being activated and industrial plants sprang up in city after city. The hopes of the prostitution underworld ran high, because large concentrations of manpower meant a greater demand for their service. Exploiters and their women flocked into communities frequented by servicemen and defense workers and did a thriving business. Prostitution activities became more and more flagrant and venereal disease increased.[7] For a time it appeared that prostitution would have a renascence comparable to its expansion before World War I.

Even before the United States entered a war in which 12.3 million Americans were in uniform at one time, there was growing citizen pressure on the federal government to suppress and where possible prevent prostitution. In order to profit from the experience of World War I, Army Chief of Staff George C. Marshall in 1940 wrote Raymond B. Fosdick to inquire about the procedures used to combat prostitution and venereal disease in 1917. Specifically, Marshall asked Fosdick for information about the machinery that had been established by the Training Camp Activities Commission in the earlier war.

The starting point for the federal government's anti-prostitution activities in World War II was a resolution that has since become known as the Eight-Point Agreement. The armed forces, the United States Public Health Service, and the American Social Health Association cooperated in formulating the resolution, first promulgated in 1940. Its formal title was "An Agreement by the War and Navy Departments, the Federal Security Agency, and State Health Departments, on Measures for the Control of the Venereal Diseases in Areas Where Armed Forces or National Defense Employees Are Concentrated." It underscored the policy of the War and Navy Departments to suppress commercialized prostitution. Although a few local military commanders maintained privately that the only solution to prostitution was to regulate it, they generally cooperated in the official policy to discourage commercialized prostitution. The Eight-Point Agreement even applied to communities that were not immediately adjacent to military or defense centers if they were frequented by military personnel.

Another vehicle for the attack on prostitution was the Interdepartmental Committee on Venereal Disease Control, organized on December 23, 1941, to coordinate the federal program against venereal disease and prostitution.

THE DIVISION OF SOCIAL PROTECTION

A part of the Interdepartmental Committee which mounted probably the most substantial anti-prostitution effort of the war years was the Division of Social Protection. It was established early in 1941, shortly before draftees began to arrive at the large Southern training camps. A report by Katherine Lenroot of the Children's Bureau to the Office of Community War Services on conditions near the camps helped lead to creation of the division.

The Office of Community War Services was the war arm of the Federal Security Agency, responsible for coordinating wartime health and welfare services and promoting recreation, social protection, and child-care programs. Just as there had been an organized effort to rehabilitate prostitutes during World War I, a similar program of rehabilitation centers developed during World War II under the Office of Community War Services. Prostitutes were treated for venereal disease, given vocational training for other occupations, helped in securing employment, and provided with case-work services for themselves and their families.[8]

The Division of Social Protection had the assignment of safeguarding the armed forces and civilians from prostitution, sex delinquency, and venereal disease.[9] Beginning in September 1941 it was directed by Eliot Ness, who had previously been Director of Public Safety in Cleveland, where he established a successful anti-prostitution program. Ness set up a network of thirteen regional offices in the United States and Hawaii.

The division's first action against prostitution was to organize a national advisory committee of leading police officials to publicize the techniques of law enforcement against prostitution.[10] In this as in many other activities the Social Protection Division brought together divergent viewpoints. The division did not enforce the law but facilitated law enforcement, established standards of operation for local community groups, and provided technical and professional advice to communities.

A subcommittee of the police advisory group provided guidance on how to cope with young girls who were drifting into prostitution. Many of these "V-girls" were teen-agers who had been attracted to military camps and became marginal prostitutes.[11] Another subcommittee set forth standards for the detention of juvenile and adult prostitutes.[12] Detroit and Washington had great success in using policewomen to combat prostitution and helped other communities in doing so.

The division also obtained information from the armed forces on rates and sources of venereal disease. Field investigators of the American Social Health Association would conduct surveys of prostitution near military and national defense areas. Armed with reports of the investigations, division representatives would confer with community authorities and military commanders about remedial action. Such programs were doubtless responsible for a continuing reduction in the armed forces' venereal disease rate. The division also cooperated with the venereal disease control authorities of the Public Health Service, which had opened fifty rapid treatment centers by 1944.

Although the original reasons for establishing the Social Protection Division stemmed from a desire to minimize venereal disease, by the end of the war social protection activity consisted ". . . of services to states and their political subdivisions in support of community action essential to prevent prostitution, eliminate conditions contributing to sex delinquency, and to provide services for the rehabilitation of sex delinquents."[13] Such a definition shifted emphasis from the prevention of prostitution in order to control venereal disease to the prevention of prostitution itself. The war experience led many officials to agree with Thomas Devine, head of the division in its last months, that "the mental health aspect of prostitution is of even greater importance than the venereal disease aspect." This viewpoint increasingly became central to the activities of the many government agencies seeking to combat prostitution.

THE MAY ACT

The wartime campaign against prostitution also involved legislation. Concern about the large numbers of military personnel away from home, especially those away for the first time, led to the May Act, which was similar to Section 17 of the Draft Act of 1917. When President Roosevelt signed it on July 11, 1941, he stressed the "united effort for total physical and moral fitness." The act prohibited "prostitution within such reasonable distance of military and/or naval establishments . . . needful to the efficiency, health, and welfare of the army or navy." It was first invoked in May 1942 in twenty-seven countries near Camp Forrest, Tennessee. The only other occasion was in July 1942 in twelve counties in North Carolina near Fort Bragg.

The Federal Bureau of Investigation periodically met with law enforcement officers, voluntary agencies, and key citizens to discuss potential offenses under the May Act. Such conferences received wide publicity, and a mere threat to invoke the act was extremely effective. The prostitution underworld, which did not fully understand the May Act, thought FBI agents were everywhere. Vigorous action by local police also helped to bring wartime commercialized prostitution to an almost complete halt. Although the May Act was continued as a permanent peacetime law in 1946, it has not been invoked since 1942.

Some critics claim the May Act increased homosexual activity, because the lack of prostitutes led military personnel to seek out men who represented the only easily accessible sexual outlets. Surveys conducted by the American Social Health Association during the war years failed to confirm this allegation, and it is possible that homosexuals did not increase but simply became more visible.

THE ARMED SERVICES

Before World War II, when venereal disease was the greatest single cause of lost manpower in the armed forces, three-fourths of all venereal infections among military personnel could be traced to prostitutes. Since May 17, 1926, disciplinary measures and loss of pay had been imposed as penalties for military personnel who contracted venereal disease. Many military personnel with venereal disease visited private physicians rather than report their condition, and other evidence suggested that fear of future punishment was not an effective deterrent. After considerable discussion within the armed services, Congress on September 27, 1944, eliminated the penalties for contracting venereal disease.

Another armed forces policy was extensive distribution of individual prophylactic kits for service personnel who might be exposed to venereal disease. In communities in which there were many opportunities for contact with prostitutes, prophylactic stations were established.

Specific action to eliminate commercialized prostitution was the responsibility of civilian agencies of law enforcement, but their degree of effectiveness frequently depended on the attitudes of local military commanders. A local commander could help to combat prostitution by placing an establishment "off limits" if he felt it was "inimical to the health and welfare of the armed forces," as General Pershing did in France in 1917. A commander could also influence local officials to take necessary action. In some cases during World War II a whole community was placed off limits.

A few military commanders did not really believe it was possible to suppress prostitution, notably overseas where the

1940 Eight-Point Agreement was not really effective. In many countries American military personnel found themselves unable to date girls their own age. Especially in the Orient, boys and girls went to separate schools and did not socialize with each other. Many GIs thus found that the only girls they could date were outside the established pattern of social behavior.

Prostitution existed in segregated areas in many countries. Some commanding officers tacitly accepted such segregation in spite of the American government's anti-prostitution policy. One difficulty encountered overseas in attempts to combat prostitution was that military police could not post an off-limits notice on any private establishment in a foreign country. The commander could publish a list of off-limits places and post it on bulletin boards, but few soldiers or sailors sought to memorize the names and addresses of prohibited establishments. A prostitute who picked up a customer in an off-limits place generally took him to a hotel or rooming house and made the task of military enforcement authorities even more difficult.

In North Africa after the 1942 Allied invasion, American military authorities found seven thousand registered prostitutes.[14] Suppression of prostitution was considered but was abandoned as impractical because the civil authorities were unsympathetic and because there were so many prostitutes. It was decided to place certain areas off limits to American troops but to provide free access to selected houses which would be closely supervised. The walled city in Casablanca's New Medina was open to troops early in December 1942. A number of brothels were set aside for American troops in Oran. The native quarter ("Casbah") of Algiers was placed off limits, but four large brothels and a number of smaller ones there remained available to troops. The largest brothel (the "Sphinx") was reserved for Allied officers during the evening, but enlisted men and civilians were permitted during the day. Although the brothels in North Africa were placed off limits in mid-1943, enforcement of this ruling was very lax.

During and after cessation of hostilities in Sicily, brothels in the larger communities were taken over for exclusive use of American troops. Prophylactic stations were established in or near each house, and military police were stationed not only to maintain order but to insure that each man received a prophylactic treatment before leaving.

A brothel for Fifth Army troops was maintained by the military a short distance from the Army Rest Center in Naples. Early in 1944 a number of brothels in Naples were placed off limits and a similar policy was subsequently followed as the Allied armies advanced up the boot of Italy past Rome, Livorno, Pisa, and Florence, except where military expediency made it impossible to establish such a policy. Many Italian prostitutes refused to work in brothels as they discovered they could make much more money on a free-lance basis.

Although prostitution had long been recognized as part of the continental scene, the troops massing in England in 1943 and 1944 for the invasion of France did not have much contact with commercialized prostitution. But brothels were being run for American troops in Cherbourg soon after the invasion. They were placed off limits later in 1944. As Allied troops advanced into France and Germany, several attempts were made to place other brothels off limits. Where they were maintained, segregation procedures usually were in effect so that there was one brothel for officers, another for white enlisted personnel, and a third for enlisted Negro men.

In Liberia the local government in 1942 was asked to set up native prostitutes in villages near military reservations, and soldiers were permitted to visit them. In Iran prostitution was also an established practice that was generally accepted by American commanders. Australia continued its practice of regulated prostitution, and many of the thousands of American troops who began arriving in Australia in 1942 became clients.

In the China-Burma-India theater brothels were patronized by more than half the American military personnel. In 1944

Calcutta had a large American detachment and was also a rest center for men who had been isolated in the jungles of Assam and Burma. Calcutta had a reputation as the world's leading prostitution center. British authorities decided not to attempt to regulate or even supervise the brothels, so that the off-limits listing was the only procedure available to American military commanders.

Military personnel in Manila and other Far Eastern cities came into contact with the Benny Boy, a feature of prostitution in the Far East before, during, and after World War II. The Benny Boy is a man who is dressed as a woman and uses adhesive tape to keep his genitals flat against his abdomen. The Benny Boy usually looks more feminine than the female prostitutes with whom he competes for customers. He has longer and higher hair, more makeup, and more delicate clothes. He can only be identified as a man by his larynx and feet, which are larger than a woman's. The typical American military customer, who is often drunk or near drunk, does not know the prostitute is male, even after intercourse. In the Far East, sophisticated native clients may seek out a Benny Boy for variety. There is no imputation of homosexuality to such a contact.

Soldiers' popular music sometimes reflected an interest in prostitution. During World War II one of the leading folk songs of American military personnel overseas was "Lili Marlene." Although its published lyrics were relatively sedate, the song's informal lyrics dealt with prostitution. The variants of "Lili Marlene" included lyrics that were first sung in Elizabethan and Jacobean England. Ironically, the song was first written in 1915 by Hans Leip, a German soldier on his way to the Russian front. ("In front of the barracks . . . was a street lantern . . . so that's where we shall meet again . . . Lili Marlene.") World War II also saw the revival by American forces of "Mademoiselle from Armentieres," a folk song of the American forces overseas in World War I. Many of the unofficial lyrics that were spontaneously developed for this and similar songs of World War II dealt with prostitutes.

VOLUNTARY AGENCIES

Among the voluntary agencies which have cooperated most extensively with the military are the USO and the American Social Health Association. On February 4, 1941, the United Service Organizations (USO) was established as a membership corporation composed of the Young Men's Christian Association, the Young Women's Christian Association, the Salvation Army, the National Catholic Community Service, the National Jewish Welfare Board, and the National Travelers Aid Association. In its contract with the federal government, USO was charged with the wartime responsibility of "fostering and furthering the religious, spiritual, welfare, educational, and recreational needs of the men and women in the armed forces and defense industries of the United States."[15]

USO had many of the same functions as the recreation programs of the Training Camp Activities Commission in World War I. It contributed to minimizing prostitution by the many services it made available to military personnel in 1,277 communities in the United States and overseas. The scope of USO is suggested by the 33.6 million persons who used its services in 1944. Attendance for USO buildings ranged from three million to 25 million per month. Some impression of their activities can be obtained from the number of persons using selected USO facilities during 1944: handicraft and art, 575,161; photography, 441,955; sports, 15,154,345; musical instruments, 743,560; and books loaned or distributed, 3,982,506.

The USO camp shows became a familiar sight at military installations in this country and overseas. At their peak in 1945, camp shows' curtains were rising seven hundred times a day. On December 31, 1947, President Truman wrote: "The USO has now fulfilled its commitment and discharged its wartime responsibility completely and with signal distinction."

Other organizations cooperated in the attempt to eliminate prostitution. Hotel, restaurant, and tavern trade associations, and taxicab owner groups were among those that did so.

Typical of the zeal that characterized such efforts was an experience in Washington in 1944. A middle-aged man who had a major role in the federal anti-prostitution campaign entered a restaurant and asked for a table for two. Fifteen minutes after he had been seated, his wife came to the table to join him. The manager refused to permit her to sit down, saying that it was the policy of the restaurant to refuse service to any woman who joined a man after he had been seated.

The American Social Health Association, the country's only nongovernmental agency concerned with prostitution, has cooperated with the military over the years. Its surveys of communities seek to evaluate the amount and kind of commercialized prostitution. Between 1939 and 1969, the association conducted 7,745 such surveys in 1,478 communities throughout the United States. The surveys were conducted in every city in the continental United States with a population of 100,000 or more; in two-thirds of the cities with a population of 50,000 to 100,000; and in more than 450 smaller communities representing the majority of all urbanized areas.

The first systematic studies of commercialized prostitution in the United States were conducted by George J. Kneeland in Chicago and New York City. His studies helped to pave the way for the periodic reports on prostitution in various communities that were begun by the association before the United States entered World War I. By trial and error over the decades, investigative procedures were developed to cope with changing circumstances. Bascom Johnson was the director of the association's Legal Division which was responsible for the surveys of prostitution until shortly after World War II. Paul M. Kinsie, formerly an associate of Kneeland and long the director of investigations for the association and for its Division of Legal and Social Protection, was largely responsible for the shaping and adaptation of the procedures used.

The association conducts investigations only in communities in which it has been invited to do so. Requests for surveys are received from the United States Public Health Service; state, county, and city health officers; the armed forces; citizen leaders; voluntary agencies; and other community officials. They may call for an investigation if there is already a prostitution problem or if they suspect there may be one. Some cities, because of their size and importance, are studied on a regular basis. The association conducts its studies of prostitution in communities near military installations and those visited by servicemen, in accordance with the Eight-Point Agreement.

THE POSTWAR YEARS

As early as 1942 a decrease in prostitution was found in 526 out of 680 communities studied by the American Social Health Association. By 1945 commercialized prostitution in the United States had reached an all-time low as a result of the high degree of law enforcement by local, county, and state authorities. Long before demobilization, however, rumors were current that the May Act and other law enforcement against prostitution would cease by the end of the war.

In almost all military theaters of operation there was a sharp upsurge in prostitution immediately after the end of hostilities in 1945. The increase resulted from the many soldiers, sailors, and airmen who found themselves with free time on their hands and without the urgency of a wartime situation to absorb their energies. Relaxation of discipline also contributed to an atmosphere in which there was greater susceptibility to opportunities for contact with commercialized vice. For these and other reasons, demobilization brought with it much prostitution near overseas military installations.

Although the Eight-Point Agreement, expressing the federal government's stand against prostitution, was reaffirmed in April 1946 and again in November 1948, Congress did not appropriate funds for the Social Protection Division after 1946. At a May 11, 1948, meeting, the Interdepartmental Venereal Disease Control Committee, including representatives of the armed forces, the Public Health Service, the American Social Health Association, and the Veterans' Administration, discussed prostitution's effect on the health and welfare of servicemen and civilians. This committee unanimously passed a resolution asking the American Social Health Association to assume the Social Protection Division's former responsibilities.

With the end of wartime restrictions, from 1945 through 1948 there was a rebirth of commercialized prostitution in many American cities. The wartime interest "in the united effort for total physical and moral fitness" waned in the years that followed. Many brothels reopened, and bars, taverns, and nightclubs in many cities became focal points for prostitutes. This trend began reversing itself around 1950 as the result of better law enforcement, which profited from the World War II lesson that only when intermediaries and auxiliary personnel were dealt with was there any substantial diminution in prostitution. Relatively few of the other lessons learned during the war have been integrated into subsequent military or civilian anti-prostitution programs.

An Armed Forces Disciplinary Control Board was established in each army area and naval district in March 1950. The board's regular discussions of conditions inimical to the health and moral welfare of service personnel are attended by representatives of all services and local law enforcement agencies. Representatives of the American Social Health Association and of local liquor control authorities are usually present. The major weapon of the board is its ability to place an establishment off limits. The board usually invites the proprietor of the place to appear at a subsequent meeting in order to respond to allegations.

The Korean War in the early 1950's again posed problems for American commanders because Korea had segregated prostitution. A typical brothel in Korea contained a madam ("Mama San") and five women. The many soldiers who wished to find a brothel had little difficulty in doing so. Others who visited Manila on leave patronized the world's largest brothel, which had over a hundred women.

Okinawa's several thousand prostitutes relied on American

troops for much of their business during the 1950's. Its brothels were far enough away from native villages not to be offensive but were close enough to the military post for easy access. The Okinawa situation was representative of many overseas military garrison communities.

The war in Vietnam appears to have given rise to controlled prostitution for the benefit of American servicemen, though hardly for the first time in the history of the United States at war.[16] Vietnamese General Ky early stated that he would try to open brothels for American troops, and a brothel quarter was built exclusively for American soldiers in the community of An Khe. A twenty-five-acre area of "boum-boum parlors" was surrounded by barbed wire.[17] Each of the thirty-five parlors was built of concrete and consisted of a bar with eight cubicles in the rear. A "short time" cost from $2 to $5. Although the prostitution quarter ("Sin City" or "Disneyland") is run by the Vietnamese, American military police patrol the area to check the pass of every soldier entering it. The Vietnamese girls who work in the area must get a special entertainer's card and receive a weekly medical examination. One high-ranking American officer, in explaining the tacit American endorsement of the arrangement, said, "We wanted to get the greatest good for our men with the least harm."

An American soldier who served a year in Vietnam described his visit to An Khe: "Before I got a pass, I had to pick up a rubber and pass an exam on how to use it. I went to a native barber shop where I got a great haircut, manicure, some great pot, and a blow job. I relaxed a few hours with the pot and then went out to Disneyland and went to one of the houses. I had a drink and the Mama San told me I could get a boum-boum for 300 piastres or a sop-sop [fellatio] for 500. I got a boum-boum. Not bad, though it only took a few minutes. When I left the compound, the MP at the gate told me to wash myself to avoid clap or syphilis. I went back to the company and got a pro-treatment. The whole deal had cost me about seven bucks, and I had enough pot to last for a couple of weeks."[18]

In the Saigon area there are more than one hundred illegal brothels. The 160 cabarets and forty-seven dance halls operating at the height of the war employed more than fifty thousand bar girls and taxi-dancers. When the Nguyen Van Thieu government in November 1967 threatened to close down the cabarets and dance halls, a delegation of their employees said they would take to the streets in opposition.

Some of the "rest and recreation" centers for Vietnam servicemen appear to have institutionalized officially condemned mores by providing access to prostitutes. More than three thousand American servicemen visit Taipei on Taiwan each month on "rest and recreation" leaves or furloughs. The "R-and-R" center distributes a pamphlet of advice to military personnel. Information in the pamphlet includes guidance on how to rent a girl: "Her company can be bought from the bar for a 24-hour period for U.S. $15. . . . Do not purchase the company of a girl for more than 24 hours. They seldom look as good in the morning as they did the previous night. . . ."[19] The pamphlet advises a serviceman who is renting a girl to get a signed contract from the bar manager he pays. Some impression of the number of contacts with prostitutes which are occurring in Taipei can be inferred from the approximately 1,100 girls who work out of its bars.

In a daring departure from official Defense Department policy, the senior army medical officer in Vietnam recommended in 1969 that post exchanges there own the brothels. Brigadier General David E. Thomas felt that such a plan would eliminate subterfuges and reduce the high rate of venereal disease. GIs contract venereal disease in Vietnam at a rate of 200 cases per 1,000 persons, in contrast to the United States rate of 32 per 1,000. Some 47 per cent of the Vietnam cases involve military personnel who get venereal disease more than once during their tour.

General Thomas reported that 57 per cent of a large sample of prostitutes examined at the Vung Tau rest center had venereal disease. The General observed that "If the girls are properly examined at frequent intervals and if the soldier is examined to make sure that he isn't bringing VD in with him, and if he is made to take proper precautions after intercourse, then you can't help but reduce the incidence [of VD] among that percentage of soldiers who will use the controlled establishment."[20]

X. INTERNATIONAL CONTROL

$\mathcal{T}$he long history of cooperation between governments and among private groups with respect to prostitution goes back to the 1899 International Conference for the Suppression of Traffic in Women held in England. The International Agreement for the Suppression of the White Slave Traffic in 1904 pledged authorities in thirteen countries to coordinate their activities. The Second International Convention for the Suppression of the White Slave Traffic in 1910 bound its signatories to punish any person who helped a girl under twenty to enter a career as a prostitute, or who procured an adult by force or fraud. The white slave traffic has always been incorrectly designated, because a considerable proportion of the women sold into prostitution were not Caucasoid. The United States Congress has prohibited interstate (Mann Act) and international traffic (Bennet Act) in persons.

The All-American Conference on Venereal Disease was held in Washington in 1920. Over 450 delegates from the Americas adopted standards in venereal disease control and legal and protective measures concerned with prostitution. Article 23C, incorporated into the League of Nations' covenant in 1920, gave the League general supervision over agreements on international traffic in women and children. The next year the League appointed an advisory committee on such traffic.

In 1921 Grace Abbott, head of the United States Children's Bureau, became interested in the international traffic in women and children and encouraged the Social Section of the League of Nations to assume responsibility for the project. A committee of experts included representatives of France, Italy, Uruguay, Sweden, and Japan. John D. Rockefeller, Jr., provided funds to underwrite its investigations. Bascom Johnson and Paul M. Kinsie acted as director and assistant director, respectively, of field studies. The first study was begun on May 3, 1923. Investigation began in the country of demand and worked back to the country of source. One hundred twenty-three cities in twenty-five countries were visited, in South America, North Africa, and most of Europe. The data were given to the committee of experts between 1923 and 1927, and the committee helped each country prepare appropriate legislation dealing with prostitution and immigration. Its final report appeared in 1927 in three parts:

1. The existing traffic in girls who had been lured into the profession and in experienced prostitutes.

2. The international traffic in persons.

3. An appendix on existing laws on prostitution and immigration in each country.

The main traffic in prostitution, the committee found, came from Austria, France, Germany, Hungary, Italy, Poland, Rumania, Spain, and Turkey. The prostitutes went to Latin American countries (Argentina, Brazil, Mexico, Panama, and Uruguay) and to some extent to the United States. Egypt and other countries in North Africa also received prostitutes. Counterfeit passports and visas, pretense of marriage, and promises of employment were subterfuges used to get prostitutes from one country to another. The report stated forcefully that so long as licensed and tolerated brothels were permitted, it was almost impossible to eliminate third persons who profited from traffic in women and children.

The report aroused much discussion in the United States, though the strict immigration quota laws of 1924 had made it only a secondary target for prostitutes from abroad. The expense of getting a prostitute into the United States was so great that many traffickers used this country only as a last resort.

Movement of prostitutes from one country to another received so much publicity from the League report that a major effort was made to suppress the traffic. Effective action was difficult because so many women and children appeared to have genuine offers of employment or marriage from the country to which they were going. The "fiancé" who dupes his "intended" is at least as old as Fanny Hill.[1] The prostitute arriving in a new country seldom knew its language, was without friends and relatives, and thus was at the mercy of those who imported her.[2]

From 1930 to 1933 the League of Nations maintained a Commission of Enquiry into the traffic in women and children in fifteen countries in the Far East. In 1933 the International Convention for the Suppression of the Traffic in Women declared it a punishable offense to lead a woman across national boundaries for immoral purposes. The League's Committee on the Traffic in Women and Children drew great attention in 1934 with a resolution calling for the elimination of licensed houses in all countries. The League prepared a 1937 draft convention for this purpose, but World War II intervened before an international conference could conclude it.

The United Nations Economic and Social Council, by Resolution 43(IV) of March 29, 1947, instructed its Secretary General to update the League of Nations draft convention of 1937. This study led to the 1949 Convention for the Suppression of the Traffic in Persons and the Exploitation of the Prostitution of Others, which was adopted by the U.N. General Assembly as Resolution IV on December 2, 1949, and went into effect

July 25, 1951. The convention, which consolidates earlier instruments, has three innovations, compared to previous international instruments:

(1) Any form of exploitation of others is prohibited, whether or not the person exploited is of age or consents.

(2) Regulation of prostitution by government authorities is prohibited.

(3) Governments are to cooperate to prevent prostitution and to work toward the reintegration into society of former prostitutes.

The convention leaves complete freedom to each country on the question of solicitation and on banning prostitution. To date, six nations have ratified it (they signed soon after the treaty's promulgation) and forty-one have acceded (they became parties to the convention after the initial period of signing). The convention has failed to get a significant number of accessions for a variety of reasons. The fact that the United States has not signed is usually said to be a reflection of the complexities of our state and federal relations rather than a rejection of the principles of the convention.

One reason for the convention's comparative lack of acceptance is that some countries did not feel they could carry out its provisions. Others felt that syphilis was no longer a central problem, so that concerted action against prostitution was less necessary. The major nongovernmental organizations working in the field of international human rights made little effort to mobilize and influence public opinion in favor of the convention.

The countries which have bound themselves by the convention, in the order of their doing so, are

Israel	1950
Yugoslavia	1951
Union of South Africa	1951
Norway	1952
Poland	1952
Pakistan	1952
Cuba	1952
Philippines	1952

India	1953
Haiti	1953
Union of Soviet Socialist Republics	1954
Soviet Socialist Republic of Ukraine	1954
Bulgaria	1955
Rumania	1955
Iraq	1955
Hungary	1955
Mexico	1956
Soviet Socialist Republic of Byelorussia	1956
Libya	1956
Argentina	1957
Czechoslovakia	1958
Ceylon	1958
Japan	1958
Brazil	1958
Albania	1958
Republic of Arabia	1959
Syria	1959
France	1960
Korea	1962
Guinea	1962
Spain	1962
Upper Volta	1962
Algeria	1963
Mali	1964
Belgium	1965
Malawi	1965
Singapore	1966
Kuwait	1968
Venezuela	1968

The official United Nations position, which can be described as abolitionist, has more recently been set forth in a report of the Study on Traffic in Persons and Prostitution, prepared by the U.N. Secretariat at the request of the Social Commission.[3] The report advocates that licensed or tolerated houses of prostitution be closed, irrespective of prevailing conditions and national characteristics. But it also emphasizes the need for a flexible course because of the complex nature of prostitution. The report recommends a program of prevention, rehabilitation, and suppression of prostitution, and prevention and treatment of venereal disease. The plan is left to the discretion of individual countries and appropriate government and private groups. Within the United Nations, the Social Defense Section of the Social Development Division is the group concerned with prostitution.

One voluntary agency working in the field is the International Bureau for the Suppression of Traffic in Persons, in London. Founded in 1899, it is one of the oldest private organizations concerned with prostitution and has affiliated national committees in various countries. Another leading group is the International Abolitionist Federation, founded in 1875, with headquarters in Geneva. Its British branch is the Josephine Butler Society. Founded in 1870, it has long suggested that the prevailing legislation against prostitutes is a violation of English law because it deprives accused women of legal safeguards and of guarantees of personal security established by law.

A newer agency is the International Union Against the Venereal Diseases and the Treponematoses, established in 1923, with headquarters in Paris. In considering the social aspects of venereal disease, the union has always been concerned with the suppression of commercialized prostitution. It has consultative status with the United Nations, as does the International Abolitionist Federation.

There have been efforts to encourage the United Nations to explore the incidence of slavery throughout the world, with special reference to the shipment of women for purposes of prostitution. Many reports have documented the mysterious disappearance of young women who went to various countries as dancers or students. Such women may be forced into prostitution but be unable or reluctant to contact their consulate, because of guilt, fear of recriminations, beatings, or dependence on drugs. A number of African, Asian, and Latin countries have not cooperated in efforts to establish the existence of a slave traffic in women because their proclaimed absence of such slavery is a national status symbol.

In 1963 the Secretary General of the United Nations appointed Dr. Mohamed Awad as Special Rapporteur on slavery. Dr. Awad collected information on the subject and recommended the appointment of a standing committee. But member nations were reluctant to take any action and the question was referred to the Human Rights Commission, which has not undertaken any subsequent inquiry or program.[4]

COUNTRIES BORDERING THE UNITED STATES

The countries bordering the United States pose some genuine difficulties with respect to enforcing U.S. laws against prostitution. The Mexican border has long represented a serious problem, but the United States has no jurisdiction over Mexican affairs. Many American men go from San Diego to Tia Juana, from Brownsville to Matamoras, and from Nogales in Arizona to Nogales in Mexico. Mexican prostitutes generally charge $5, while American prostitutes in the border communities charge $15 or $20. There appear to be practically no American women working as prostitutes in the brothels along the border. Although the United States and Mexico participate in various programs designed to improve health conditions in border communities, these efforts have not been especially successful, in marked contrast to the energetic efforts of Canadian authorities in reducing prostitution in Windsor, Montreal, and Vancouver.

One of the most active Mexican prostitution centers is Juarez, just across the border from El Paso. Some 1,400 registered prostitutes work in the red light district near Juarez Avenue. The women are supposed to have daily inspections and penicillin injections. California in 1969 passed a law which specifies that state residents under eighteen who wish to cross the Mexican border must be accompanied by a parent or guardian, have written consent, or have a passport. A tourist official in Mexico, discussing the possibility of more drastic action to block Americans from crossing the border, said, "It would not deal with the problem. We have a saying, 'You cannot hide the sun with a finger.' "

Cuba was notorious for its many brothels and their "circuses." It had a number of brothels which featured "nymphets," ranging in age from twelve to fifteen, who were from upper-class families and would permit a client to do anything except actual sexual penetration. This restriction was designed to insure that the girls would have an intact hymen for their husbands. The girls were well trained in noncoital methods of bringing their clients to a climax. Many American tourists used to visit Cuba because of its widely publicized prostitution. A number of American women went to Cuba to work as prostitutes; some Cuban prostitutes came to the United States posing as Puerto Ricans. Since the rise to power of Fidel Castro, the Cuban market for prostitutes has declined, and some have gone to Miami and other American communities.

OTHER COUNTRIES

The experiences of other countries may have some relevance for prostitution in the United States, even though each country's institutions are to a great extent culture-bound and linked to other aspects of the social structure.

Just as the British system of narcotics control has been compared with the American system, the British abolitionist approach to prostitution has often been contrasted to ours. England has suffered little of the organized exploitation of prostitutes that has characterized the United States in earlier decades. Prostitution itself is not a criminal offense, but soliciting on the streets was made punishable by fine in the Street Offenses Act of 1959. All arrests are made by uniformed police officers, and the prostitute seldom tries to conceal her identity. A woman unable to pay a fine is allowed up to one week to raise the money.

In England, pimps, madams, racketeers, and other third parties are given heavy fines and long jail sentences. In a brothel raid it is not the prostitute but the landlord who is arrested. Tests for venereal disease are not mandatory because such an examination is regarded as an invasion of civil rights. There is no red light district in London, though Soho has a concentration of "burlesque" houses and a substantial proportion of London's seventeen thousand prostitutes. They solicit from doorways by smiling or, if bolder, asking a passerby if he would like to "see the show" or "come in." Many of the doorways are controlled by pimps. Although many prostitutes used to be relatively free agents who could stake their claim to a street and patrol it, they are now more likely to work out of doorways that are "owned" by exploiters. While this "tidying up" has made prostitution less of a public embarrassment in England, one unanticipated effect has been that exploiters have been given new control over prostitutes.

In spite of obvious differences between the two countries, many Americans would probably be sympathetic to the English attitude toward prostitution. The United States prohibitionist approach is unique in its punishment of both prostitutes and clients. It may be that such laws and the American determination to eliminate prostitution reflect the Puritan heritage and similar qualities that earlier manifested themselves in prohibition.

The experience of communist countries is relevant to any evaluation of the future of prostitution. Beginning with Russia, every communist country has been determinedly anti-sexual and has insisted that its citizens submerge sex into larger shared civic goals and activities. Marxist thinkers have also uniformly regarded prostitution as a form of exploitation to be eliminated. The experience of Russia over almost a half-century ought therefore to provide some clues to what might happen under conditions which optimize a government's ability to put its policies into effect.

No statistics on the incidence of prostitution have ever been published in Russia. Officially, prostitution has been eliminated in the Soviet Union, for the conditions that create and nourish it have, officially, disappeared.[5] These conditions presumably include women's inequality and lack of rights, the considerably lower payment for their labor, intolerable conditions of poverty, and the enslavement of workers.

The fight against prostitution during the first years of Soviet rule was carried out under the banner of a campaign against the conditions that pushed women into prostitution.[6] At the end of 1919 a Commission Against Prostitution was organized under the auspices of the People's Commissariat of Health (*Narodniy Kommissariat Zdravokhranenia*); later an Interdepartmental Commission Against Prostitution was established under the People's Commissariat of Social Security (*Narodniy Kommissariat Sotsialnogo Obespecheniya*). Provincial councils to deal with prostitution were set up on the local level. A Central Council Against Prostitution was established to supervise and coordinate the work of the provincial groups.

In 1924 the Commissariat of Health began to establish a large network of health-and-work clinics for women in Moscow, Leningrad, Gorki, Rostov-on-Don, Kiev, Tbilisi, Baku, Irkutsk, and Tashkent. Special homes and assistance were made available to homeless women. The fight against the keeping of "houses of ill repute" and against complicity in prostitution was intensified.

Prostitution is not and never has been criminally punishable in the USSR. Activities connected with prostitution that are classed as criminal offenses include maintenance of "houses of immoral conduct," procuring, and luring women into prostitution. Nevertheless, the USSR has been and is presently waging a *de facto* struggle against female prostitution. Formerly prostitutes were convicted by administrative trial, outside the law courts, as socially dangerous elements. Since 1957 prostitutes have been tried for leading an "antisocial, parasitic way of life," or receiving support by ways other than work.

The existence of prostitution in the USSR can be gleaned

from occasional reports. One such article comments on a prostitute, who is not described as such. "Once again Toska is living off her admirers." That "big-town chick—don't you think she'll find admirers in the new place where she's going?" The "new place" is Bodaybo in Siberia. The article observes that the miners' wives have asked that "Bodaybo be spared having such Toskas sent there." The name Toska has already become a common noun in Siberia. Exile to Siberia is a last resort and is used only when the peoples' courts have failed to deal effectively with a prostitute.[7] Another article flatly identifies "the Pimenovs—mother and daughter—who had set up a house of ill repute in their own home, and were judged by a public court."[8]

The existence of prostitution has also been confirmed by officials. Thus A. N. Burmistrov, a member of the Moscow Department for the Protection of Public Order, has stated: "A woman drinks and brings men she hardly knows home with her for the night. Finally her dissipated way of life begins to attract the attention of the police. It is discovered that her growing daughter sleeps (and sometimes does not sleep!) in the same room where the drinking and other forms of amusement take place. The years pass, and we learn that the girl who has grown up under these conditions has been arrested in the hotel room of a man whom she had just met on the street. Or she was summoned to the police department because of the neighbors' complaints about her dissolute way of life."[9]

Russia, even today, appears to have procurers and pimps. One "king of the underworld" in Riga recently said to a potential client, "I can introduce you to an enchanting blonde. You will spend a splendid evening with her. I get three rubles for fixing it up."

Soviet optimism about eliminating prostitution was shared by the Communist government of Hungary. In 1949 some of the country's key officials predicted that they would wipe out prostitution within a year. Licensed houses were closed by government edict, but prostitution continued to thrive in secret brothels and even in state-run hostels. Some prostitutes were removed from the streets for rehabilitation, but many of them created "health problems" in the shops and factories where they were forced to work against their will. Hungarian prostitutes have ignored the Budapest newspaper *Nexszava's* confident announcement in 1949 that prostitution would soon end: "After all, prostitution belongs only to the social structure of capitalism. It cannot exist under socialism, where the evils of capitalism have been eliminated." Prostitution continues to flourish in Hungary because most prostitutes are able to demonstrate that they engage in other work.

Some communist countries unofficially permit prostitution but try to make it less visible to foreigners. In Warsaw, for example, prostitutes have special facilities in the major hotels, except for those hotels frequented by foreigners.[10]

XI. THE FUTURE

𝒫rostitution in America or any other country cannot be considered as an isolated social phenomenon, for it reflects the economic and social structure as well as the influence of the family, religion, and many other factors. Most of all, it reflects larger trends in male-female relationships. Although a number of forces are at work that could bring about the possibility of an increase in prostitution, some contrary trends could diminish its practice considerably.

CHANGING ATTITUDES

Curiously enough, among the elements contributing to a possible increase in prostitution in America is the nation's extended involvement in Southeast Asia. Servicemen overseas on war duty have traditionally been good customers for prostitution, and the war in Vietnam has exposed many American men to contact with prostitutes. The great increase in nonmilitary travel abroad is providing other men with opportunities for meeting foreign prostitutes. For some men, our culture's libidinization and voyeurism may encourage and help to trigger latent interests in prostitution. In this connection, the prostitute's high visibility in the mass media serves as a reminder of her availability.

Another trend working toward a possible increase in prostitution is the development of a number of commercially sponsored though technically private sex clubs, which have been organized for purposes of participatory sex exhibitions, mate-swapping, and "swinging" generally. The existence of a loosely organized network of such clubs could lend itself to exploitation by persons interested in extending them into prostitution centers. In the same vein, the "singles weekend" represents not only a socially sanctioned situation in which to meet a potential mate but also provides an opportunity for sexual access which implicitly recognizes that the female is as interested as the male in such access. It is not altogether impossible that the continual expansion of similar activities, combined with the increase in openness about female sexuality, will lead to a heretofore nonexistent demand from women for the services of male prostitutes.

As a result of improved contraception techniques and the liberalization of attitudes, America now has potentially more sexually active women than ever before. This changed pattern of female sexuality could have many consequences, one of which might be an increase in the number of women who are willing to work as prostitutes on a full or part-time basis.

The availability of such women, and our current enthusiasm for "touch and feel" psychotherapies in which nudity and even sexual acting-out can be part of treatment, may lead to social acceptance of therapists who are paid to engage in various kinds of sexual activity with patients. For decades there have been rumors about psychotherapists who engage in sexual relations with patients. A number of therapists have voiced their own sex fantasies to patients, others have masturbated patients, and there appears to be a greater willingness today in some quarters for a patient to accept a therapist as an active sexual partner.

Some Swedish physicians have urged that prostitutes be available by prescription for those persons requiring such help as part of their treatment. Sweden has also witnessed the beginning of a "sex samaritan" movement, which encourages women to help troubled men by offering themselves as sex therapists on a voluntary basis. Some impetus toward a similar goal in the United States was provided by William H. Masters and Virginia Johnson, whose Reproductive Biology Research Foundation in St. Louis provided thirteen unpaid female "partner surrogates" for forty-one single men being treated for sexual inadequacies. The report of this treatment occasioned some criticism, but Dr. Masters, arguing that the men were "social cripples," asked, "Does society want them treated? If they are not treated, it is discrimination of one segment of society over another."[1]

On the other side of the ledger, one of the forces working to diminish prostitution is the development of major programs to treat narcotic addicts in such states as New York, California, and Illinois. Because many women originally enter prostitution in order to get money for narcotics, any decline in the number of female narcotics users would be likely to lead to a drop in the incidence of those seeking money by prostitution. Indeed, it is said that the number of prostitutes might be reduced by as much as one-third to one-half if there were a sharp decline in the number of women addicts. Comparative success in treating addicts with drugs like methadone and cyclazocine, which block the effect of heroin, may further cut down the incidence of addiction. Therapeutic communities of former addicts, such as Synanon and Daytop Village, have been widely publicized. A variety of new approaches to treatment is being investigated in many parts of the country.

Massive and planned social change of the kind originally contemplated in the anti-poverty program may also have profound consequences in reducing the number of women who turn to prostitution as a means of livelihood. Many Negro and Puerto Rican women are now being helped toward acquiring work skills that, it is hoped, will make prostitution seem not merely an unattractive but an unnecessary alternative. As women in such minority groups utilize new opportunities and educational facilities, and in the process develop a strong sense of group identity and pride, many may come to see prostitution as an expression of the debasement of their group and reject it as an occupation.

Working against a future increase in prostitution is the fact that the nature of marriage has changed in the last several decades, and there is now greater acceptance of the notion that a wife should be able to satisfy her husband's sexual needs. If she cannot do so, the couple is expected to adjust or adapt to the situation. A vast literature has developed to guide, instruct, and edify spouses on techniques that will help them to become more desirable and effective sexual partners. Whatever the quality of this literature, the implication behind it is that an intelligent couple can, and indeed ought to, provide lasting sexual satisfaction for each other. If wives remain sexually provocative to their husbands, there should, logically, be something of an accompanying decline in prostitution.

A related change which could have an effect on attitudes toward prostitution is the decreasing gap between tender and sensual love. In an America where advanced contraceptive methods are readily available and where sex has become a much less solemn and foreboding activity than it once was, a man can now more readily accept his wife as a person with whom he can experience sex for recreation as well as procreation. In the past, many men felt that sex activity conducted in a relatively lighthearted manner was not appropriate for their wives, who were presumably reserved for earnest and significant encounters. But husbands and wives are more likely now to accept the views that sexual relationships with a spouse can cover a wide range of emotions and still be meaningful. As such attitudes become more prevalent, some functions previously served by prostitution may well decline.[2] There will doubtless still be prostitution catering to highly exotic sexual practices, such as extreme fetishism or sado-masochism, but this is an appeal to a relatively small group of clients.

American attitudes toward interracial sex and marriage are now more accepting—another fact which may work against prostitution. Until recently, prostitution had been the major source of interracial sex.[3] In the last few years relations with minority-group members, including sexual activity, have become more acceptable to many whites. For some men, relations with minority-group women could replace the forbidden—and therefore all the more enticing—interracial sex provided by prostitution.

Enforcement of anti-prostitution laws is not likely to be relaxed in the face of the tremendous publicity currently being given to the "sexual revolution" or "the new morality." Mass media have been announcing the existence of this new "promiscuity" so enthusiastically that many people are undoubtedly ready to believe that the United States is no less than a continuing saturnalia. Many citizens may feel that it is important to maintain anti-prostitution laws as a defense against latent impulses toward free sexual expression. Although operating on an unconscious level, such considerations could be important in diminishing the extent of prostitution.

Prostitution will probably become less popular, too, as basic concepts of mental health become accepted by the general public. In fact, if an honest approach to the significance of the sexual aspects of human behavior were the rule, prostitution might all but vanish. The new "situation ethics," which has attracted so many young people, stresses that sex should not be used exploitatively; and wider acceptance of this view could not but help to downgrade prostitution.

SOME VIEWPOINTS

To date the movement to legalize prostitution has not generated anything like major support or momentum. Although the League for Sexual Freedom and similar groups have actively sought to eliminate laws against prostitution, they have not achieved much success.

A new element in the discussion of prostitution has been provided by the Women's Liberation Movement, some of whose theoreticians have recently echoed a traditional argument of prostitutes in hailing the prostitute for her "honesty." Ti-Grace Atkinson, a Women's Lib leader, has concluded that "prostitutes are the only honest women because they charge for their services, rather than submitting to a marriage contract which forces them to work for life without pay."[4] Miss Atkinson has urged that laws against prostitution be repealed.

It is, however, unlikely that American society will repeal its laws against prostitution, at least in the immediate future. So long as sexual intercourse is invested with emotional meanings, it will be difficult for Americans to regard the sale of sexual access as just another service. The purveyors of the service will continue to be regarded with ambivalence and suspicion, and their work will never be considered merely a routine job.

One way of approaching prostitution would be to examine those cultures that do not have it in order to see what social conditions seem to be connected with its absence. The Tikopia, for example, are a society without prostitution.[5] Before marriage male and female are almost completely promiscuous, but sexual relations after marriage are limited to partners. Divorce is relatively easily achieved. This relative freedom in the relations between the sexes seemingly makes prostitution unnecessary. The United States is probably several generations removed from such freedom as the Tikopia enjoy, even if American attitudes appear to be liberalizing.

Moreover, the Tikopia way of life may simply not be valid for an industrial and highly urbanized society. For no modern industrial society has been able to destroy all vestiges of prostitution. Even the communist countries have not been successful in eliminating it. If they cannot do so, with their greater machinery for suppressing behavior they deem undesirable, the United States is hardly likely to do better.

This being the case, the question then arises, if there will always be prostitutes and clients, why shouldn't civilized people accept it? But a major issue about prostitution is whether it serves a true social function, and whether fulfillment of this function makes it impossible for prostitutes to achieve any reasonable amount of human happiness. It could be argued, for example, that slavery was functional in the United States before the Civil War; yet however functional it might have been, it clearly violated the slaves' humanity. Similarly, the American dream of making equality meaningful for all would clearly seem to be violated by segregating a group of women whose primary work is meeting the sexual needs of men on an anonymous cash basis. Respect for human beings and for the ideal of giving every person an opportunity to achieve, in John Dewey's phrase, the greatest quality as well as quantity of experience, is clearly inconsistent with condoning prostitution.

It seems to be impossible for women prostitutes to operate in other than exploitative situations—without, that is, pimps and others who derive profit from them. Such exploiters, and the association of prostitution with a variety of different crimes, further contributes to the undesirability of prostitution as a career. But perhaps the least desirable feature of prostitution as a vocation is that the prostitute becomes less valued as she grows older. In most other occupations a worker acquires experience which is increasingly important to the employer. As the prostitute grows older, she becomes less desirable to clients and her earning power declines rather than increases.

Popular opposition to prostitution rests partly on the fact that there seems to be no way of effectively restricting prostitution to one section of a community, as Abraham Flexner observed more than a half-century ago.[6] Some proponents of legalized prostitution had hoped that the Eros Center in Hamburg, which opened in 1967, would provide a model segregated prostitution district and inspire a similar enterprise in this country. But the 136 women in Eros Center have not reduced the more than 4,700 known prostitutes in Hamburg. Nor has Eros Center reduced the violence and crime in the St. Pauli area of the city; in fact, both have increased since 1967. Prostitution around the Reeperbahn and Herbert Strasse in Hamburg has also increased and if anything become more overt. Most of the women who work in Eros Center have a "protector," and many have a pimp as well. Although many other cities in West Germany have tried to restrict prostitution to specific areas, none has succeeded in doing so. About three-fourths of the prostitutes in West Germany have a pimp or other third party who profits from their work. There is also a heavy concentration of procurers from other countries in West Germany.[7]

CAN POLICY CHANGE?

One reason for the low priority given prostitution as a social problem is a feeling that attitudes toward it are difficult and perhaps finally impossible to change. Capital punishment provides an example of another field in which public attitudes were once hardened but in which a shift has taken place. New York State eliminated capital punishment in 1965 mainly because a few people conducted a systematic campaign to change attitudes. The year 1968 was the first on record in which no executions occurred in the United States. If attitudes toward capital punishment can change so radically, beliefs about prostitution may also be modified. One reason for the shift in attitudes toward capital punishment is the United Nations' recommendation of its abolition. Since the United Nations has implicitly rebuked the United States for being the only country now punishing prostitutes, a major shift in American views could occur if the issue of prostitution became important to opinion leaders. A closer analogy is that of abortion, another issue involving sexual behavior on which a major change in public attitudes has occurred.

A number of states have now adopted liberal abortion laws. New York, where the opposition to reform was most intense, adopted the most liberal law in the country in 1970.

The hopelessness that surrounds much discussion of prostitution and what to do about it used to characterize official and unofficial attitudes toward drug addiction as recently as ten years ago.[8] But in the last decade public and governmental opinion has become aroused, many new programs have been developed, and a wide range of innovative ideas is now being explored. New York State, with more than half the country's drug addicts, did not have a program or even one bed available for them in 1959; today it has thousands of beds and an annual budget of more than $100 million for treatment and rehabilitation. An aroused public opinion, such as occurred in the case of addiction after a half-century of inertia, may suggest a model for a similar breakthrough in prostitution.

As reformers in the field of addiction have had to accept interim goals while public opinion evolves, it may be possible to take some intermediate steps toward an ultimately more humane and civilized approach to prostitution. The model of addiction suggests what could be a useful contemporary viewpoint toward prostitution. Modern approaches to the drug problem stress a lack of sympathy for addiction and drug abuse but a sympathetic attitude toward the addict, offering him every assistance. Educational programs seek to deter future drug users, and control procedures attempt to make illicit drugs unavailable. At the same time the addict is regarded as a person with an illness who should get every kind of help and support in coping with it.

A similarly enlightened attitude toward prostitution would include disapproval for the practice but every possible assistance to the women who work in it. A realistic goal would be to maximize opportunities for those women who wish to leave prostitution. It would be unrealistic to force all women who are identified as prostitutes to submit to treatment. Treatment might be mandatory for prostitutes who have venereal disease or are juveniles. Other women would enter treatment voluntarily. The great range of personality and background found among prostitutes makes it unlikely that any one program would meet the needs of all. The problem calls for extensive experimentation with different approaches to rehabilitation to determine the kinds of women who respond best to each approach. A panel composed of specialists in resocialization might determine the most constructive approach to each case. An administrative procedure for handling such cases outside the usual system of criminal justice is a possibility that ought to be explored.

The best time to try to cope with incipient prostitution is doubtless around the time of adolescence. Girls who experience a diffusion of identity or a negative identity, and who have problems with intimacy, may, as we have seen, move into prostitution as a way of coping with events or internal psychological pressures. An emotionally disturbed promiscuous adolescent, young female delinquent, or unwed mother often appears to be drifting toward prostitution. Programs designed to identify and help such persons are likely to be successful if introduced before the girl has become entrenched in a career of prostitution. Working with girls who exhibit such characteristics could prove far more rewarding than have previous attempts to rehabilitate older prostitutes. Such girls might receive an intensive period of preparation for treatment and rehabilitation.

A thoughtful rehabilitation program is needed because vocational training by itself is unlikely to enable a former prostitute to hold a job. Milieu therapy, perhaps in a halfway-house situation, may be one way of effecting a radical change in personality and outlook. The discipline and routine of an ordinary job may be overwhelming for a prostitute who has a low threshold of frustration and has not received special preparation.

In the rehabilitation of narcotics addicts one particularly effective approach is to employ former addicts as therapeutic personnel. Many have developed vocations as dedicated therapists and, at the same time, contributed toward the opening of new career possibilities for other addicts. They have the respect of addicts because there can be no doubt that they know the score and have firsthand experience of what they are talking about. Similarly, former prostitutes might make excellent therapists in the rehabilitation of women "in the life." Such an approach might generate as much public support as Daytop and Synanon were able to develop for drug addicts. Indeed, some of the female members of those same institutions who have been prostitutes might serve as a beginning cadre.

Resocialization of prostitutes in various European countries has had a success rate that in recent years has ranged from 33 to 75 per cent. France, Spain, and Italy have successfully used fairly large halfway houses, and England has had a favorable experience with smaller facilities. Most countries have reported that prostitutes under twenty-two and over twenty-eight are most likely to respond to retraining and re-education. The experiences of those European countries that have mounted effective programs to reintegrate the prostitute into the community can provide valuable clues.

The most effective of these European resocialization programs have helped the former prostitute to enter a new "friendly circle" to replace the group from which she had been withdrawn. Both residential and nonresidential treatment has been successful. Every effort is made to train the woman for work which involves graded increases in responsibility. Women who have experienced years of submission need to strengthen their personalities by identification with a shared responsibility. Resocialization centers avoid placing the women in traditional jobs for "reclaimed women," such as laundry and domestic work.

War experience has proved that private and government agencies can work together effectively to implement sound rehabilitation programs. Creative experimentation in the rehabilitation of prostitutes is long overdue. Such programs need to be established and carefully evaluated. Some approaches will undoubtedly fail, others will have only partial success. But we must begin to provide facilities on almost a compensatory basis, recognizing that we have neglected prostitution since World War II. Such programs would explore the feasibility of retraining pimps as well as prostitutes. The relationship of prostitute to pimp makes it important for the latter to be included in any efforts at resocialization.

In recent years there has been a vigorous controversy over the nature and direction of instruction in family-life education and sex education. Although the subject is still controversial and is not fully accepted in some quarters, there is reason to believe that it will become more firmly established in the near future. As it reaches more young people, such instruction should help the next generation to be more realistic and honest about prostitution. Perhaps long before then, enlightened approaches to the problem of prostitution will ease the heavy social, criminal, and judicial burden which it has long placed on so many American communities.

NOTES

CHAPTER I : VIEWS OF PROSTITUTION

1. T. W. Galloway, *Sex and Social Health*, New York: American Social Health Association, 1924.
2. Community Council of Greater New York, Committee on Delinquency and Correction, *Report on the Examination of Laws, Court and Police Procedures Dealing with Prostitution*, New York: The Council, 1958.
3. Law enforcement agencies may record a prostitution arrest as a violation of laws regulating prostitution, vagrancy, loitering, and similar activities. It is therefore possible only to approximate the number of arrests for the complex of activities considered under prostitution. The best source for trend data is the series of annual volumes of *Uniform Crime Reports for the United States*, published by the Federal Bureau of Investigation. The Bureau has not itself made any estimates of the number of prostitutes.
4. A. C. Kinsey, W. R. Pomeroy, and C. E. Martin, *Sexual Behavior in the Human Male*, Philadelphia: W. B. Saunders, 1948, 595–604.
5. These studies have been summarized annually by the Association, which in 1960 changed its name from the American Social Hygiene Association. For the sake of consistency, the modern term is used even during the period when it did not apply.
6. C. Winick, "Atonie: The Unemployed and Marginal Worker," in G.

Fisk, ed., *The Frontiers of Management Psychology*, New York: Harper and Row, 1964, 269–286.

7. B. Reitman, *The Second Oldest Profession*, New York: Vanguard, 1936.

8. K. Davis, "Prostitution," in R. K. Merton and R. A. Nisbet, eds., *Contemporary Social Problems*, New York: Harcourt, Brace, 1961, 262–288.

9. G. M. Haber, "Prostitution as an Occupation in the United States," unpublished manuscript, 1960.

10. E. F. Frazier, *The Negro Family in the United States*, Chicago: University of Chicago Press, 1939.

11. M. Strunk, *Public Opinion, 1935–1946* (under the editorial direction of H. Cantril), Princeton: Princeton University Press, 1951.

12. A. Flexner, *Prostitution in Europe*, New York: Century, 1914.

13. R. H. Everett, "Can We Regulate Prostitution?," *Federal Probation*, 1947, 11, 39–42.

14. United Nations Department of Economic and Social Affairs, *Study on Traffic in Persons and Prostitution*, New York: International Documents Service, Columbia University Press, 1959.

15. H. Benjamin, "Prostitution," in A. Ellis and A. Arbanel, eds., *Encyclopedia of Sexual Behavior*, New York: Hawthorn Books, 1961, 869–882; H. Benjamin and A. Ellis, "An Objective Examination of Prostitution," *International Journal of Sexology*, 1954, 8, 100–105.

16. E. R. A. Seligman, *The Social Evil, with Specific Reference to Conditions in the City of New York*, 2nd ed., New York: Putnam, 1912.

17. J. M. Murtagh and S. C. Harris, *Cast the First Stone*, New York: McGraw-Hill, 1957.

18. L. D. Morrison, "Prostitution and the Police," *Journal of Social Hygiene*, 1951, 37, 365–372.

19. American Medical Association, Report of Reference Committee on Hygiene and Public Health, *Journal of the American Medical Association*, December 22, 1945, 29, 1201–1202; M. Glasgow, "Prostitution: An Analysis," *Medical Woman's Journal*, 1943, 50, 35–40.

20. T. C. Esselstyn, "Prostitution in the United States," *Annals of the American Academy of Political and Social Science*, 1968, 376, 123–135.

21. M. Ploscowe, *Sex and the Law*, New York: Prentice-Hall, 1951; Kinsey, *et al.*, *Sexual Behavior in the Human Male;* A. C. Kinsey, W. B. Pomeroy, C. E. Martin, and P. H. Gebhard, *Sexual Behavior in the Human Female*, Philadelphia: W. B. Saunders, 1953; W. H. Masters and V. E. Johnson, *Human Sexual Response*, Boston: Little, Brown, 1966.

22. C. Winick, "Celebrities' Errancy as a Subject for Journalism," *Gazette*, 1962, 7, 329–334.

23. C. Cunnington, *Women*, London: Burke, 1950.
24. W. Morehouse, "Moments of Magic on Broadway," *New York Times Magazine*, September 17, 1961, 32.
25. R. Lubove, "The Progressive and the Prostitute," *Historian*, 1962, 24, 308–330.
26. C. Winick, "Teenagers, Satire, and *Mad*," *Merrill-Palmer Quarterly*, 1962, 8, 183–203; Winick, "Thoughts and Feelings of the General Population as Expressed in Free-Association Typing," *American Imago*, 1962, 19, 67–84; O. Klapp, *Heroes, Villains, and Fools*, New York: Prentice-Hall, 1962, 150–152.
27. A. L. Kadis and C. Winick, "The Role of the Deviant in the Therapy Group," *International Journal of Social Psychiatry*, 1960, 6, 277–287.
28. C. Winick, "A Content Analysis of Orally Communicated Jokes," *American Imago*, 1963, 20, 271–291; G. Legman, *Rationale of the Dirty Joke*, New York: Grove Press, 1968.
29. J. Laver, *Manners and Morals in the Age of Optimism, 1848–1914*, New York: Harper and Row, 1966, 272.

CHAPTER II : THE PROSTITUTE

1. O. Brim, "Personality as Role Learning, "in I. Iscoe and H. W. Stevenson, eds., *Personality Development in Children*, Austin: University of Texas Press, 1960; H. S. Becker and J. Carper, "The Elements of Identification with an Occupation," *American Sociological Review*, 1956, 21, 341–348; M. Samit, "Measuring a City's PQ," *Markets of America*, 1958, 22, 155–156; H. Wilensky, "Orderly Careers and Social Participation," *American Sociological Review*, 1961, 26, 525–526.
2. W. Reckless, "A Sociologist Looks at Prostitution," *Federal Probation*, 1943, 7, 12–16.
3. N. Algren, *A Walk on the Wild Side*, New York: Farrar, Straus, 1956.
4. R. Mason, *The World of Suzie Wong*, New York: Signet, 1957.
5. C. Isherwood, *The Berlin Stories*, New York: James Laughlin, 1946; S. Kale, *The Fire Escape*, New York: Doubleday, 1960.
6. J. Jones, *From Here to Eternity*, New York: Scribner, 1951.
7. J. D. Ball and G. H. Thomas, "A Sociological, Neurological, Serological and Psychiatric Study of a Group of Prostitutes," *American Journal of Insanity*, 1918, 74, 647–666.
8. League of Nations, Advisory Committee on Social Questions, *Prostitutes: Their Early Lives*, New York: United Nations, Sales Section, 1938, "Enquiry into Measures for Rehabilitation of Adult Prostitutes," Part 1; H. Hironimous, "Survey of 100 May Act Violators," *Federal Probation*, 1943, 7, 31–34.
9. A. T. Bingham, "Determinants of Sex Delinquency Among Adolescent Girls," *Journal of Criminal Law and Criminology*, 1923, 13, 494–586;

cf. note 8, *supra;* F. Q. Holsopple, *Social Non-Conformity in 420 Delinquent Girls,* Philadelphia: United States Interdepartmental Social Hygiene Board, 1919; P. A. Mertz, "Mental Deficiency in Prostitutes," *Journal of the American Medical Association,* May 31, 1919, 72, 1597–1599; B. Thompson, *Sister of the Road: The Autobiography of Box-Car Bertha,* New York: Macaulay, 1937.

10. K. B. Davis, "A Study of Prostitutes," in G. J. Kneeland, *Commercialized Prostitution in New York City,* New York: Century, 1913, 163–228; C. Aronovici, *Unmarried Girls with Sex Experience,* Philadelphia: Bureau for Social Research of the Serbert Institute, 1915.

11. S. Glueck and E. T. Glueck, *Five Hundred Delinquent Women,* New York: Alfred A. Knopf, 1934.

12. Cf. note 10, *supra;* P. Durban, "Facteurs Sociaux et Atmosphère Aétiologique de la Prostitution," *L'Hygiène Mentale* (Supplément de L'Encéphale), 1951, 40, 13–27, 48–54; M. Bergeron, A. Grasset, and B. Roger, "Deux Ans de Fonctionnement d'un Centre d'Observation pour Vagabonds Juvéniles," *Année Med-psychologique,* 1950, 108, 612–615; M. Schachter and S. Cotte, "Etude de la Prostitution Juvénile à la Lumière du Test de Rorschach," *Archives Internationales de Neurologie,* 1951, 70, 4–18; S. Krishnaswamy, "A Study of the Responses of Sex-Delinquents, Prostitutes and Non-Delinquent Girls," *International Journal of Sexology,* 1954, 8, 97–99.

13. S. Shoham and G. Rahav, "Social Stigma and Prostitution," *Annales Internationales de Criminologie,* 1967, 6, 470–513.

14. C. Winick, "The Drug Addict and His Treatment," in H. Toch, ed., *Legal and Criminal Psychology,* New York: Holt, Rinehart, and Winston, 1961, 357–380.

15. J. K. Skipper, Jr., and C. H. McCaghy, "Stripteasers: The Anatomy and Career Contingencies of a Deviant Occupation," paper presented to the 1969 annual meeting, American Sociological Association.

16. P. H. Gebhard, W. B. Pomeroy, C. E. Martin, and C. V. Christenson, *Pregnancy, Birth, and Abortion,* New York: Harper, 1958, 187–188.

17. W. W. Sanger, *History of Prostitution,* New York: Harper, 1958.

18. D. Maurer, "Prostitutes and Criminal Argots," *American Journal of Sociology,* 1939, 44, 546–550.

19. C. Pollock, *Harvest of My Years,* Indianapolis: Bobbs-Merrill, 1943, 59–60.

20. D. J. Winslow, "The Occupational Superstitions of Negro Prostitutes in an Upstate New York City," *New York Folklore Quarterly,* 1968, 24, 294–301.

21. Flexner, *Prostitution in Europe;* N. R. Jackman, R. O'Toole, and G. Geis, "Self-Image of the Prostitute," *Sociological Quarterly,* 1963, 4, 150–161.

22. C. Winick, "Narcotic Addiction and Its Treatment," *Law and Contemporary Problems*, 1957, 22, 9–33.
23. A. Loos, *Gentlemen Prefer Blondes*, London, Brentano, 1926; S. Lewis, *Elmer Gantry*, New York: Harcourt, Brace, 1927.
24. W. Faulkner, *Sanctuary*, New York: Random House, 1931.
25. S. Cousins, *To Beg I Am Ashamed*, New York: Vanguard, 1938.
26. F. Wertham, *Seduction of the Innocent*, New York: Rinehart, 1954, 54–74, 186–187.
27. J. C. Oates, *Them*, New York: Vanguard, 1969.
28. V. Nabokov, *Lolita*, New York: Putnam, 1958.
29. H. Deutsch, *The Psychology of Women*, New York: Grune and Stratton, 1944, I, 255–264.
30. Cf. note 7, *supra*.
31. Holsopple, *Social Non-Conformity in 420 Delinquent Girls*.
32. Hironimous, "Survey of 100 May Act Violators."
33. A. S. Maerov, "Prostitution: A Survey," *Psychiatric Quarterly*, 1965, 39, 675–701.
34. H. Ellis, *Studies in the Psychology of Sex*, Philadelphia: F. A. Davis, 1911, VI, 118–120.
35. M. Sherif and H. Cantril, *The Psychology of Ego-Involvements*, New York: John Wiley, 1947, 380–388.
36. L. Eidelberg, *The Dark Urge*, New York: Pyramid Books, 1961; K. Abraham, "Hysterical Dream-States," in *Selected Papers of Karl Abraham*, London, Hogarth Press and The Institute of Psychoanalysis, 1948, 90–124.
37. W. Pomeroy, "Some Aspects of Prostitution," *Journal of Sex Research*, 1965, 1, 177–187.
38. Aronovici, *Unmarried Girls with Sex Experience;* Holsopple, *Social Non-Conformity in 420 Delinquent Girls;* T. Kemp, *Prostitution: An Investigation of Its Causes, Especially with Regard to Hereditary Factors*, Copenhagen: Levin and Munksgaard, 1936; Hironimous, "Survey of 100 May Act Violators."
39. K. Niemineva, "A Study of Factors Influencing Fertility of Prostitutes," *International Journal of Sexology*, 1952, 6, 77–83.
40. Gebhard, *et al.*, *Pregnancy, Birth, and Abortion*.
41. G. Legman, personal communication, 1965.
42. League of Nations, *Prostitutes: Their Early Lives;* Hironimous, "Survey of 100 May Act Violators."
43. K. Menninger, *Love Against Hate*, New York: Harcourt, Brace, 1942, 290–291.
44. L. Fishman, "A Pathography of Auguste Comte," *Psychoanalytic Review*, 1950, 37, 66–70.
45. Ball and Thomas, "A Sociological, Neurological, Serological and Psychiatric Study of a Group of Prostitutes"; T. Kemp, *Physical*

and Psychological Causes of Prostitution and the Means of Com-
bating Them, Geneva: League of Nations Advisory Committee on
Social Questions, Part IV, Official No. C. 26, 1943; A. Deutsch, "The
Prostitution Racket Is Back," *American Mercury*, September 1946,
63, 270–277; W. Keane, *The Subject People Don't Talk About*, New
York: American Social Health Association, 1958.

46. W. Lentino, "Medical Evaluation of a System of Legalized Prostitution," *Journal of the American Medical Association*, May 7, 1955, 158,
20–23; "Is Prostitution Still a Significant Health Problem?," *Medical Aspects of Human Sexuality*, October 1968, 2, 39–46.

47. Dr. William J. Brown, Chief of the Venereal Disease Branch of the
Communicable Disease Center, Public Health Service, provided
information on this case in a personal communication, April 1, 1970.

48. R. Y. Thornton, "You're in the Fight Against Prostitution," *Journal
of Social Hygiene*, 1954, 40, 111–116.

49. U.S. Public Health Service, *Background Information on the Status
of Syphilis and Other Trepanematoses*, Washington: The Service,
1962.

50. Study conducted by the New York City Health Department, 1968.

51. O. W., *No Bed of Roses: The Diary of a Lost Soul*, New York: Macaulay, 1930; *God Have Mercy on Me!*, New York: Macaulay, 1931.

52. G. F. Melody, "Chronic Pelvic Congestion in Prostitutes," *Medical
Aspects of Human Sexuality*, November 1969, 3, 103–104.

53. Economic Opportunity Council of San Francisco, *Drugs in the
Tenderloin*, San Francisco: The Council, 1967, 17.

54. C. Winick, "Maturing out of Narcotic Addiction," *United Nations
Bulletin on Narcotics*, 1962, 14, 1–7; "The Life Cycle of the Narcotic
Addict and of Addiction," *United Nations Bulletin on Narcotics*,
1964, 16, 1–11.

55. Ball and Thomas, "A Sociological, Neurological, Serological and
Psychiatric Study of a Group of Prostitutes"; H. Greenwald, *The
Call Girl: A Social and Psychoanalytic Study*, New York: Bal-
lantine, 1958.

56. H. S. Additon, *Work Among the Delinquent Women and Girls*,
Philadelphia: The American Academy of Political and Social Science, 1918; W. C. Reckless, *The Crime Problem*, New York: Apple-
ton-Century-Crofts, 1961, 118, 653.

57. I. L. Reiss, *Premarital Sexual Standards in America*, Glencoe: Free
Press, 1960.

58. Federal Security Agency Social Protection Division, *Techniques of
Law Enforcement in the Use of Police Women, with Special Reference to Social Protection*, Washington: Government Printing Office,
1945; R. J. Milliken, "The Role of the Police Woman's Bureau in
Combating Prostitution," *Federal Probation*, 1943, 7, 20–22.

59. M. Van Waters, "Study and Treatment of Persons Charged with Prostitution," *Federal Probation*, 1943, 7, 27–30.
60. M. F. Rappaport, "Toward a New Way of Life," *Journal of Social Hygiene*, 1945, 31, 590–599; "After 10 Years," *Journal of Social Hygiene*, 1953, 39, 209–215.
61. R. A. Koch, "The San Francisco Separate Women's Court," *Journal of Social Hygiene*, 1944, 30, 288–295.
62. P. W. Tappan, *Delinquent Girls in Court*, New York: Columbia University Press, 1947; P. M. Horn, "We Don't Call Them Criminals," *Saturday Evening Post*, June 24, 1961, 234, 17–19, 79–81.
63. M. Marsh, *Prostitutes in New York City: Their Apprehension, Trial, and Treatment*, New York: Welfare Council of New York, 1941.
64. C. H. Rolph (pseud.), ed., *Women of the Streets: A Sociological Study of the Common Prostitute*, edited for and on behalf of the British Social Biology Council, London: Secker & Warburg, 1955.
65. G. B. Barker, "The Problem of the Young Offender in a Psychiatric Hospital," unpublished manuscript, 1963.
66. G. Mortensson and E. Vestergaard, "Efterundersogelse af 300 Unge Prostituerede Kvinder," *Nordisk Tidsskkrift for Kriminalvidenskab*, 1965, 53, 246–258; F. Bernocchi, "Risultati di un Esperienza di Recupero della Prostituta," *Igiene Mentale*, 1963, 7, 105–178.
67. M. Schachter, "Prostitution as a 'Gratuitous Act': A Contribution to the Psychopathology of Rebellious Youth," *Archivos de Criminologia, Neuropsiquiatria y Disciplinas Conexas*, 1961, 9/34, 294–304; E. H. Erikson, "The Problem of Ego Identity," *Journal of the American Psychoanalytic Association*, 1965, 4, 56–121.
68. W. Healy, A. F. Bronner, and A. M. Bowers, *Structure and Meaning of Psychoanalysis*, New York: Knopf, 1930, 389; O. Fenichel, "Neurotic Acting Out," *Psychoanalytic Review*, 1945, 32, 197–206; *The Psychoanalytic Theory of Neurosis*, New York: Norton, 1945, 156, 486-487; Maerov, "Prostitution: A Survey."
69. M. Schmideberg, "Some Clinical Implications of the Sense of Bodily Reality," *Journal of the Hillside Hospital*, 1953, 2, 207–212.
70. E. G. Glover, *The Psychopathology of Prostitution*, London: Institute for the Scientific Treatment of Delinquency, 1945; G. Vella and A. Petizio, "Contribute alla Conoscenza del Compartamento della Prostituta," *Quaderni di Criminologia Clinica*, 1960, 2/3, 317–344; S. Deri, "Differential Diagnosis of Delinquents with the Szondi Test," *Journal of Projective Techniques*, 1954, 18, 33–41; E. Fancher, *A Szondi Study of Prostitutes*, unpublished manuscript, 1949; M. H. Hollender, "Prostitution, the Body, and Human Relatedness," *International Journal of Psychoanalysis*, 1964, 42, 404–413.
71. E. R. Geleerd, F. J. Hacker, and D. Rapaport, "Contribution to the Study of Amnesia and Allied Conditions," *Psychoanalytic Quar-*

terly, 1945, 14, 199–220; A. M. Johnson and S. A. Szurek, "The Genesis of Antisocial Acting Out in Children and Adults," *Psychoanalytic Quarterly*, 1952, 21, 323–343.

72. S. Rado, "Fear of Castration in Women," *Psychoanalytic Quarterly*, 1933, 2, 425–475.

73. A. Parry, *Tattoo: Secrets of a Strange Art as Practiced Among the Natives of the United States*, New York: Scribner, 1933; "Tattooing Among Prostitutes and Perverts," *Psychoanalytic Quarterly*, 1934, 3, 476–482.

74. L. Goitein, "The Potential Prostitute," *Journal of Criminal Psychopathology*, 1942, 3, 359–367; G. Barag, "Zum Psychoanalyze der Prostitution," *Imago*, 1937, 23, 330–362; H. H. Hart, "The Meaning of Circumstantiality," *Samiksa*, 1953, 7, 271–284.

75. N. N. Chatterji, "A New Theory of Paranoia," *Samiksa*, 1955, 9, 29–62.

76. A. Katan, "The Role of Displacement in Agoraphobia," *International Journal of Psychoanalysis*, 1951, 32, 41–50.

77. G. Van der Heide, "A Case of Pollakiuria Nervosa," *Psychoanalytic Quarterly*, 1941, 10, 267–283; A. Adler, *The Neurotic Constitution*, New York: Moffat, Yard, 1917.

78. E. Bergler, "Psychopathology of Compulsive Smoking," *Psychiatric Quarterly*, 1946, 20, 297–321.

79. An unpublished report on male prostitution by Edward Sagarin of City College of New York has been very helpful in the preparation of this section.

80. W. M. Butts, "Boy Prostitutes of the Metropolis," *Journal of Clinical Psychopathology*, 1947, 8, 673–691.

81. J. B. Rioux, "Heroin Addiction in a Male Adolescent," *American Journal of Psychotherapy*, 1956, 10, 296–308; D. L. Gerard and C. A. Kornetsky, "A Social and Psychiatric Study of Adolescent Opiate Addicts," *Psychiatric Quarterly*, 1954, 28, 113–125.

82. K. Kaiser and E. Schramm, "Der Homosexuelle Mann als Opfer von Kapitalverbrechen," *Kriminalistik*, 1962, 16, 255–266; P. Weissman, "Structural Considerations in Overt Male Bisexuality," *International Journal of Psychoanalysis*, 1962, 43, 159.

83. H. Call, "Male Prostitution on the West Coast," in H. Benjamin and R. E. L. Masters, *Prostitution and Morality*, New York: Julian Press, 1964, 311–337; D. E. J. MacNamara, "Male Prostitution in American Cities: A Socioeconomic or Pathological Phenomenon?," paper presented to the March 1965 meeting of the American Orthopsychiatric Association.

84. MacNamara, "Male Prostitution in American Cities."

85. R. W. Deisher, V. Eisner, and S. I. Sulzbacher, "The Young Male Prostitute," *Pediatrics*, 1969, 43, 936–941.

86. J. Rechy, *City of Night*, New York: Grove Press, 1963.

87. T. Painter and G. Legman, "Homosexual Prostitution in the United States," unpublished manuscript, 1940.
88. P. Gandy and R. Deisher, "Young Male Prostitutes: The Physician's Role in Social Rehabilitation," *Journal of the American Medical Association*, 1970, 212, 1661–1666.

CHAPTER III : THE MADAM

1. A Kuprin, *Yama*, New York: Bernard Guilbert Guerney, 1922; C. Slade, *Sterile Sun*, New York: Vanguard, 1934; and *Mrs. Party's House*, New York: Vanguard, 1948; M. Mitchell, *Gone with the Wind*, New York: Macmillan, 1936.
2. P. Adler, *A House Is Not a Home*, New York: Rinehart, 1953; B. Davis, *Call House Madam*, San Francisco: Martin Tudordale, 1942.
3. G. Draper, "Strange Campaign of an Ex-Madam," *San Francisco Chronicle*, April 2, 1962, 1, 9.
4. S. Stanford, *Lady of the House*, New York: Putnam, 1968, 168.
5. S. Longstreet, *Sportin' House*, Los Angeles: Sherburne, 1966; *Nell Kimball: Life of an American Madam*, New York: Macmillan, 1970.

CHAPTER IV : THE PIMP

1. Reitman, *The Second Oldest Profession*.
2. H. B. Woolston, *Prostitution in the United States*, New York: Century, 1921.
3. S. Ferenczi, "Zuhälter and Femme Entretenante," in *Final Contributions to the Problems and Methods of Psychoanalysis*, New York: Basic Books, 1955, 217.
4. M. Choisy, *Psychoanalysis of the Prostitute*, New York: Pyramid Books, 1962, 44–53.
5. H. Deutsch, *Psychoanalysis of the Neuroses*, London: Hogarth Press and The Institute of Psychoanalysis, 1951.
6. B. Bosselman, *Self-Destruction: A Study of the Suicidal Impulse*, Springfield, Ill.: Charles C. Thomas, 1958, 44–45.

CHAPTER V : BIT PLAYERS

1. American Medical Association, Resolution on Control of Venereal Diseases, *Journal of the American Medical Association*, June 20, 1942, 119, 656; Editorial: "Examination and Certification of Prostitutes," *Journal of the American Medical Association*, June 9, 1951, 146, 564.
2. Lentino, "Medical Evaluation of a System of Legalized Prostitution."
3. B. Johnson, "Prostitution and Quackery in Relation to Syphilis Control," *Journal of Social Hygiene*, 1940, 26, 6–11.

CHAPTER VI : WAYS OF PLYING THE TRADE

1. Adler, *A House Is Not a Home*.
2. K. Cetynski, *House of Dolls*, New York: Simon and Schuster, 1955.
3. F. Henriques, *Prostitution in Europe and the New World*, London: MacGibbon and Kee, 1963.
4. C. Winick, "The Silent Language of the Classes," unpublished manuscript, 1956.
5. R. S. and H. M. Lynd, *Middletown*, New York: Harcourt, Brace, 1929, 113; *Middletown in Transition*, New York: Harcourt, Brace, 1937, 163.
6. Kuprin, *Yama*.
7. J. Joyce, *Ulysses*, Paris: Shakespeare and Company, 1926.
8. J. Steinbeck, *Cannery Row*, New York: Viking, 1945.
9. P. M. Kinsie, "Commercialized Prostitution," *The Police Chief*, June 1959, 26, 19.
10. From the files of the American Social Health Association.
11. Longstreet, *Sportin' House*, 172.
12. Kneeland, *Commercialized Prostitution in New York City*.
13. Longstreet, *Sportin' House*, 176.
14. H. McGowan, *Big City Madam*, New York: Lancer, 1965, 94–102.
15. S. Harris, "Key Club–Sin Club," *True Confessions*, September 1963, 71, 6–7, 15–16, 71.
16. W. Clarke, "Prostitution and Alcohol," *Journal of Social Hygiene*, 1917, 3, 75–90.
17. P. M. Kinsie, *The Prostitution Racket*, New York: American Social Health Association, 1945.
18. G. Gorer, *Hot Strip Tease*, London: Cresset Press, 1937.
19. Kinsey, *et al.*, *Sexual Behavior in the Human Female*, 660–661.
20. A. Wheelis, *The Seeker*, New York: Random House, 1960.
21. V. McManus, *Not for Love*, New York: Putnam, 1960, 166–180.
22. J. O'Hara, *Butterfield 8*, New York: Harcourt, Brace, 1935.
23. M. Fry, *Sex, Vice and Business*, New York: Ballantine, 1959.
24. J. Stearn, *Sisters of the Night*, New York: Messner, 1956.
25. J. H. Bryan, "Apprenticeships in Prostitution," *Social Problems*, 1965, 12, 287–296.
26. J. H. Bryan, "Occupational Ideologies of Call Girls," *Social Problems*, 1966, 13, 441–449.
27. T. Hirschi, "The Professional Prostitute," *Berkeley Journal of Sociology*, 1962, 7, 33–49.

CHAPTER VII : THE CLIENT

1. Home Office, Scottish Home Department, *Report of the Committee*

on Homosexual Offenses and Prostitution, London: Her Majesty's Stationery Office, 1957.
2. A. C. Kinsey, "Social Level and Sexual Outlet," in R. Bendix and S. N. Lipset, eds., *Class Status and Power*, Glencoe: Free Press, 1953, 300–308.
3. W. F. Snow, "Men's Attitudes Toward Prostitutes," unpublished manuscript, 1925.
4. McManus, *Not for Love*, 169–170.
5. P. H. Gebhard, paper presented to the December 1967 meeting, American Association for the Advancement of Science.
6. M. J. Karpf, "The Effect of Prostitution on Marital Sex Adjustment," *Marriage and Family Living*, 1953, 15, 65–71.
7. E. B. Hitschmann, *Great Men: Psychoanalytic Studies*, New York: International Universities Press, 1956, 212–213.
8. R. Gover, *One Hundred Dollar Misunderstanding*, New York: Grove Press, 1962.
9. L. A. Kirkendall, "Circumstances Associated with Teenage Boys' Use of Prostitution," *Marriage and Family Living*, 1960, 22, 145–149; *Premarital Intercourse and Inter-personal Relationships*, New York: Julian Press, 1961.
10. J. Boswell, *The Letters of James Boswell*, ed., C. B. Tinker, Oxford: Clarendon Press, 1924.
11. W. Ehrmann, *Premarital Dating Behavior*, New York: Henry Holt, 1959.
12. P. Kronhausen and E. Kronhausen, *Sex Histories of American College Men*, New York: Ballantine, 1960.
13. Davis, "Prostitution."
14. A. Ellis, "Why Married Men Visit Prostitutes," *Sexology*, 1959, 25, 344–347.
15. T. C. N. Gibbens and M. Silberman, "The Clients of Prostitutes," *British Journal of Venereal Disease*, 1960, 36, 113–117.
16. K. Menninger, "Observations of a Psychiatrist in a Dermatology Clinic," *Bulletin of the Menninger Clinic*, 1942, 11, 141 147.
17. C. Winick, "The Role of Behavioral Science in Venereal Disease Programs," *Medical Digest* (Bombay), 1963, 31, 111–122.
18. C. Winick, "Prostitutes' Clients' Perception of the Prostitutes and of Themselves," *International Journal of Social Psychiatry*, 1962, 8, 289–297.
19. R. M. Loewenstein, "A Contribution to the Psychoanalytic Theory of Masochism," *Journal of the American Psychoanalytic Association*, 1957, 5, 197–234.
20. Winick, "A Content Analysis of Orally Communicated Jokes."
21. S. Freud, "Notes upon a Case of Obsessional Neurosis," *The Standard Edition of the Complete Psychological Works of Sigmund*

Freud, X, London: Hogarth Press, 1955; "On the Universal Tendency to Debasement in the Sphere of Love," *Standard Edition,* XI, 177–190; "A Special Type of Object Choice Made by Men," *Standard Edition,* XI, 163–175; E. Jones, "Psychosexual Impotence and Anaesthesia," in *Papers on Psychoanalysis,* London: Bailliere, Tindall, and Cox, 1938, 392–406; B. Karpman, "Passive Parasitic Psychopathy," *Psychoanalytic Review,* 1947, 34, 102–118, 198–222.

22. J. C. Flugel, *The Psychoanalytic Study of the Family,* London: Hogarth Press, 1948; B. Kotkov, "Unresolved Sexual Phantasies in Group Psychotherapy," *Psychoanalytic Review,* 1957, 44, 313–322.

23. B. Lewin, "Phobic Symptoms and Dream Interpretation," *Psychoanalytic Quarterly,* 1952, 21, 295–322.

24. E. Simmel, "Alcoholism and Addiction," *Psychoanalytic Quarterly,* 1948, 17, 6–31.

25. T. W. Adorno, E. Frenkel-Brunswik, D. J. Levinson, and R. N. Sanford, *The Authoritarian Personality,* New York: Harper, 1950.

26. L. Kennedy, *The Trial of Stephen Ward,* London: V. Gollancz, 1964.

27. E. Bergler, "Obscene Words," *Psychoanalytic Quarterly,* 1936, 5, 226–248; "Some Recurrent Misconceptions Concerning Impotence," *Psychoanalytic Review,* 1940, 27, 450–466.

CHAPTER VIII : THE LAW

1. J. Skolnick, *Justice Without Trial,* New York: Wiley, 1966, 115–163.

2. W. R. LaFave, *Arrest: The Decision to Take a Suspect into Custody,* Boston: Little, Brown, 1965, 450–465.

3. C. Winick, I. Gerver, and A. Blumberg, "The Psychology of Judges," in Toch, *Legal and Criminal Psychology,* 121–145.

4. B. Johnson, "The Unofficial Grand Jury," *Journal of Social Hygiene,* 1939, 25, 215–220.

5. Much of this discussion of Nevada statutes derives from a memorandum prepared by Judge Morris Ploscowe, for which we are grateful. See Nevada Revised Statutes, 1966, 201:390, 201:380, 201:420, 266:350, 269:75.

6. 66 Nev. 60, 303 P. 2nd 611 (1949).

7. 201:300, *et seq.*

8. W. B. Huie, *The Revolt of Mamie Stover,* New York: Duell, Sloan and Pearce, 1951.

9. W. E. Quisenberry, "Eight Years After the Houses Closed," *Journal of Social Hygiene,* 1953, 39, 312–322.

10. F. Braden, "Steady Pressure on the Prostitution Racket: A Chief of Police Needs Support," *Journal of Social Hygiene,* 1952, 193–203.

11. P. M. Kinsie, "Sex Crimes and the Prostitution Racket," *Journal of Social Hygiene*, 1950, 36, 250–252.
12. W. C. Waterman, *Prostitution and Its Repression in New York City, 1900–1931*, New York: Columbia University Press, 1932.
13. W. Reckless, *Vice in Chicago*, Chicago: University of Chicago Press, 1933.
14. H. Powell, *Ninety Times Guilty*, New York: Harcourt, Brace, 1939.
15. E. Reid and O. Demaris, *The Green Felt Jungle*, New York: Pocket Books, 1964, 92–110.

CHAPTER IX : PROSTITUTION AND THE MILITARY

1. U. Sinclair, *The Autobiography of Upton Sinclair*, London: W. H. Allen, 1963.
2. Longstreet, *Sportin' House*, 241.
3. R. B. Fosdick, *European Police Systems*, New York: Century, 1915.
4. R. B. Fosdick, *Chronicle of a Generation: An Autobiography*, New York: Harper, 1958, 142–186.
5. W. F. Snow and B. Johnson, "Prostitution in the United States," unpublished manuscript, 1940.
6. W. Clarke, "Social Hygiene in War," *Rocky Mountain Medical Journal*, 1943, 40, 591–595.
7. Federal Security Agency Social Protection Division, *Social Services to Delinquent Women*, Atlanta: Social Security Board Region VII, 1945.
8. Federal Security Agency Social Protection Division, *Challenge to Community Action*, Washington: Government Printing Office, 1945.
9. Federal Security Agency Social Protection Division, *Techniques of Law Enforcement Against Prostitution*, Washington: Government Printing Office, 1943.
10. Federal Security Agency Social Protection Division, *Techniques of Law Enforcement in the Treatment of Juveniles and Prevention of Juvenile Delinquency*, Washington: Government Printing Office, 1944.
11. Federal Security Agency Social Protection Division, *Recommendations on Standards for Detention of Juveniles and Adults*, Washington: Government Printing Office, 1945.
12. E. Ness, "Federal Government's Program in Attacking the Problem of Prostitution," *Federal Probation*, 1953, 7, 17–19.
13. T. Devine, "Our Strength Is in United Action," *Journal of Social Hygiene*, 1945, 31, 508–514.
14. U.S. Army Medical Department, *Preventive Medicine in World War II*, V: *Communicable Diseases*, Washington: Office of the Surgeon

General, 1960. This volume is the basic source of the discussion of World War II which follows.

15. United Service Organizations, *Operation USO: Report of the President*, February 4, 1941–January 9, 1948.
16. *Die Zeit* (Hamburg), October 1, 1965.
17. *Time*, May 6, 1966.
18. The rate of exchange is about eighty piastres to a dollar.
19. S. Gruson, " 'R and R' Tours on Taiwan: American Servicemen Bring a Mixed Blessing to the Island," *New York Times*, February 14, 1968.
20. *San Francisco Chronicle*, October 24, 1969, 1.

CHAPTER X : INTERNATIONAL CONTROL

1. J. Cleland, *Memoirs of a Woman of Pleasure*, New York: Putnam, 1963.
2. B. Johnson, "The Attitudes of Governments Toward Foreign Prostitutes," *Journal of Social Hygiene*, 1928, 14, 129–138.
3. United Nations, *Study on Traffic in Persons and Prostitution*.
4. S. Barclay, *Bondage: The Slave Traffic in Women Today*, New York: Funk and Wagnalls, 1968. The thirty-fourth session of the General Assembly, International Criminal Police Organization (Interpol), at its meeting in Rio de Janeiro in June 1965, prepared an international agreement which would make it impossible to hire women in other countries on the basis of contracts liable to lead them into prostitution.
5. *Bolshaya Meditsinskaya Entsiklopedia* (Moscow), 1962, 26, 1050–1051.
6. *Bolshaya Sovetskaya Entsiklopedia* (Moscow), 1955, 35, 1833–1855.
7. *Literaturnaya Gazeta* (Moscow), 32, March 14, 1963.
8. *Izvestia* (Moscow), April 3, 1963.
9. *Molodoy Kommunist* (Moscow), April 1963.
10. *Süddeutsche Zeitung* (Munich), April 11, 1970, quoting a report in *Orbis*, the official publication of the Polish travel organization.

CHAPTER XI : THE FUTURE

1. W. H. Masters and V. E. Johnson, *Human Sexual Inadequacy*, Boston: Little, Brown, 1970; *Time*, May 25, 1970, 51.
2. W. Young, *Eros Denied*, New York: Grove Press, 1964, 152.
3. J. Dollard, *Caste and Class in a Southern Town*, New Haven: Yale University Press, 1937, 137–142.
4. *New York Times*, May 29, 1970, 30.
5. R. Firth, *We, the Tikopia*, London: Allen and Unwin, 1936.
6. Flexner, *Prostitution in Europe*.

7. C. Arnelunxen, "Moderne Erscheinungs formen der Zühälterei," *Neue Polizei* (Dusseldorf), 1967, 21, 12–16.

8. C. Winick, "Tendency Systems and the Effects of a Movie Dealing with a Social Problem," *Journal of General Psychology*, 1963, 68, 289–305.

INDEX

309

A NOTE ON THE AUTHORS

CHARLES WINICK is Professor of Sociology at the City University of New York and has been research director for the American Social Health Association. He has been active in investigating deviant behavior, including a large study of prostitutes' clients, drug use among prostitutes, and changing sex roles in the United States. He has also consulted for the United States Senate Subcommittee on Juvenile Delinquency, the Joint Commission on Mental Health of Children and Youth, the World Health Organization, and other agencies concerned with social problems. His concept of the "maturing out" of narcotics addiction has provoked discussion and research. Mr. Winick is the author of *Practicum of Group Psychotherapy* and, most recently, *The New People*. His writings appear in *Medical Opinion and Review*, *Social Problems*, *Public Opinion Quarterly*, *Journal of Social Psychology*, *American Sociological Review*, *Law and Contemporary Problems*, and *Medical Aspects of Human Sexuality*, among other publications.

PAUL M. KINSIE is the world dean of students of prostitution. As a result of his participation in field work for every important study of the subject since 1917, he is well acquainted with persons working in all phases of prostitution. During World War I he surveyed prostitution near military installations for the Commission on Training Camp Activities. He conducted interviews in ten American cities for sociologist Howard B. Woolston's study of *Prostitution in the United States* (1921). During the 1920's he was field director for the League of Nations Committee of Experts for the Traffic in Women and Children, working in Latin America, Europe, and Africa. In the 1930's he conducted special investigations for the Immigration and Naturalization Service. During World War II, Mr. Kinsie assisted a number of government programs concerned with prostitution. For many years he directed the Division of Legal and Social Protection of the American Social Health Association.